MILE BY MILE

First published in Great Britain
2017 by Aurum Press Ltd
74–77 White Lion Street
Islington
London N1 9PF

Mile by Mile on the LNER, *Mile by Mile on the LMSR* and *Travelling on the Southern Railway: The Journey Mile by Mile* all originally published in 1947 and 1948 by Stuart N. Pike.

Pages 146–173 © Aurum Press

Please note that S.N. Pike's original numbering of the maps has been faithfully reproduced, and the absence in these original three guides of any maps numbered from 1 onwards does not mean any maps have been omitted.

Introductions text by Peter Herring

A catalogue record for this book is available from the British Library.

ISBN: 978 1 78131 641 2
Ebook ISBN: 978 1 78131 672 6

10 9 8 7 6 5 4 3 2 1
2021 2020 2019 2018 2017

Edited by Nick Freeth
Designed by Paul Turner and Sue Pressley, Stonecastle Graphics
Great Western Railway maps by Reginald Piggott; research by Matt Thompson

Printed in China

MILE BY MILE

AN ILLUSTRATED JOURNEY ON BRITAIN'S RAILWAYS

LNER · LMSR · SOUTHERN RAILWAY · GREAT WESTERN RAILWAY

AS THEY WERE IN 1947

S.N. PIKE MBE

With introductions by Peter Herring

Aurum
Press

The Making of *Mile by Mile*

It appears to have been a labour of love. No one commissioned Stuart Nelson Pike to draw his astonishingly detailed annotated maps of the main lines out of London. Virtually nothing was omitted as he enhanced the trackside data with information on nearby places of interest, from castles to coal mines, rivers to Roman roads. Every station, signal box, bridge, tunnel and water trough was recorded, coupled with notes on speed records and the like. The maps are dated 1947, the eve of nationalisation and the coming of British Railways, and much of what Stuart Pike recorded has since vanished. At a time when the view from a train window offers little of lineside interest, *Mile by Mile* presents a fascinating historical record and a chance to reminisce.

Stuart Pike charted the route of the London, Midland & Scottish Railway from Euston to Liverpool, that of the London & North Eastern Railway linking Kings Cross and Edinburgh, and the paths of the lines out of Waterloo to Portsmouth, Southampton, Swanage, Weymouth, Ilfracombe and Plymouth. This last, wider coverage could be explained by him living in Southern Railway territory, by the Thames in Shepperton, Middlesex.

Little has been discovered about Stuart Pike. He was one of six children of the painter Sidney Pike (1858-1923) and appears to have inherited his father's drawing skills. He served with distinction in the Royal Flying Corps during the First World War, later rising to the rank of Squadron Leader in the Royal Air Force Volunteer Reserve. He was awarded the MBE in 1944.

However, there was one glaring omission among Stuart Pike's 1947 pamphlets, and that was the Great Western Railway. There is no indication why; perhaps he simply couldn't find the time.

When railway enthusiast Nick Dodson discovered long-forgotten copies of *Mile by Mile*, he determined that these unique publications should be made available once more – and made complete. Adhering to Stuart Pike's style, cartographer Reginald Piggott and railway expert Matt Thompson undertook the assignment of illustrating and describing the GWR routes from Paddington to Bristol and Penzance, and their work was added to a new edition.

With a redesigned layout, fresh text and photographs, Aurum Press is now bringing the wonderfully evocative world of Stuart Pike's *Mile by Mile* to a new audience.

Editor's footnote:
Like Stuart Pike himself, we have omitted the possessive apostrophe from 'Kings Cross', even though it often appears in other railway books and maps.

Contents

Introduction

Britain's railways have weathered five major upheavals, most recently the privatisation of the 1980s. Before that, in 1963, Dr Richard Beeching delivered his report 'The Reshaping of British Railways'. Though containing many sound recommendations, it is still vilified for the 'Beeching Axe' that saw one-third of lines close.

Before Beeching came the Modernisation Plan of 1955. Its aim was to turn around the fortunes of an ailing state system, but it too is identified with a single measure: the elimination of steam traction. That state system had been created in 1948 by the post-war Labour government as part of a broad programme of nationalisation. British Railways was formed from the four war-ravaged elements of the earliest, and most fundamental of those upheavals, the government-enforced Grouping of 1923. With hindsight, if some degree of regulation and rationalisation had been imposed before 1923, the 'Beeching Axe' might have been less bloody.

The Grouping was the consequence of over a century of slow, then steady but finally often irrational growth. From colliery and mine railways, first horse-drawn then steam-powered, came the 25-mile (40.2km) Stockton & Darlington Railway of 1825, the first to carry passengers along with freight. It was the work of Northumberland-born George Stephenson, and his *Locomotion No.1* hauled the first train. Doubts remained, though, about the merits of steam haulage, and it was a further five years before trains ran over the first inter-city railway from Liverpool to Manchester. The inaugural service was hauled by another Stephenson engine, *Rocket*. This, however, was more the work of George's gifted son, Robert. *Rocket*, with its multi-tube, horizontal boiler, became the template for all subsequent steam locomotive design.

During the 1830s railway building began in earnest. A key figure was Joseph Locke, who had greatly assisted George Stephenson in the construction of the Liverpool & Manchester, and went on to build the Grand Junction, Lancaster & Carlisle and London & Southampton Railways. Opened in 1837, the Grand Junction connected Birmingham

◄ LMSR Pacific no.6208 *Princess Helena Victoria* passes Edge Hill on the route of the Liverpool to Manchester Railway, heading for the West Country. Following the introduction of 'Coronation' 4-6-2s, 'Princess Royals' often drew Merseyside expresses.

6

and Wolverhampton with Stafford, Crewe and Warrington, and had a junction with the Liverpool & Manchester. At Birmingham's Curzon Street station, the GJR shared platforms with the London & Birmingham Railway, which had been engineered by Robert Stephenson: a coming together that created Britain's first trunk line. Through services between the north-west and the capital began in 1838.

All these lines were constructed to a track gauge, originally determined by George Stephenson, of 4 feet 8½ inches (1,435mm). For the engineer appointed to oversee the construction of a railway from London to Bristol that distance was unacceptable. Isambard Kingdom Brunel's Great Western would employ a broad gauge of 7 feet (2,134mm) that promised greater stability and consequently faster speeds. Its locomotives would be larger, stronger and more powerful; its carriages more spacious, comfortable and smoother-riding.

Brunel was proved correct, and the route westwards from Paddington remains a

▲ Platform 8 on the arrivals side of Paddington station. GWR staff stand beside a train of clerestory-roofed stock. The Brunel-designed terminus opened in May 1854; the fourth of its glazed spans was added in 1915.

masterpiece of engineering. He was, however, hopeless at designing locomotives and, acknowledging this, appointed Daniel Gooch as his locomotive superintendent in 1837. The extraordinary thing was that Gooch – himself a protégé of Robert Stephenson – was just twenty years old. This prodigy would design the locomotives that brought Brunel's vision for the GWR to life, and that vision would later survive the inevitable and irresistible conversion from broad to standard gauge.

The Great Western had begun operating from Paddington to Maidenhead in 1838, with the complete route to Bath and Bristol opening in 1841. The 1840s were to be the railways' decade of greatest growth, as a national network rapidly took shape. William Cubitt and his son, Joseph, constructed another of the main lines into London, the Great Northern, and the latter went on to collaborate

on the London & South Western and build the London, Chatham and Dover Railway.

Railways had become a fashionable investment, and attracted their fair share of both entrepreneurs and charlatans. Nicknamed the 'Railway King', George Hudson personified the era of 'Railway Mania.' He was involved in many schemes, chiefly around Yorkshire and the north-east, and went on to become chairman of the Midland Railway. Many who bought into and benefited from Hudson's grand ambitions turned a blind eye to his dubious business practices. His career began to unravel in 1848, when he was accused of fraudulently paying share dividends out of capital rather than revenue. It was the start of a fall from grace that eventually saw him imprisoned.

Arguably the greatest visionary of the period was Lancashire-born Edward Watkin. From taking on the secretaryship of the Trent Valley Railway in 1845, by 1881 he had become a director of nine different railway companies and trustee of a tenth. Watkin's ambition was not limited to Britain. His roles with the Great Central Railway, London's Metropolitan Railway and the South Eastern Railway led him to envisage a through service from Manchester and Liverpool via a Channel Tunnel to Paris. The scheme got as far as to see work begin on the tunnel.

Opened in 1899, the GCR marked the end of main-line railway construction in Britain. Looking back, it is clear many railways were built with genuine purpose – to give a good example, the growth of major cities and their suburbs required an expansion of local lines – but others were a result of misguided ambition, senseless rivalry and greed. Many never made a profit, and some duplicated existing routes and competed to serve the same communities.

Throughout this period, both locomotive and rolling stock design evolved. Engines grew in size and power, and – in the hands of the Midland's Samuel Johnson, the Lancashire & Yorkshire's John Aspinall, the South Eastern & Chatham's Harry Wainwright and the Great Northern's Patrick Stirling among others – became objects of engineering beauty. Trains became more comfortable and faster, with many prestige expresses being introduced. Luxury Pullman cars were first imported from the United States in 1874 by the Midland Railway, and, in December 1881, the London, Brighton & South Coast Railway inaugurated the first all-Pullman service from London to Brighton, the forerunner of the celebrated 'Brighton Belle.'

For the most part, railways were a matter of national and company pride, mirrored in the increasing grandeur of principal stations. Poor inter-company coordination had been greatly reduced and, thanks to the introduction of third-class fares in addition to first and second, long-distance rail travel had not only become available but affordable. There was some strong competition: between the Great

Western and the London & South Western for boat train traffic from Plymouth, for example; and between the GWR and the London & North Western from London to Birmingham.

The fiercest rivalry, however, came on the London to Edinburgh route, where the West and East Coast companies competed, albeit unofficially, to achieve the fastest runs. In 1885, the East Coast offered the quickest time: seven hours, representing a modest average speed of 43.7mph (70.3kph). In the summer of 1888, the West Coast finally responded, and 'racing' began in earnest, with simultaneous 10.00 a.m. departures from Euston and Kings Cross. The schedules were 8 hours 30 minutes and 8 hours 15 minutes respectively, but drivers were encouraged to 'thrash' their engines and arrivals were invariably early. Attracting wide interest – reports appeared in newspapers, bookmakers took bets and results were cabled each day to the *New York Herald* – the racing continued until early August that year, when the companies called a truce and agreed fixed schedules.

The competitive spirit was reignited with the opening of the Forth Bridge in 1890. The battleground was now the London to Aberdeen run, especially its overnight services. Added spice came from the convergence of both East and West Coast routes at Kinnaber Junction, where the Caledonian Railway – one of the West Coast operators – controlled the signals.

Competition peaked during August 1895 and again attracted the interest of the press, which coined the headline 'Race to the North.' Unlike 1885, company correspondence made no pretence that this was not a contest. Excited crowds turned out to see the spectacle even during the early hours of the morning, but interest was not confined to record breaking: the dangers were also being debated. On 19 August, approaching Edinburgh, the East Coast train took a 15mph (24.1kph)

▼ 'A3' Pacific no.4472 *Flying Scotsman* leaves Kings Cross with the inaugural 'Flying Scotsman' on 1 May 1928. It covered 393 miles (632.4km) non-stop – a record for a scheduled service. Crew changeovers took place via a corridor in the tender.

speed restriction at Portobello at 81.5mph (131.16kph) and was still travelling at 64mph (103kph) entering Waverley station.

Soon after, the chairmen of the North British and Great Northern Railways agreed the rivalry had gone far enough. The last word was left to the West Coast. Consisting of only three coaches, on the night of 22-23 August its service reached Aberdeen at 4.32 a.m. It had covered the 539.7 miles (868.56km) from London in 8 hours 32 minutes, an average speed of 63.3mph (101.87kph). The achievement remains unsurpassed.

During the 1900s, with no fewer than 149 companies operating over 24,000 route miles (38,624.2km), Britain's railways reached their zenith. While electric trams were offering competition within some towns and cities, over long distances road transport was still in its infancy. Railways could enjoy a monopoly in passenger and freight traffic, although their 'common carrier' status, requiring them to accept any consignment, could prove burdensome.

The outbreak of war in August 1914 brought far-reaching changes and sowed the seeds of what was to follow in the 1920s. All railways came under the control of the government's Railway Executive, a control that was retained until 1921. When hostilities ended in 1918, the inevitable decline in maintenance standards had taken its toll of locomotives, rolling stock and track. Many engines had been requisitioned for service in France and Belgium, some never to return. There had been huge increases in traffic and consequently expenditure, but government payments to the companies remained based on 1913 revenues. They were wholly inadequate to restore pre-war standards, and the situation was not helped by a breakdown in labour relations – leading, in 1919, to a national rail strike.

It was clear to the government and to many railway executives that a return to the pre-war position was untenable, and that there had to be some form of amalgamation. It had not gone unnoticed that wartime unification had successfully brought together a disparate collection of companies. Could such a move work in peacetime, and how should it be organised?

There were two clear options: one based on geographical divisions; the other on 'corridors' centred on the principal trunk routes out of London. The latter would preclude old rivalries threatening the integration of services, even if it meant Scotland's railways being run hundreds of miles away in London. This was the chosen option, and it was at the core of the Transport Act that entered the statute books on 16 August 1921.

Reluctant to leave their fates to civil servants, some companies pre-empted matters by forging their own alliances, the merger of the Lancashire & Yorkshire and London & North Western Railways in 1922 being the most significant. Full amalgamation began with the Great Western Railway, followed by the incorporation of the London & North Eastern, London Midland & Scottish and Southern Railways on 1 January 1923.

Over 30 companies were excluded from the Grouping, including several Welsh narrow gauge lines, although the Vale of Rheidol and Welshpool & Llanfair – still operating to this day – became part of the GWR. Many were omitted not for being too minor but because they were utterly impoverished. Some owned little more than their trackbeds, relying on larger neighbours for locomotives and rolling stock. The newly created foursome did not want to be saddled with their debts.

It was anticipated that the 'Big Four', as they were dubbed, would quickly implement line closures – but surprisingly, only 40 miles (64.37km) lost their passenger services between 1923 and 1926. The pace increased after 1930 with 580 miles (933.4km) closing in two years up to the end of 1931. Altogether, between 1923 and nationalisation in 1948, 1,264 miles (2,034km) closed to passengers, although most were kept open for freight.

This quartet of companies would be responsible for the running of Britain's railways for the ensuing quarter of a century. The stories of what they inherited, how they developed and what finally befell them are told in the subsequent chapters of *Mile by Mile*.

11

▼ The 2 feet 6 inches (762mm) gauge Welshpool & Llanfair Light Railway was absorbed into the GWR, and is now a tourist line. In GWR livery, 1902 built 0 6 0 tank no.823 *The Countess* stands with a mixed train at its Raven Square terminus.

The LNER Story

A southbound freight train passed at speed by a streamlined Gresley Pacific on its way to Leeds, Newcastle-upon-Tyne or Edinburgh summed up the twin faces of the LNER – where records were set for high-speed running and, less spectacularly, for hauling coal.

Gresley Pacifics, storming out of London's Kings Cross station with express trains destined for Scotland, Tyneside or the West Riding, encapsulated the prestige, glamour, engineering advances – and apparent profitability – of 1930s rail travel. It was a false image in two respects. Though well-managed – and, with 6,590 route miles (10,605.5km), the second largest of the 'Big Four' – the LNER was impoverished for much of its existence. Moreover, passengers accounted for just forty per cent of its business. This was soon evident

on the journey northwards, with shunting engines handling coal trains from Yorkshire and the East Midlands. In its first year, the LNER conveyed 102 million tons of coal, thirty-seven per cent of the nation's output.

Compared to the LMSR, the LNER's creation was an amicable affair. A merger between the three major southern constituents, the Great Northern, Great Central and Great Eastern Railways, had been proposed in 1909 but rejected as being too large a monopoly. Thirteen years on it was a government edict.

Opened in 1850, with its terminus at Kings Cross, the Great Northern was the senior. The Great Central was the junior, a monument to the ambition of its chairman, Sir Edward Watkin. Founded in 1846 as the cross-country Manchester, Sheffield & Lincolnshire Railway, the company was renamed when Watkin

▲ On 5 March 1935, 'A3' Pacific no.2750 *Papyrus* is cheered on its departure from Kings Cross for Newcastle-upon-Tyne. During the journey, *Papyrus* reached a speed of 108mph (173.8kph), a record for a non-streamlined locomotive.

◀ The first 'A4' Pacific, no.2509 *Silver Link*, leaves Kings Cross on 27 September 1935 with a trial run of the 'Silver Jubilee' express. Public services to Newcastle-upon-Tyne began on 30 September, averaging 67mph (107.8kph) for the 268.25 mile (431.7km) journey.

15

launched his scheme for a 'London Extension'; it began operating as the GCR in 1897 with the first trains arriving at its Marylebone terminus two years later.

From its headquarters at Liverpool Street, the Great Eastern served Cambridgeshire, Essex, Suffolk and Norfolk. While its main line trains broke no records, the intensity and efficiency of its North London suburban services was admirable. The largest (and most successful) component of the LNER was the North Eastern Railway, whose 1,770 route miles (2,848.5km) included the historic route of the Stockton & Darlington Railway. Two main Scottish companies came into the LNER fold, the North British and the Great North of Scotland Railway. With 1,460 route miles (2,349.6km) the NBR was the second largest of the LNER's constituent companies, and had

▲ A 'then and now' display on 30 June 1938, publicising new rolling stock for the 'Flying Scotsman.' 'Stirling Single' No.1 (1870) draws some vintage six-wheelers, with 'A4' no.4498 *Sir Nigel Gresley* at the head of their modern counterparts.

earned a reputation as one of the worst-run railways in Britain.

Matters had improved by the time the NBR's William Whitelaw became first chairman of the LNER, with Ralph Wedgwood appointed its general manager, a post he would hold for sixteen years. Both the NER's Sir Vincent Raven and the GCR's John Robinson were supremely qualified for the vacancy of locomotive superintendent but, with both approaching retirement, the vote went to the Great Northern's Nigel Gresley. It was a decision the board would not regret.

In *Mile by Mile* the emphasis is on the London to Edinburgh line which, after climbing out of Kings Cross and through the suburbs, continued through Hitchin and Huntingdon to Peterborough. From here, the LNER served the East Midlands, Lincoln and resorts such as Skegness which, as a famous LNER poster declared, was 'SO Bracing'. At Doncaster, departure point for Sheffield, Leeds, Bradford and Hull, the route north switched to NER rails. York, headquarters of the North Eastern Railway, offered connections for Scarborough, Whitby, Harrogate and again Leeds.

Passing through Darlington and Durham and across the River Tyne into Newcastle, the route skirted the Northumberland coast before crossing the border at Berwick-upon-Tweed and entering ex-NBR territory for the remainder of the 393-mile (632.4km) journey to Edinburgh Waverley. From here, the LNER served Perth, Aberdeen, Inverness and Carlisle and, from the ex-NBR terminus at Glasgow Queen Street, Fort William and the West Highland fishing port of Mallaig.

At the Grouping, the LNER inherited 7,419 locomotives. They were generally of a good standard, which was fortunate since finances severely restricted renewals. In the dying days of the GNR, with trainloads testing the existing 4-4-2 Atlantics, Gresley had unveiled a brace of Pacifics, 'A1' class nos.1470 *Great Northern* and 1471 *Sir Frederick Banbury*. Their success saw a further ten delivered under LNER auspices, beginning with one of the world's most celebrated locomotives, no.1472 (4472) *Flying Scotsman*.

It was *Flying Scotsman* that, in 1928, achieved the first authenticated 100mph (160.9kph) for steam traction, by which point the 'A1s' were being rebuilt with new valve gear and higher-pressure boilers. Reclassified 'A3', no.4472 was appropriately at the head of the inaugural non-stop 'Flying Scotsman' from Kings Cross to Edinburgh on 1 May that year.

During the 1930s, Gresley had the resources to fulfil his ideas – not always successfully, it has to be added. In 1935, the 'A3' evolved into the streamlined 'A4' Pacifics which powered luxury expresses such as the 'Silver Jubilee' and 'Coronation', reducing journey times to Newcastle-upon-Tyne and Edinburgh to four and six hours. Thirty-five were built at Doncaster and, on 3 July 1938, one earned a permanent place in history, as no.4468 *Mallard* set a still unbroken speed record for steam traction of 126mph (202.7kph).

Many observers, though, consider Gresley's finest achievement to be the 'V2' 2-6-2 which was introduced in 1936 to haul a new Anglo-Scottish fast freight service, the 'Green Arrow.' The 'V2s' handled prodigious loads, especially during wartime – on one occasion a single 'V2' took a 26-coach train from Peterborough to Kings Cross.

Sir Nigel Gresley died in 1941 to be succeeded by Edward Thompson. For some, Thompson's shabby rebuilding of the magnificent 'P2' 2-8-2s was evidence of the bitterness he felt towards Gresley. Others claim Thompson was simply being practical. Wartime offered him few opportunities, and his one true success was the 'B1' 4-6-0, with 410 outshopped between 1942 and 1952.

In 1945, the reins were taken over by Arthur Peppercorn, who, in the short time before nationalisation, produced two Pacific designs worthy of Sir Nigel himself, the 'A1' and the 'A2'. One 'A2' survives, no.60532 *Blue Peter*, but it was over forty years before the power of an 'A1' could again be experienced in the shape of no.60163 *Tornado*, completed in 2008 – the first main line steam locomotive to be built in Britain since 1960.

▼ No.4468 *Mallard* was the first 'A4' fitted with the Kylchap double-chimney exhaust system, and demonstrated its benefits on 3 July 1938 by setting a world speed record for steam of 126mph (202.7kph) between Grantham and Peterborough.

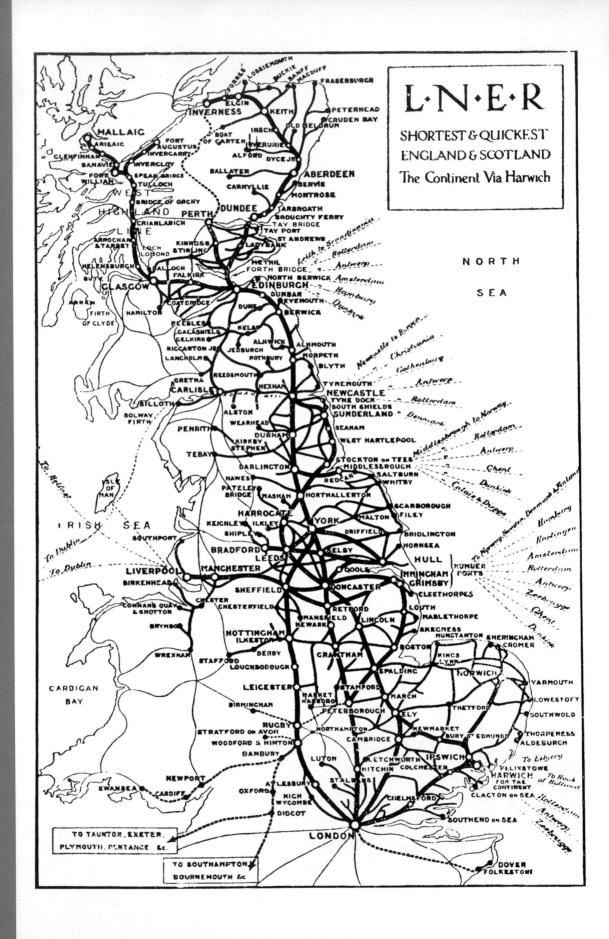

MILE by MILE

ON THE L.N.E.R.

by

S. N. PIKE, M.B.E.

KINGS CROSS EDITION
L.N.E.R.

The journey between London and the North described detail :—

- GRADIENTS OF THE LINE
- SPEED TESTS AND MILEAGES
- VIADUCTS, BRIDGES AND EMBANKMENTS
- TUNNELS, CUTTINGS AND CROSSOVERS
- STREAMS, RIVERS AND ROADS
- TOWNS, VILLAGES AND CHURCHES
- MINES, FACTORIES AND WORKS

with an account of features of interest and beauty to be seen from the train.

Published by
STUART N. PIKE,
Shepperton - on - Thames
Middlesex, England

ERRATA

Map 14 (Page 16) : *The true position of mileposts 165, 166 and 167 is slightly north of where indicated on this map, milepost 167 being north of the Goole Canal, not south of the bridge as shown.*

Map 16 (Page 18) : *The correct name of the Junction 2 miles north of York is Skelton Junct., not Poppleton as shown.*

20

Author's Note

The pleasures and thrills of the journey between Kings Cross and Edinburgh are limitless. Every mile of the trip embraces some special feature of interest or beauty to compel the attention of the passenger.

The object of this little book is to encourage the passenger to anticipate his progress, and to enable him to know, to a nicety, what he next will see from the window at any and every stage of the journey. It is such a pity to sacrifice this experience to idle slumber, or to concentration on a magazine that would the better be enjoyed at home.

The beautiful countryside rushes by; beneath the tranquil surface, right beside the line, miners are toiling for the black diamonds essential to feed the great industrial plants we pass.

I acknowledge, with grateful thanks, certain information given me by Officials of the L.N.E.R. Railwaymen of every grade have contributed their share to make this publication as complete as possible. Railwaymen are justly proud of the vast organisation they serve; it is their wish that passengers should enjoy to the full the journeys they make with such speed and safety. The information and advice they have so readily placed at my disposal has been gladly offered with that end in view.

Shepperton, 1947.   *S. N. P.*

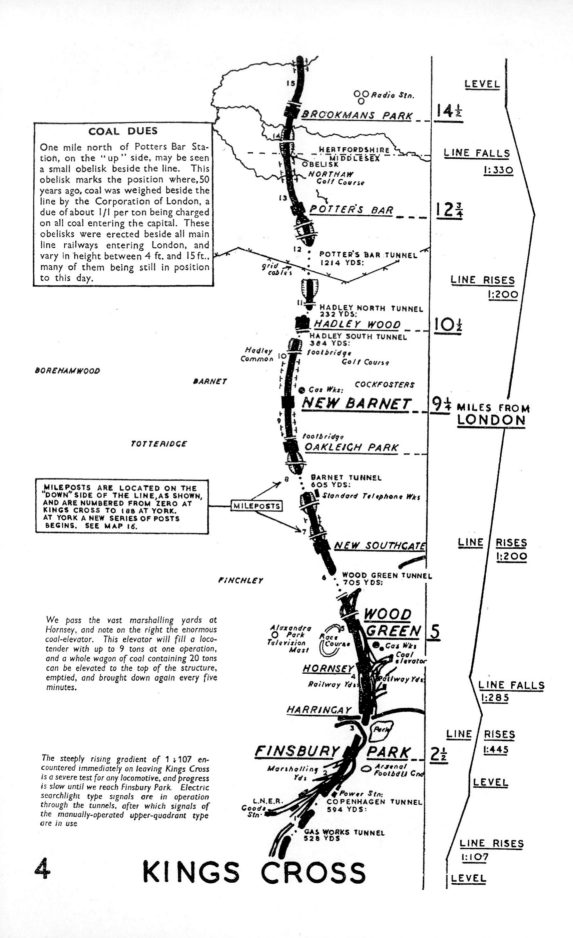

COAL DUES

One mile north of Potters Bar Station, on the "up" side, may be seen a small obelisk beside the line. This obelisk marks the position where, 50 years ago, coal was weighed beside the line by the Corporation of London, a due of about 1/1 per ton being charged on all coal entering the capital. These obelisks were erected beside all main line railways entering London, and vary in height between 4 ft. and 15 ft., many of them being still in position to this day.

MILEPOSTS ARE LOCATED ON THE "DOWN" SIDE OF THE LINE, AS SHOWN, AND ARE NUMBERED FROM ZERO AT KINGS CROSS TO 188 AT YORK. AT YORK A NEW SERIES OF POSTS BEGINS. SEE MAP 16.

MILEPOSTS

We pass the vast marshalling yards at Hornsey, and note on the right the enormous coal-elevator. This elevator will fill a loco-tender with up to 9 tons at one operation, and a whole wagon of coal containing 20 tons can be elevated to the top of the structure, emptied, and brought down again every five minutes.

The steeply rising gradient of 1 : 107 encountered immediately on leaving Kings Cross is a severe test for any locomotive, and progress is slow until we reach Finsbury Park. Electric searchlight type signals are in operation through the tunnels, after which signals of the manually-operated upper-quadrant type are in use

Radio Stn.

BROOKMANS PARK

HERTFORDSHIRE
MIDDLESEX
OBELISK
NORTHAW
Golf Course

POTTER'S BAR

POTTER'S BAR TUNNEL
1214 YDS.

grid
cables

HADLEY NORTH TUNNEL
232 YDS.

HADLEY WOOD

HADLEY SOUTH TUNNEL
384 YDS.
footbridge
Golf Course

Hadley
Common

BOREHAMWOOD

BARNET

Gas Wks.

COCKFOSTERS

NEW BARNET

footbridge
OAKLEIGH PARK

TOTTERIDGE

BARNET TUNNEL
605 YDS.

Standard Telephone Wks.

NEW SOUTHGATE

WOOD GREEN TUNNEL
705 YDS.

FINCHLEY

WOOD
GREEN

Alexandra
Park
Television
Mast

Race
Course

Gas Wks.
Coal
elevator

HORNSEY
Railway Yds.

Railway Yds.

HARRINGAY

Park

FINSBURY PARK

Arsenal
Football Gnd.

Marshalling
Yds.

Power Stn.
COPENHAGEN TUNNEL
594 YDS.

L.N.E.R.
Goods
Stn.

GAS WORKS TUNNEL
528 YDS.

LEVEL

14½

LINE FALLS
1:330

12¾

LINE RISES
1:200

10½

9¼ MILES FROM LONDON

LINE RISES
1:200

5

LINE FALLS
1:285

LINE RISES
1:445

2½

LEVEL

LINE RISES
1:107

LEVEL

4

KINGS CROSS

COLUMN 4 TO BE FILLED IN BY PASSENGER

LONDON—EDINBURGH

EXACT DISTANCES BETWEEN STATIONS—EXPRESS TRAIN RUNNING TIMES

(1) STATION	(2) Distance Between Stations		(3) Express Train Running Times	(4) Actual Running Times			(5) NOTES and Average Speeds over each Section
	Miles	Yards	Minutes	Minutes	Early	Late	
KING'S CROSS to HATFIELD	17	1,199	27				From a standing start the heavily laden express encounters a severe 1 : 107 gradient through the Gasworks and Copenhagen tunnels, to be followed by a steep 1 : 200 climb for 6 miles from milepost 4 to Potters Bar, where the summit is reached. From here we rush through Hatfield at really high speed. Average speed 39.0 m.p.h., the low figure being due to the difficult start. (See Maps 4 and 5.)
HATFIELD to HITCHIN	14	424	14				The summit on this section is at Woolmer Green Box, near milepost 24. The junction of the lines at Langley are passed at 65 to 70 m.p.h. Water is taken on at the Troughs at milepost 27 at this speed, which we maintain through Hitchin. Average speed 61 m.p.h. (See Maps 5 and 6.)
HITCHIN to HUNTINGDON	26	1,672	26				This is a really fast section of the line, and, except for a slowing down for curves near Offord, a very high speed is maintained. Average speed 62.3 m.p.h. (See Maps 6 and 7.)
HUNTINGDON to PETERBOROUGH	17	863	19				An exceptionally fast section of the line. The necessity for approaching Peterborough at a minimum pace reduces our average speed to 55.2 m.p.h. (See Maps 7 and 8.)
PETERBOROUGH to GRANTHAM	29	165	44				From a standing start at Peterborough we encounter a series of rising gradients from milepost 85 for the next 15 miles. Over the summit we pass through Great Ponton at very high speed, slowing down slightly for Grantham. Average speed 39.5 m.p.h. (See Maps 8, 9 and 10.)
GRANTHAM to NEWARK	14	1,138	14				Very high speeds are attained on the falling gradients. Average over the section 63.2 m.p.h. (See Maps 10 and 11.)
NEWARK to RETFORD	18	902	24				Between Newark and milepost 128 the line is dead level, but rising gradients up to Askham tunnel lower the average. Speed is sharply reduced approaching Retford. Average speed 46.2 m.p.h. (See Maps 12 and 13.)

(Continued on page 13)

5

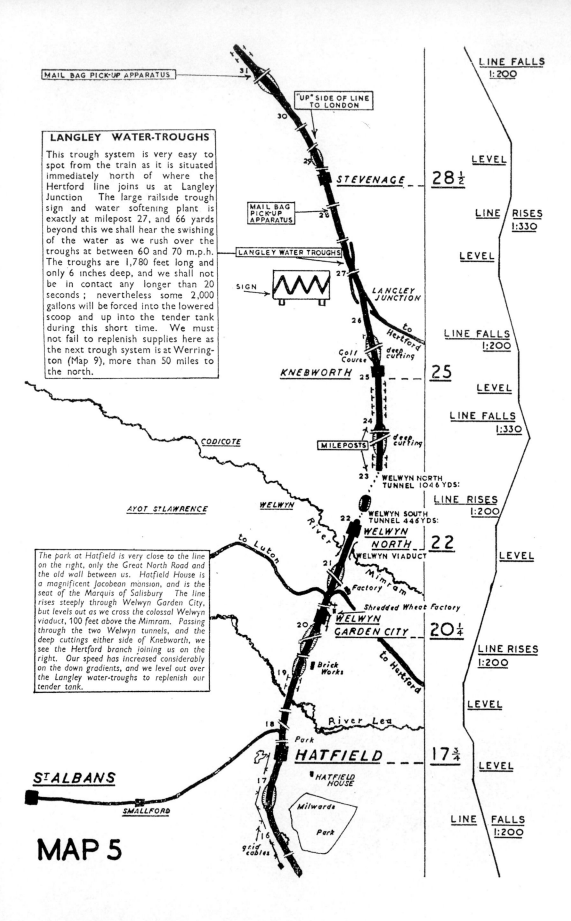

MAIL BAG PICK-UP APPARATUS

"UP" SIDE OF LINE TO LONDON

MAIL BAG PICK-UP APPARATUS

LANGLEY WATER TROUGHS

SIGN

STEVENAGE ___ 28½

LINE FALLS 1:200

LEVEL

LINE RISES 1:330

LEVEL

LANGLEY WATER-TROUGHS

This trough system is very easy to spot from the train as it is situated immediately north of where the Hertford line joins us at Langley Junction The large railside trough sign and water softening plant is exactly at milepost 27, and 66 yards beyond this we shall hear the swishing of the water as we rush over the troughs at between 60 and 70 m.p.h. The troughs are 1,780 feet long and only 6 inches deep, and we shall not be in contact any longer than 20 seconds ; nevertheless some 2,000 gallons will be forced into the lowered scoop and up into the tender tank during this short time. We must not fail to replenish supplies here as the next trough system is at Werrington (Map 9), more than 50 miles to the north.

LANGLEY JUNCTION

to Hertford

deep cutting

Golf Course

KNEBWORTH 25 ___ 25

LINE FALLS 1:200

LEVEL

LINE FALLS 1:330

24

CODICOTE

MILEPOSTS

deep cutting

23 ... WELWYN NORTH TUNNEL 1046 YDS:

AYOT St LAWRENCE

WELWYN

River

WELWYN SOUTH TUNNEL 446 YDS:

LINE RISES 1:200

22 WELWYN NORTH 22

WELWYN VIADUCT

LEVEL

The park at Hatfield is very close to the line on the right, only the Great North Road and the old wall between us. Hatfield House is a magnificent Jacobean mansion, and is the seat of the Marquis of Salisbury The line rises steeply through Welwyn Garden City, but levels out as we cross the colossal Welwyn viaduct, 100 feet above the Mimram. Passing through the two Welwyn tunnels, and the deep cuttings either side of Knebworth, we see the Hertford branch joining us on the right. Our speed has increased considerably on the down gradients, and we level out over the Langley water-troughs to replenish our tender tank.

to Luton

Mimram

Factory

21

Shredded Wheat Factory

20 WELWYN GARDEN CITY ___ 20¼

to Hertford

LINE RISES 1:200

19

Brick Works

LEVEL

18

River Lea

St ALBANS

SMALLFORD

Park

HATFIELD ___ 17¾

LEVEL

17

HATFIELD HOUSE

Milwards Park

LEVEL

16

LINE FALLS 1:200

grid cables

MAP 5

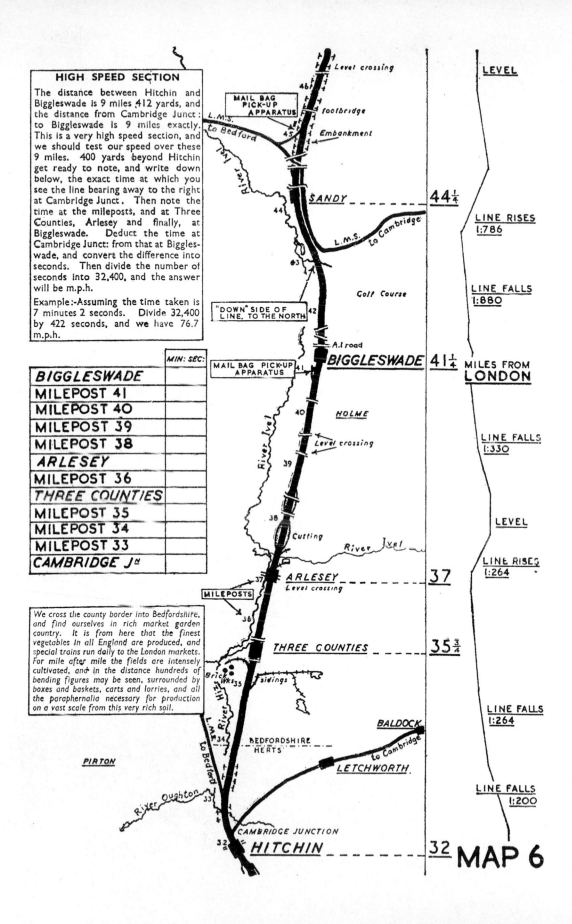

HIGH SPEED SECTION

The distance between Hitchin and Biggleswade is 9 miles 412 yards, and the distance from Cambridge Junct: to Biggleswade is 9 miles exactly. This is a very high speed section, and we should test our speed over these 9 miles. 400 yards beyond Hitchin get ready to note, and write down below, the exact time at which you see the line bearing away to the right at Cambridge Junct. Then note the time at the mileposts, and at Three Counties, Arlesey and finally, at Biggleswade. Deduct the time at Cambridge Junct: from that at Biggleswade, and convert the difference into seconds. Then divide the number of seconds into 32,400, and the answer will be m.p.h.

Example:-Assuming the time taken is 7 minutes 2 seconds. Divide 32,400 by 422 seconds, and we have 76.7 m.p.h.

	MIN: SEC:
BIGGLESWADE	
MILEPOST 41	
MILEPOST 40	
MILEPOST 39	
MILEPOST 38	
ARLESEY	
MILEPOST 36	
THREE COUNTIES	
MILEPOST 35	
MILEPOST 34	
MILEPOST 33	
CAMBRIDGE Jⁿ	

We cross the county border into Bedfordshire, and find ourselves in rich market garden country. It is from here that the finest vegetables in all England are produced, and special trains run daily to the London markets. For mile after mile the fields are intensely cultivated, and in the distance hundreds of bending figures may be seen, surrounded by boxes and baskets, carts and lorries, and all the paraphernalia necessary for production on a vast scale from this very rich soil.

Level crossing
MAIL BAG PICK-UP APPARATUS
footbridge
L.M.S. to Bedford
Embankment
River Ivel
SANDY 44¼
L.M.S. To Cambridge
Golf Course
"DOWN" SIDE OF LINE, TO THE NORTH
A.1 road
MAIL BAG PICK-UP APPARATUS
BIGGLESWADE 41¼ MILES FROM **LONDON**
River Ivel
HOLME
Level crossing
Cutting
River Ivel
MILEPOSTS
ARLESEY 37
Level crossing
THREE COUNTIES 35¾
Brick Wks Sidings
BALDOCK
to Cambridge
BEDFORDSHIRE HERTS
LETCHWORTH
PIRTON
River Oughton
River Hiz
L.M.S. To Bedford
CAMBRIDGE JUNCTION
HITCHIN 32

LEVEL
LINE RISES 1:786
LINE FALLS 1:880
LINE FALLS 1:330
LEVEL
LINE RISES 1:264
LINE FALLS 1:264
LINE FALLS 1:200

MAP 6

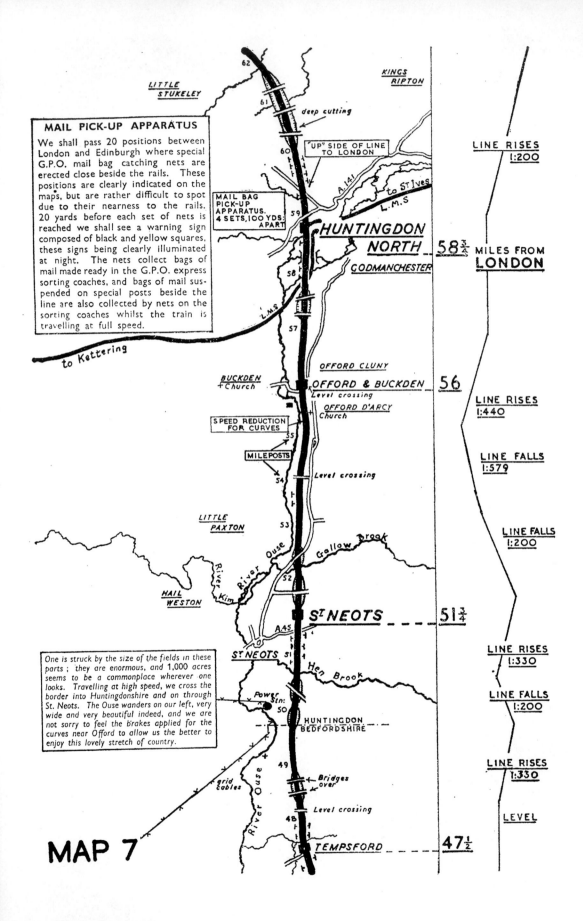

MAIL PICK-UP APPARATUS

We shall pass 20 positions between London and Edinburgh where special G.P.O. mail bag catching nets are erected close beside the rails. These positions are clearly indicated on the maps, but are rather difficult to spot due to their nearness to the rails. 20 yards before each set of nets is reached we shall see a warning sign composed of black and yellow squares, these signs being clearly illuminated at night. The nets collect bags of mail made ready in the G.P.O. express sorting coaches, and bags of mail suspended on special posts beside the line are also collected by nets on the sorting coaches whilst the train is travelling at full speed.

LITTLE STUKELEY

KINGS RIPTON

deep cutting

"UP" SIDE OF LINE TO LONDON

MAIL BAG PICK-UP APPARATUS. 4 SETS, 100 YDS. APART

A.141

to St Ives

L.M.S

HUNTINGDON NORTH 58¾

GODMANCHESTER

LINE RISES 1:200

MILES FROM **LONDON**

L.M.S

to Kettering

OFFORD CLUNY

BUCKDEN + Church

OFFORD & BUCKDEN 56

Level crossing

OFFORD D'ARCY Church

LINE RISES 1:440

SPEED REDUCTION FOR CURVES

MILEPOSTS

Level crossing

LINE FALLS 1:579

LITTLE PAXTON

Gallow Brook

LINE FALLS 1:200

River Kim

River Ouse

HAIL WESTON

St NEOTS 51¾

One is struck by the size of the fields in these parts; they are enormous, and 1,000 acres seems to be a commonplace wherever one looks. Travelling at high speed, we cross the border into Huntingdonshire and on through St. Neots. The Ouse wanders on our left, very wide and very beautiful indeed, and we are not sorry to feel the brakes applied for the curves near Offord to allow us the better to enjoy this lovely stretch of country.

A.45

St NEOTS

Hen Brook

LINE RISES 1:330

Power Stn:

HUNTINGDON BEDFORDSHIRE

LINE FALLS 1:200

grid cables

River Ouse

Bridges over

Level crossing

LINE RISES 1:330

LEVEL

MAP 7

TEMPSFORD 47½

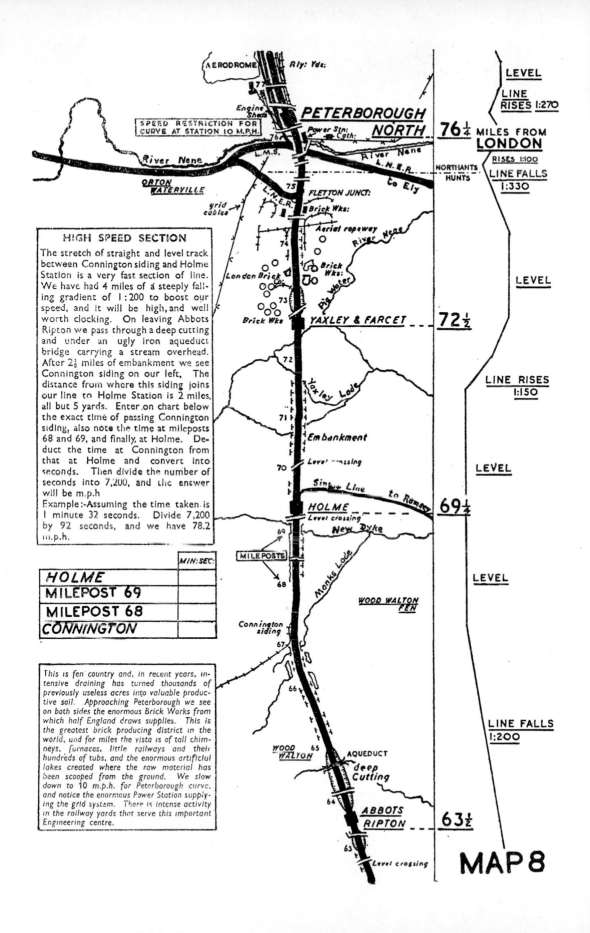

AERODROME Rly: Yds:

PETERBOROUGH NORTH

SPEED RESTRICTION FOR CURVE AT STATION 10 M.P.H.

Engine Sheds

Power Stn: Cath:

76¼ MILES FROM **LONDON**

LEVEL
LINE RISES 1:270

RISES 1:100
LINE FALLS 1:330

NORTHANTS HUNTS

River Nene

L.M.S.

River Nene

L.N.E.R.

to Ely

76¼

ORTON WATERVILLE

75

grid cables

L.N.E.R.

FLETTON JUNCT:

Brick Wks:

Aerial ropeway

River Nene

74

London Brick Co:

Brick Wks:

Pig Water

LEVEL

73

Brick Wks

YAXLEY & FARCET

72½

HIGH SPEED SECTION

The stretch of straight and level track between Connington siding and Holme Station is a very fast section of line. We have had 4 miles of a steeply falling gradient of 1:200 to boost our speed, and it will be high, and well worth clocking. On leaving Abbots Ripton we pass through a deep cutting and under an ugly iron aqueduct bridge carrying a stream overhead. After 2½ miles of embankment we see Connington siding on our left. The distance from where this siding joins our line to Holme Station is 2 miles, all but 5 yards. Enter on chart below the exact time of passing Connington siding, also note the time at mileposts 68 and 69, and finally, at Holme. Deduct the time at Connington from that at Holme and convert into seconds. Then divide the number of seconds into 7,200, and the answer will be m.p.h

Example:-Assuming the time taken is 1 minute 32 seconds. Divide 7,200 by 92 seconds, and we have 78.2 m.p.h.

72

Yaxley Lode

LINE RISES 1:150

71

Embankment

70

Level crossing

LEVEL

Single Line to Ramsey

HOLME

69¼

Level crossing

New Dyke

LEVEL

	MIN: SEC:
HOLME	
MILEPOST 69	
MILEPOST 68	
CONNINGTON	

69

MILEPOSTS

68

Monks Lode

WOOD WALTON FEN

Connington siding

67

This is fen country and, in recent years, intensive draining has turned thousands of previously useless acres into valuable productive soil. Approaching Peterborough we see on both sides the enormous Brick Works from which half England draws supplies. This is the greatest brick producing district in the world, and for miles the vista is of tall chimneys, furnaces, little railways and their hundreds of tubs, and the enormous artificial lakes created where the raw material has been scooped from the ground. We slow down to 10 m.p.h. for Peterborough curve, and notice the enormous Power Station supplying the grid system. There is intense activity in the railway yards that serve this important Engineering centre.

66

LINE FALLS 1:200

WOOD WALTON

65

AQUEDUCT

deep Cutting

64

ABBOTS RIPTON

63½

63

Level crossing

MAP 8

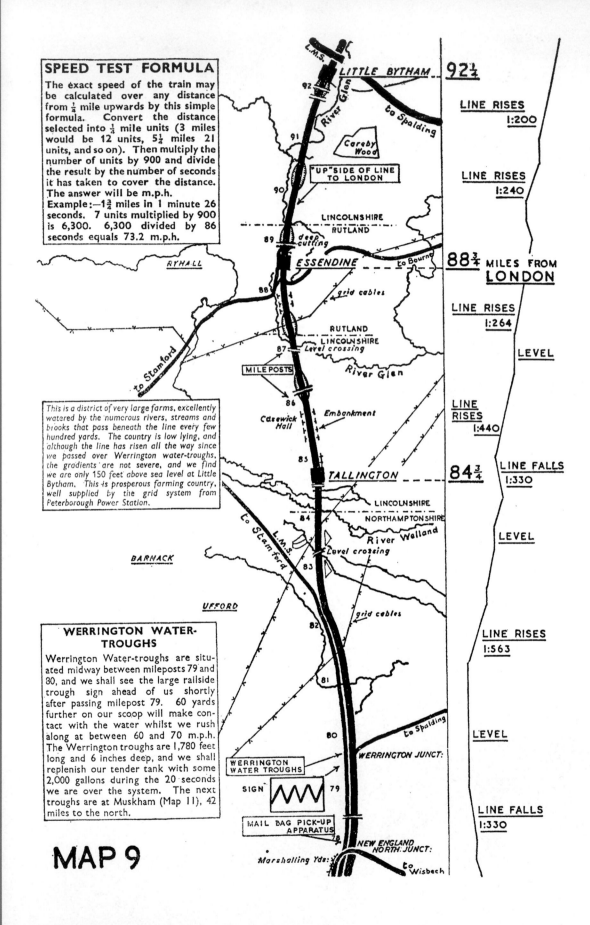

SPEED TEST FORMULA

The exact speed of the train may be calculated over any distance from ¼ mile upwards by this simple formula. Convert the distance selected into ¼ mile units (3 miles would be 12 units, 5¼ miles 21 units, and so on). Then multiply the number of units by 900 and divide the result by the number of seconds it has taken to cover the distance. The answer will be m.p.h.

Example:—1¾ miles in 1 minute 26 seconds. 7 units multiplied by 900 is 6,300. 6,300 divided by 86 seconds equals 73.2 m.p.h.

This is a district of very large farms, excellently watered by the numerous rivers, streams and brooks that pass beneath the line every few hundred yards. The country is low lying, and although the line has risen all the way since we passed over Werrington water-troughs, the gradients are not severe, and we find we are only 150 feet above sea level at Little Bytham. This is prosperous farming country, well supplied by the grid system from Peterborough Power Station.

WERRINGTON WATER-TROUGHS

Werrington Water-troughs are situated midway between mileposts 79 and 80, and we shall see the large railside trough sign ahead of us shortly after passing milepost 79. 60 yards further on our scoop will make contact with the water whilst we rush along at between 60 and 70 m.p.h. The Werrington troughs are 1,780 feet long and 6 inches deep, and we shall replenish our tender tank with some 2,000 gallons during the 20 seconds we are over the system. The next troughs are at Muskham (Map 11), 42 miles to the north.

MAP 9

LITTLE BYTHAM — 92¼

LINE RISES 1:200

River Glen — to Spalding

Careby Wood

"UP" SIDE OF LINE TO LONDON

LINE RISES 1:240

LINCOLNSHIRE
RUTLAND

deep cutting

ESSENDINE — to Bourn — 88¾ MILES FROM LONDON

RYHALL

grid cables

LINE RISES 1:264

RUTLAND
LINCOLNSHIRE

Level crossing

River Glen

LEVEL

MILE POSTS

To Stamford

Casewick Hall

Embankment

LINE RISES 1:440

TALLINGTON — 84¾

LINE FALLS 1:330

LINCOLNSHIRE
NORTHAMPTONSHIRE

River Welland

LEVEL

BARNACK

To Stamford
L.M.S.

Level crossing

UFFORD

grid cables

LINE RISES 1:563

to Spalding

WERRINGTON JUNCT:

LEVEL

WERRINGTON WATER TROUGHS

SIGN — 79

WERRINGTON WATER TROUGHS

MAIL BAG PICK-UP APPARATUS

NEW ENGLAND NORTH JUNCT:

LINE FALLS 1:330

Marshalling Yds:

to Wisbech

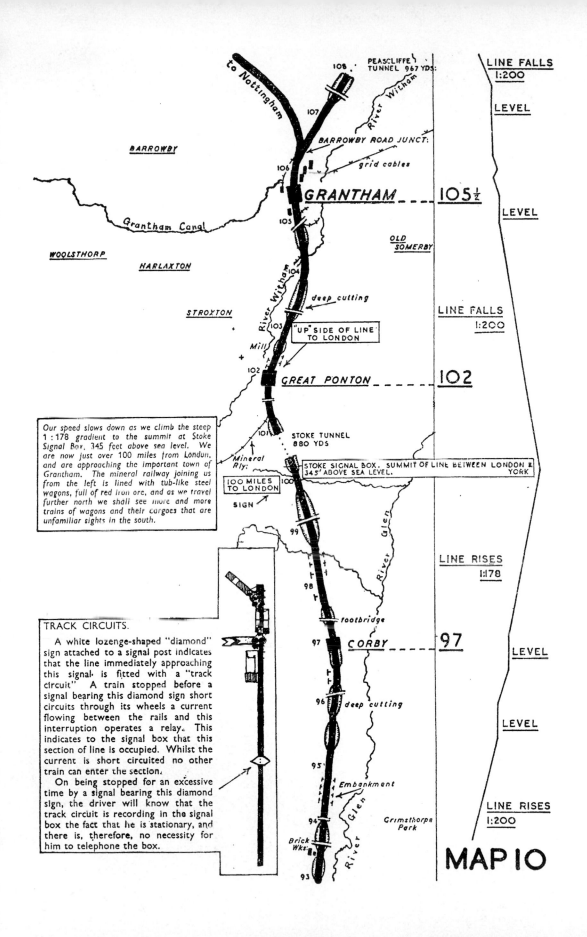

to Nottingham

PEASCLIFFE
TUNNEL 967 YDS:

108

107

River Witham

BARROWBY ROAD JUNCT:

grid cables

106

BARROWBY

GRANTHAM

105

Grantham Canal

OLD
SOMERBY

WOOLSTHORP

HARLAXTON

104

deep cutting

STROXTON

103

"UP" SIDE OF LINE
TO LONDON

River Witham

Mill

102

GREAT PONTON

+

101

STOKE TUNNEL
880 YDS:

Mineral
Rly:

100

100 MILES
TO LONDON

SIGN

STOKE SIGNAL BOX. SUMMIT OF LINE BETWEEN LONDON &
345' ABOVE SEA LEVEL.   YORK

River Glen

99

98

97   **CORBY**

footbridge

96   deep cutting

95

Embankment

94

River Glen

Grimsthorpe
Park

Brick
Wks:

93

Our speed slows down as we climb the steep
1 : 178 gradient to the summit at Stoke
Signal Box, 345 feet above sea level. We
are now just over 100 miles from London,
and are approaching the important town of
Grantham. The mineral railway joining us
from the left is lined with tub-like steel
wagons, full of red iron ore, and as we travel
further north we shall see more and more
trains of wagons and their cargoes that are
unfamiliar sights in the south.

TRACK CIRCUITS.

A white lozenge-shaped "diamond"
sign attached to a signal post indicates
that the line immediately approaching
this signal is fitted with a "track
circuit". A train stopped before a
signal bearing this diamond sign short
circuits through its wheels a current
flowing between the rails and this
interruption operates a relay. This
indicates to the signal box that this
section of line is occupied. Whilst the
current is short circuited no other
train can enter the section.

On being stopped for an excessive
time by a signal bearing this diamond
sign, the driver will know that the
track circuit is recording in the signal
box the fact that he is stationary, and
there is, therefore, no necessity for
him to telephone the box.

LINE FALLS
1:200

LEVEL

LEVEL

105½

LEVEL

LINE FALLS
1:200

102

LINE RISES
1:178

97

LEVEL

LEVEL

LINE RISES
1:200

MAP 10

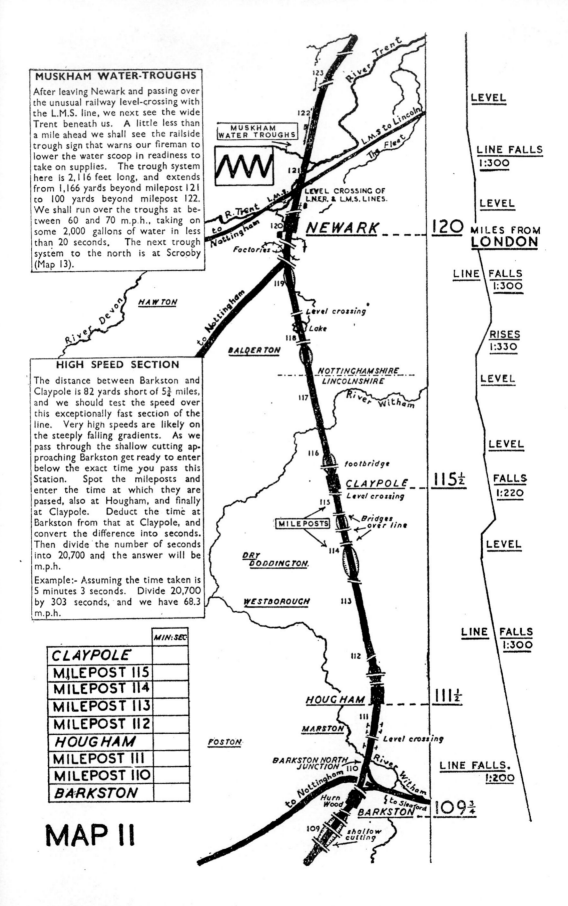

MUSKHAM WATER-TROUGHS

After leaving Newark and passing over the unusual railway level-crossing with the L.M.S. line, we next see the wide Trent beneath us. A little less than a mile ahead we shall see the railside trough sign that warns our fireman to lower the water scoop in readiness to take on supplies. The trough system here is 2,116 feet long, and extends from 1,166 yards beyond milepost 121 to 100 yards beyond milepost 122. We shall run over the troughs at between 60 and 70 m.p.h., taking on some 2,000 gallons of water in less than 20 seconds. The next trough system to the north is at Scrooby (Map 13).

30

HIGH SPEED SECTION

The distance between Barkston and Claypole is 82 yards short of 5¾ miles, and we should test the speed over this exceptionally fast section of the line. Very high speeds are likely on the steeply falling gradients. As we pass through the shallow cutting approaching Barkston get ready to enter below the exact time you pass this Station. Spot the mileposts and enter the time at which they are passed, also at Hougham, and finally at Claypole. Deduct the time at Barkston from that at Claypole, and convert the difference into seconds. Then divide the number of seconds into 20,700 and the answer will be m.p.h.

Example:- Assuming the time taken is 5 minutes 3 seconds. Divide 20,700 by 303 seconds, and we have 68.3 m.p.h.

	MIN:SEC.
CLAYPOLE	
MILEPOST 115	
MILEPOST 114	
MILEPOST 113	
MILEPOST 112	
HOUGHAM	
MILEPOST 111	
MILEPOST 110	
BARKSTON	

MAP 11

LONDON—EDINBURGH

EXACT DISTANCES BETWEEN STATIONS—EXPRESS TRAIN RUNNING TIMES

(1) STATION	(2) Distance Between Stations		(3) Express Train Running Times	(4) Actual Running Times			(5) NOTES and Average Speeds over each Section
	Miles	Yards	Minutes	Minutes	Early	Late	
RETFORD to DONCASTER	17	611	19				Falling gradients approaching Scrooby water-troughs send us over the water pick-up at 65 m.p.h. The line rises steeply to milepost 150, but we again make fine speed to the outskirts of Doncaster. Average speed 55.2 m.p.h. (See Maps 12 and 13.)
DONCASTER to YORK	32	308	42				The 6 miles of level track between mileposts 158 and 166 is a high speed section, and well worth " clocking." We slow down for the curve and swing bridge at Selby and also for the curve at Chaloner's Whin Junction. The sharp curve at York is approached slowly. Average speed 46.0 m.p.h. (See Maps 14, 15 and 15.)
YORK to THIRSK	22	352	25				12 miles of dead level and dead straight track allows for really fast travelling. By the time we reach Tollerton, speeds are in excess of 75 m.p.h. The standing start at York, however, reduces our average to 53.4 m.p.h. (See Maps 16 and 17.)
THIRSK to NORTHALLERTON	7	1,320	8				The line rises very slightly. This section is covered at an average of 58.1 m.p.h. (See Maps 17 and 18.)
NORTHALLERTON to DARLINGTON	14	308	15				The Wiske Water-troughs are taken at high speed. Speed is reduced approaching Darlington and we average 57.0 m.p.h. over this 14¼ miles. (See Map 18.)
DARLINGTON to FERRY HILL	12	1,496	16				The line rises 1 : 220 and 1 : 203 until we reach the summit by milepost 55, 292 feet above sea level. We average 47.4 m.p.h. over this section. (See Maps 18 and 19.)
FERRY HILL to DURHAM	9	330	12				Severe rising and falling gradients and speed restrictions limit our speed on this section, and we average 46.2 m.p.h. (See Maps 19 and 20.)
DURHAM to NEWCASTLE	14	66	19				This is not a fast section of the line and our average works out at 44.2 m.p.h. The approach to Newcastle over the King Edward Bridge is taken very slowly. (See Maps 20 and 21.)

(Continued on page 37)

31

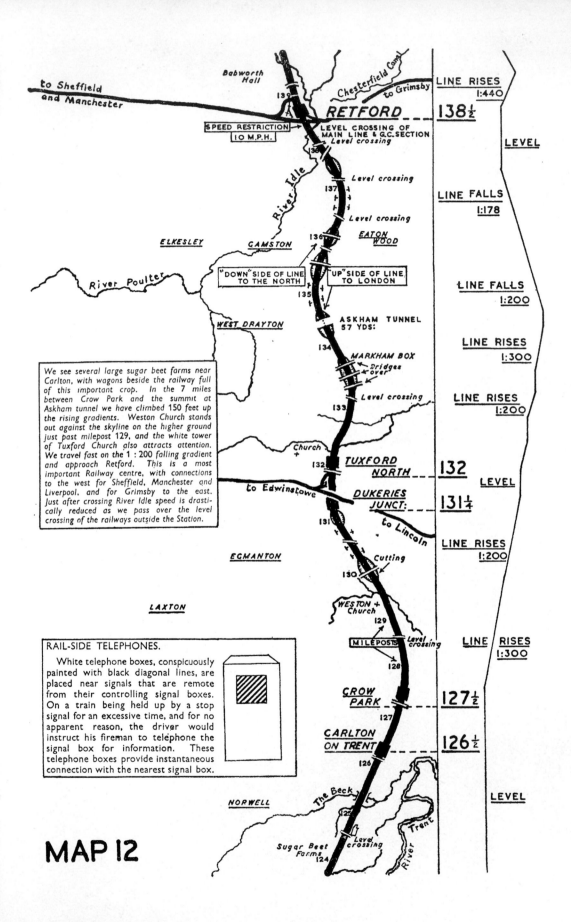

Babworth Hall

to Sheffield and Manchester

Chesterfield Canal

to Grimsby

LINE RISES
1:440

RETFORD 138½

SPEED RESTRICTION
10 M.P.H.

LEVEL CROSSING OF
MAIN LINE & G.C. SECTION

Level crossing

138

LEVEL

River Idle

Level crossing

137

LINE FALLS
1:178

Level crossing

ELKESLEY

CAMSTON

EATON
WOOD

136

LINE FALLS
1:200

River Poulter

"DOWN" SIDE OF LINE
TO THE NORTH

"UP" SIDE OF LINE
TO LONDON

135

WEST DRAYTON

ASKHAM TUNNEL
57 YDS:

LINE RISES
1:300

134

MARKHAM BOX

Bridges
over

LINE RISES
1:200

We see several large sugar beet farms near
Carlton, with wagons beside the railway full
of this important crop. In the 7 miles
between Crow Park and the summit at
Askham tunnel we have climbed 150 feet up
the rising gradients. Weston Church stands
out against the skyline on the higher ground
just past milepost 129, and the white tower
of Tuxford Church also attracts attention.
We travel fast on the 1 : 200 falling gradient
and approach Retford. This is a most
important Railway centre, with connections
to the west for Sheffield, Manchester and
Liverpool, and for Grimsby to the east.
Just after crossing River Idle speed is drastically reduced as we pass over the level
crossing of the railways outside the Station.

Level crossing

133

Church

132

TUXFORD
NORTH 132

LEVEL

to Edwinstowe

DUKERIES
JUNCT: 131¼

to Lincoln

131

EGMANTON

LINE RISES
1:200

130

Cutting

LAXTON

WESTON +
Church 129

MILEPOSTS

Level
crossing

128

LINE RISES
1:300

RAIL-SIDE TELEPHONES.

White telephone boxes, conspicuously
painted with black diagonal lines, are
placed near signals that are remote
from their controlling signal boxes.
On a train being held up by a stop
signal for an excessive time, and for no
apparent reason, the driver would
instruct his fireman to telephone the
signal box for information. These
telephone boxes provide instantaneous
connection with the nearest signal box.

CROW
PARK 127½

127

CARLTON
ON TRENT 126½

126

LEVEL

NORWELL

The Beck

125

Level
crossing

Sugar Beet
Farms 124

River Trent

MAP 12

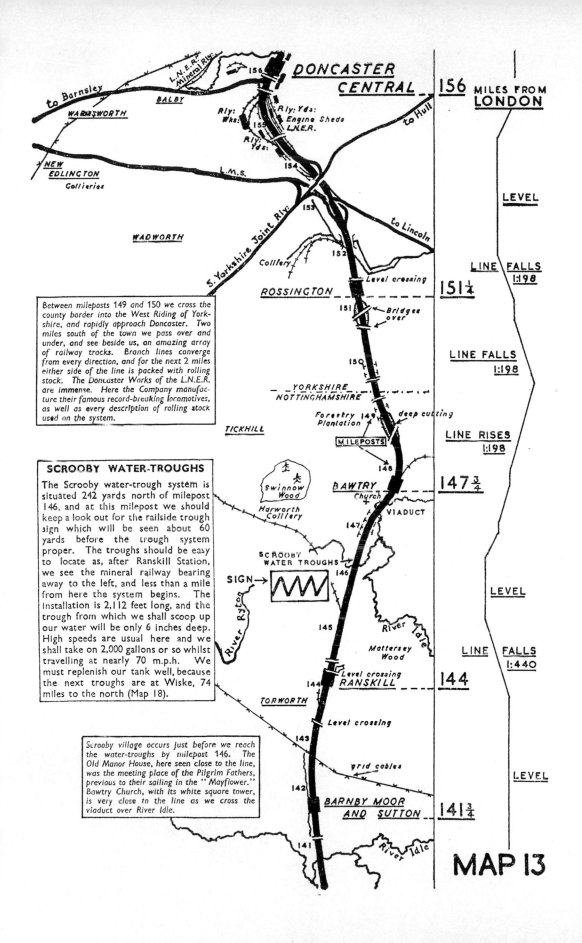

to Barnsley

L.N.E.R. Mineral Rly.

WARMSWORTH BALBY

156

DONCASTER
CENTRAL

Rly: Wks: Rly: Yds:
Engine Sheds
L.N.E.R.

Rly: Yds:

155

154

L.M.S.

NEW
EDLINGTON
Collieries

153

WADWORTH

S. Yorkshire Joint Rly.

Colliery

152

ROSSINGTON

Level crossing

151

Bridges over

150

YORKSHIRE
NOTTINGHAMSHIRE

Forestry 149
Plantation

deep cutting

MILEPOSTS

Swinnow
Wood

148

BAWTRY
Church

Harworth
Colliery

VIADUCT

147

SCROOBY
WATER TROUGHS

146

SIGN →

River Ryton

145

River Idle

Mattersey
Wood

RANSKILL
144

Level crossing

TORWORTH

143

Level crossing

grid cables

142

BARNBY MOOR
AND SUTTON

141

River Idle

156 MILES FROM
LONDON

LEVEL

LINE FALLS
1:198

151¼

LINE FALLS
1:198

LINE RISES
1:198

147¾

LEVEL

LINE FALLS
1:440

144

LEVEL

141¾

MAP 13

33

Between mileposts 149 and 150 we cross the
county border into the West Riding of Yorkshire, and rapidly approach Doncaster. Two
miles south of the town we pass over and
under, and see beside us, an amazing array
of railway tracks. Branch lines converge
from every direction, and for the next 2 miles
either side of the line is packed with rolling
stock. The Doncaster Works of the L.N.E.R.
are immense. Here the Company manufacture their famous record-breaking locomotives,
as well as every description of rolling stock
used on the system.

TICKHILL

SCROOBY WATER-TROUGHS

The Scrooby water-trough system is
situated 242 yards north of milepost
146, and at this milepost we should
keep a look out for the railside trough
sign which will be seen about 60
yards before the trough system
proper. The troughs should be easy
to locate as, after Ranskill Station,
we see the mineral railway bearing
away to the left, and less than a mile
from here the system begins. The
installation is 2,112 feet long, and the
trough from which we shall scoop up
our water will be only 6 inches deep.
High speeds are usual here and we
shall take on 2,000 gallons or so whilst
travelling at nearly 70 m.p.h. We
must replenish our tank well, because
the next troughs are at Wiske, 74
miles to the north (Map 18).

Scrooby village occurs just before we reach
the water-troughs by milepost 146. The
Old Manor House, here seen close to the line,
was the meeting place of the Pilgrim Fathers,
previous to their sailing in the "Mayflower."
Bawtry Church, with its white square tower,
is very close to the line as we cross the
viaduct over River Idle.

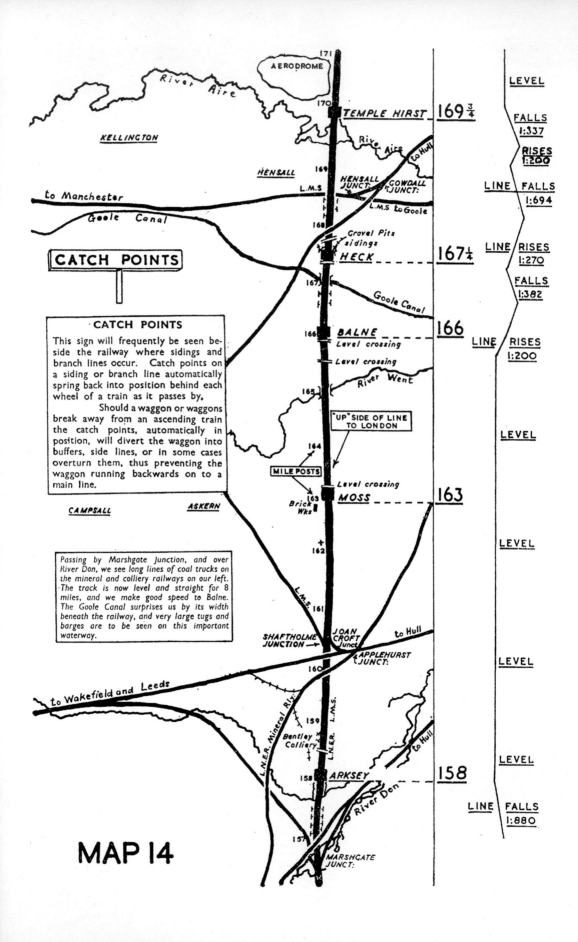

CATCH POINTS

CATCH POINTS

This sign will frequently be seen beside the railway where sidings and branch lines occur. Catch points on a siding or branch line automatically spring back into position behind each wheel of a train as it passes by.

Should a waggon or waggons break away from an ascending train the catch points, automatically in position, will divert the waggon into buffers, side lines, or in some cases overturn them, thus preventing the waggon running backwards on to a main line.

Passing by Marshgate Junction, and over River Don, we see long lines of coal trucks on the mineral and colliery railways on our left. The track is now level and straight for 8 miles, and we make good speed to Balne. The Goole Canal surprises us by its width beneath the railway, and very large tugs and barges are to be seen on this important waterway.

River Aire

AERODRAME

171

170

169¾ TEMPLE HIRST

KELLINGTON

River Aire

to Hull

169 HENSALL
L.M.S.

HENSALL GOWDALL
JUNCT JUNCT:

to Manchester

Goole Canal

L.M.S to Goole

LINE FALLS 1:694

168

Gravel Pits sidings

167½ HECK

167

Goole Canal

LINE RISES 1:270

FALLS 1:382

166 BALNE
Level crossing

166 LINE RISES 1:200

Level crossing

165 River Went

"UP" SIDE OF LINE TO LONDON

164

MILE POSTS

Level crossing

163 MOSS

CAMPSALL

ASKERN

163 Brick Wks

162

L.M.S.

161

SHAFTHOLME JUNCTION

160

JOAN CROFT Junct

to Hull

APPLEHURST JUNCT:

to Wakefield and Leeds

L.N.E.R. Mineral Rly.

159

Bentley Colliery

L.N.E.R.

L.M.S.

to Hull

158 ARKSEY

158 River Don

157

MARSHGATE JUNCT:

LEVEL

FALLS 1:337

RISES 1:200

LEVEL

LEVEL

LEVEL

LINE FALLS 1:880

MAP 14

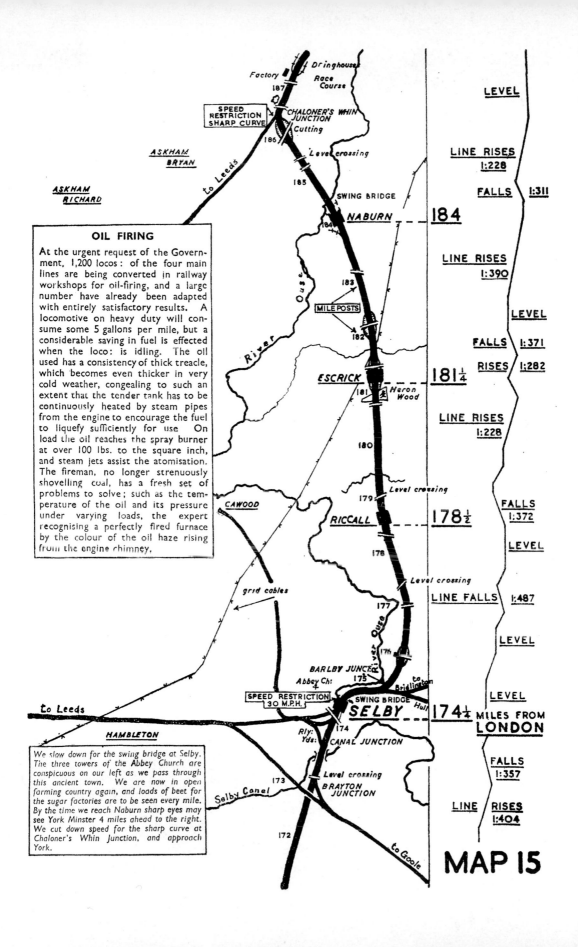

OIL FIRING

At the urgent request of the Government, 1,200 locos: of the four main lines are being converted in railway workshops for oil-firing, and a large number have already been adapted with entirely satisfactory results. A locomotive on heavy duty will consume some 5 gallons per mile, but a considerable saving in fuel is effected when the loco: is idling. The oil used has a consistency of thick treacle, which becomes even thicker in very cold weather, congealing to such an extent that the tender tank has to be continuously heated by steam pipes from the engine to encourage the fuel to liquefy sufficiently for use On load the oil reaches the spray burner at over 100 lbs. to the square inch, and steam jets assist the atomisation. The fireman, no longer strenuously shovelling coal, has a fresh set of problems to solve; such as the temperature of the oil and its pressure under varying loads, the expert recognising a perfectly fired furnace by the colour of the oil haze rising from the engine chimney,

We slow down for the swing bridge at Selby. The three towers of the Abbey Church are conspicuous on our left as we pass through this ancient town. We are now in open farming country again, and loads of beet for the sugar factories are to be seen every mile. By the time we reach Naburn sharp eyes may see York Minster 4 miles ahead to the right. We cut down speed for the sharp curve at Chaloner's Whin Junction, and approach York.

Factory
Dringhouses Race Course
187
SPEED RESTRICTION SHARP CURVE
CHALONER'S WHIN JUNCTION
Cutting
186
ASKHAM BRYAN
Level crossing
ASKHAM RICHARD
to Leeds
185
SWING BRIDGE
NABURN
184
184
183
MILE POSTS
182
River Ouse
ESCRICK
181¼
181
Heron Wood
180
CAWOOD
179
Level crossing
RICCALL
178½
178
Level crossing
grid cables
177
River Ouse
176
BARLBY JUNC:
175
Abbey Ch:
to Bridlington
SPEED RESTRICTION 30 M.P.H.
SWING BRIDGE
Hull
SELBY
174¼
to Leeds
174
Rly: Yds:
CANAL JUNCTION
HAMBLETON
173
Level crossing
BRAYTON JUNCTION
Selby Canal
172
to Goole

LEVEL

LINE RISES 1:228

FALLS 1:311

LINE RISES 1:390

LEVEL

FALLS 1:371

RISES 1:282

LINE RISES 1:228

FALLS 1:372

LEVEL

LINE FALLS 1:487

LEVEL

LEVEL

MILES FROM **LONDON**

FALLS 1:357

LINE RISES 1:404

MAP 15

35

HELPERBY

SPEED TEST FORMULA

The exact speed of the train may be calculated over any distance from ¼ mile upwards by this simple formula. Convert the distance selected into ¼ mile units (3 miles would be 12 units, 5¼ miles 21 units, and so on). Then multiply the number of units by 900 and divide the result by the number of seconds it has taken to cover the distance. The answer will be m.p.h.

Example:—1¾ miles in 1 minute 26 seconds. 7 units multiplied by 900 is 6,300. 6,300 divided by 86 seconds equals 73.2 m.p.h.

Cutting

14

LINE RISES
1:741

RASKELF — — — $201\frac{1}{2}$

1:845

13

Embankment

Light Rly to Easingwold

LINE RISES
1:666

12

200 MILES
FROM LONDON

ALNE — — — $199\frac{1}{4}$

11

ALNE

"UP" SIDE OF LINE
TO LONDON

LEVEL

10

TOLLERTON — — — $197\frac{3}{4}$

ALDWARK

YOULTON

9

River Ure

River Kyle

footbridge

HALF WAY SIGN

8

HALF WAY BETWEEN
LONDON & EDINBURGH

LEVEL

A NEW SERIES OF MILEPOSTS COMMENCES AT YORK. THEY ARE LOCATED ON THE "DOWN" SIDE OF THE LINE, AS SHOWN, AND ARE NUMBERED FROM ZERO AT YORK TO 80 AT NEWCASTLE.

MILEPOSTS

7

Level crossing

NEWTON-
UPON-OUSE

6

BENINGBROUGH — — — $193\frac{1}{2}$

From Poppleton Junction northwards we have over 12 miles of dead level and dead straight track, and high speeds are usual. Close to milepost 8 we reach a point half-way between London and our destination, Edinburgh, and a large railside sign has been erected at this spot.

5

ELECTRIC COLOUR LIGHT SIGNALS ARE IN OPERATION ON THIS SECTION FROM POPPLETON JUNCT. NORTHWARDS.

4

to Harrogate

River Ouse

3

Skelton Bridge

Approaching York, and glancing left, we see the enormous signal box which controls the loco: yard to the south of the Station. York Station platforms are sharply curved and over 500 yards long, and trains have to be despatched by a system of electric signals, the driver being entirely out of sight of more than half his train, due to the curve. On the guard operating one switch, and a platform official another, a starting indicator is illuminated enabling the train to start. Leaving York, we pass through a mile of crowded marshalling and loco: yards.

2

to Whitby

POPPLETON
JUNCTION

sidings

Water Wks:

LEVEL

River Foss

1

LINE FALLS
1:571

Marshalling
and Loco: Yds:

MAP 16

SPEED RESTRICTION
20 M.P.H.

YORK — 188

LEVEL

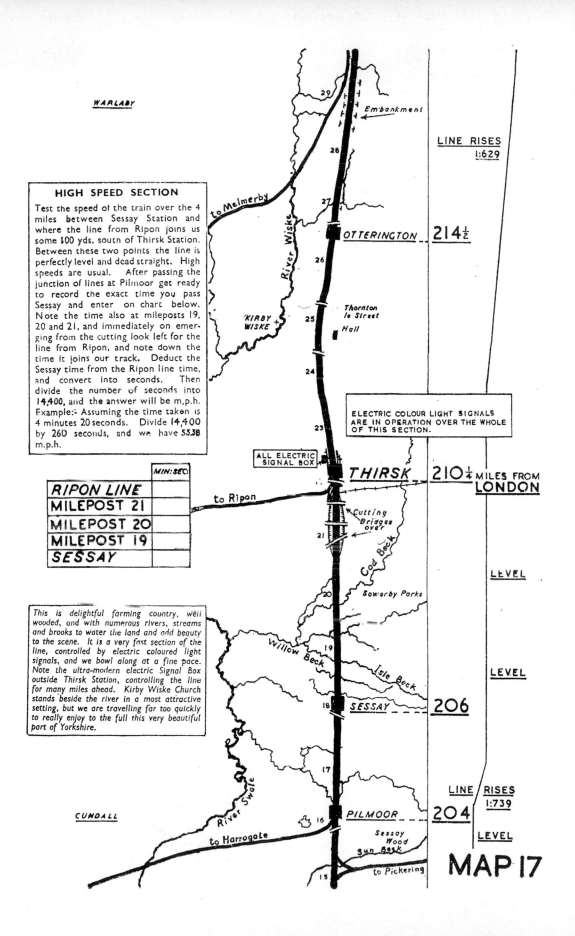

WARLABY

HIGH SPEED SECTION

Test the speed of the train over the 4 miles between Sessay Station and where the line from Ripon joins us some 100 yds. south of Thirsk Station. Between these two points the line is perfectly level and dead straight. High speeds are usual. After passing the junction of lines at Pilmoor get ready to record the exact time you pass Sessay and enter on chart below. Note the time also at mileposts 19, 20 and 21, and immediately on emerging from the cutting look left for the line from Ripon, and note down the time it joins our track. Deduct the Sessay time from the Ripon line time, and convert into seconds. Then divide the number of seconds into 14,400, and the answer will be m.p.h. Example:- Assuming the time taken is 4 minutes 20 seconds. Divide 14,400 by 260 seconds, and we have 55.38 m.p.h.

	MIN: SEC.
RIPON LINE	
MILEPOST 21	
MILEPOST 20	
MILEPOST 19	
SESSAY	

This is delightful farming country, well wooded, and with numerous rivers, streams and brooks to water the land and add beauty to the scene. It is a very fast section of the line, controlled by electric coloured light signals, and we bowl along at a fine pace. Note the ultra-modern electric Signal Box outside Thirsk Station, controlling the line for many miles ahead. Kirby Wiske Church stands beside the river in a most attractive setting, but we are travelling far too quickly to really enjoy to the full this very beautiful part of Yorkshire.

to Melmerby

River Wiske

KIRBY WISKE

Embankment

LINE RISES 1:629

OTTERINGTON 214½

Thornton le Street Hall

ELECTRIC COLOUR LIGHT SIGNALS ARE IN OPERATION OVER THE WHOLE OF THIS SECTION.

ALL ELECTRIC SIGNAL BOX

THIRSK 210¼ MILES FROM LONDON

to Ripon

Cutting Bridges over

Cod Beck

LEVEL

Sowerby Parks

Willow Beck

Isle Beck

LEVEL

SESSAY 206

River Swale

CUNDALL

to Harrogate

LINE RISES 1:739

PILMOOR 204

Sessay Wood Sun Beck

LEVEL

to Pickering

MAP 17

37

Spotting the Mileposts

Where are we now? The pleasures of a railway journey will be immensely increased if, at any given moment, we can tell to a nicety our exact position, and how far it is to the next water-troughs, the next river, junction or Station. Also the exact speed at which we are travelling.

By law, Railway Companies are required to place mile posts alongside the track every $\frac{1}{4}$ mile throughout the system, and exactly where to look for these posts is shown on every map in this book. $\frac{1}{4}$, $\frac{1}{2}$ and $\frac{3}{4}$ posts are omitted but every actual mile post is indicated. They are easily seen, and only at very high speeds will any difficulty be experienced in spotting the clearly numbered posts.

Numbering is effected in four distinct sections and, except between Berwick and Edinburgh, all the posts are on the "down" side of the line—that is, on our left hand side travelling north. Starting at zero at Kings Cross the numbers add up until we reach post 188 at York. Here another series begins numbered from zero at York to 80 at Newcastle. Newcastle starts a third series from zero to 67 at Berwick. Between Berwick and Edinburgh the posts are placed on the opposite side of the line, the "up" side, and are numbered in reverse order from 57 near Berwick down to zero at Edinburgh. The maps in this book show milepost positions as accurately as the scale will allow. By spotting the mileposts we can ascertain and check the speed of the train to very fine limits. The method of so doing is explained on all maps herein where really high speeds are to be expected.

Average Speeds

Attention is drawn to the Charts on pages 5, 13 and 27, which indicate normal express running times between principal Stations.

By checking actual times against those printed, and making entries in column 4, the passenger is able to tell whether his train running early, late, or to time. Great interest can be added to the journey by comparing the actual average speeds of the train against those given in the Charts.

On Other Pages

SEMAPHORE SIGNALS

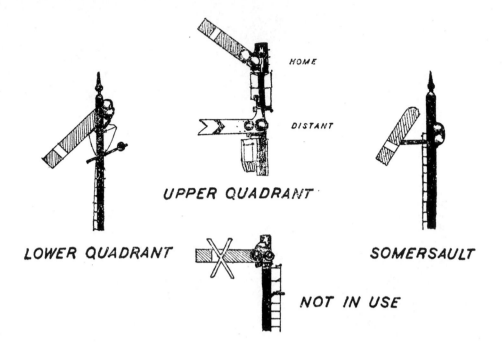

HOME

DISTANT

UPPER QUADRANT

LOWER QUADRANT

NOT IN USE

SOMERSAULT

COLOUR LIGHT SIGNALS

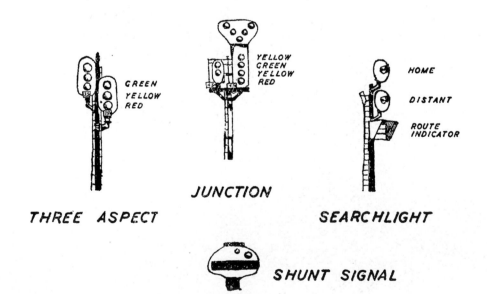

GREEN
YELLOW
RED

YELLOW
GREEN
YELLOW
RED

HOME

DISTANT

ROUTE
INDICATOR

THREE ASPECT

JUNCTION

SEARCHLIGHT

SHUNT SIGNAL

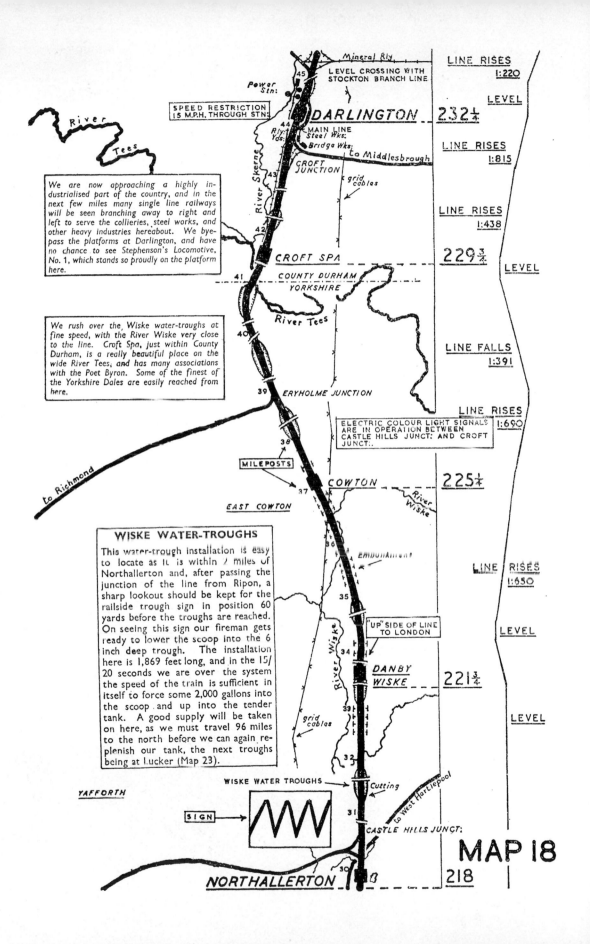

River Tees

Mineral Rly.

LEVEL CROSSING WITH
STOCKTON BRANCH LINE

Power Stn.

45

SPEED RESTRICTION
15 M.P.H. THROUGH STN.

DARLINGTON

44 Rly. Yds.
Steel Wks.
MAIN LINE
Bridge Wks.
to Middlesbrough

River Skerne

43

CROFT JUNCTION

grid cables

We are now approaching a highly industrialised part of the country, and in the next few miles many single line railways will be seen branching away to right and left to serve the collieries, steel works, and other heavy industries hereabout. We bye-pass the platforms at Darlington, and have no chance to see Stephenson's Locomotive, No. 1, which stands so proudly on the platform here.

42

CROFT SPA

41

COUNTY DURHAM
YORKSHIRE

River Tees

We rush over the Wiske water-troughs at fine speed, with the River Wiske very close to the line. Croft Spa, just within County Durham, is a really beautiful place on the wide River Tees, and has many associations with the Poet Byron. Some of the finest of the Yorkshire Dales are easily reached from here.

40

39   ERYHOLME JUNCTION

ELECTRIC COLOUR LIGHT SIGNALS
ARE IN OPERATION BETWEEN
CASTLE HILLS JUNCT: AND CROFT
JUNCT:.

38

to Richmond

MILEPOSTS

37   COWTON

EAST COWTON

River Wiske

36

Embankment

WISKE WATER-TROUGHS

This water-trough installation is easy to locate as it is within 7 miles of Northallerton and, after passing the junction of the line from Ripon, a sharp lookout should be kept for the railside trough sign in position 60 yards before the troughs are reached. On seeing this sign our fireman gets ready to lower the scoop into the 6 inch deep trough. The installation here is 1,869 feet long, and in the 15/20 seconds we are over the system the speed of the train is sufficient in itself to force some 2,000 gallons into the scoop and up into the tender tank. A good supply will be taken on here, as we must travel 96 miles to the north before we can again replenish our tank, the next troughs being at Lucker (Map 23).

35

River Wiske

"UP" SIDE OF LINE
TO LONDON

34

DANBY WISKE

33

grid cables

32

YAFFORTH

WISKE WATER TROUGHS

Cutting

To West Hartlepool

SIGN

31

CASTLE HILLS JUNCT:

30

NORTHALLERTON

LINE RISES
1:220

LEVEL

232¼

LINE RISES
1:815

LINE RISES
1:438

229¾

LEVEL

LINE FALLS
1:391

LINE RISES
1:690

225¼

LINE RISES
1:650

LEVEL

221¾

LEVEL

MAP 18

218

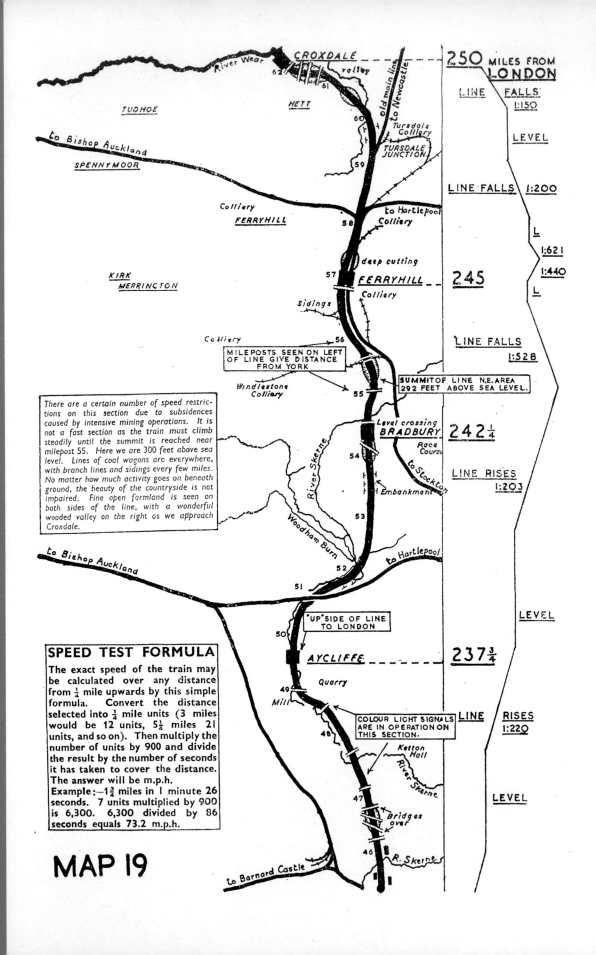

CROXDALE

River Wear

valley

old main line
to Newcastle

250 MILES FROM LONDON

LINE FALLS 1:150

TUDHOE

HETT

62

61

60

Tursdale Colliery

LEVEL

to Bishop Auckland

SPENNYMOOR

59

TURSDALE JUNCTION

LINE FALLS 1:200

Colliery
FERRYHILL

58

to Hartlepool Colliery

L 1:621

1:440

KIRK MERRINGTON

deep cutting

57

FERRYHILL

245

Colliery

L

Sidings

Colliery

56

MILEPOSTS SEEN ON LEFT OF LINE GIVE DISTANCE FROM YORK

LINE FALLS 1:528

Windlestone Colliery

55

SUMMIT OF LINE N.E. AREA 292 FEET ABOVE SEA LEVEL.

There are a certain number of speed restrictions on this section due to subsidences caused by intensive mining operations. It is not a fast section as the train must climb steadily until the summit is reached near milepost 55. Here we are 300 feet above sea level. Lines of coal wagons are everywhere, with branch lines and sidings every few miles. No matter how much activity goes on beneath ground, the beauty of the countryside is not impaired. Fine open farmland is seen on both sides of the line, with a wonderful wooded valley on the right as we approach Croxdale.

Level crossing
BRADBURY

242¼

Race Course

River Skerne

54

to Stockton

LINE RISES 1:203

Embankment

53

Woodham Burn

to Bishop Auckland

52

to Hartlepool

51

"UP" SIDE OF LINE TO LONDON

LEVEL

50

SPEED TEST FORMULA

The exact speed of the train may be calculated over any distance from ¼ mile upwards by this simple formula. Convert the distance selected into ¼ mile units (3 miles would be 12 units, 5¼ miles 21 units, and so on). Then multiply the number of units by 900 and divide the result by the number of seconds it has taken to cover the distance. The answer will be m.p.h.

Example:—1¾ miles in 1 minute 26 seconds. 7 units multiplied by 900 is 6,300. 6,300 divided by 86 seconds equals 73.2 m.p.h.

AYCLIFFE

237¾

Quarry

49

Mill

48

COLOUR LIGHT SIGNALS ARE IN OPERATION ON THIS SECTION.

LINE RISES 1:220

Ketton Hall

River Skerne

47

Bridges over

LEVEL

46

R. Skerne

MAP 19

to Barnard Castle

42

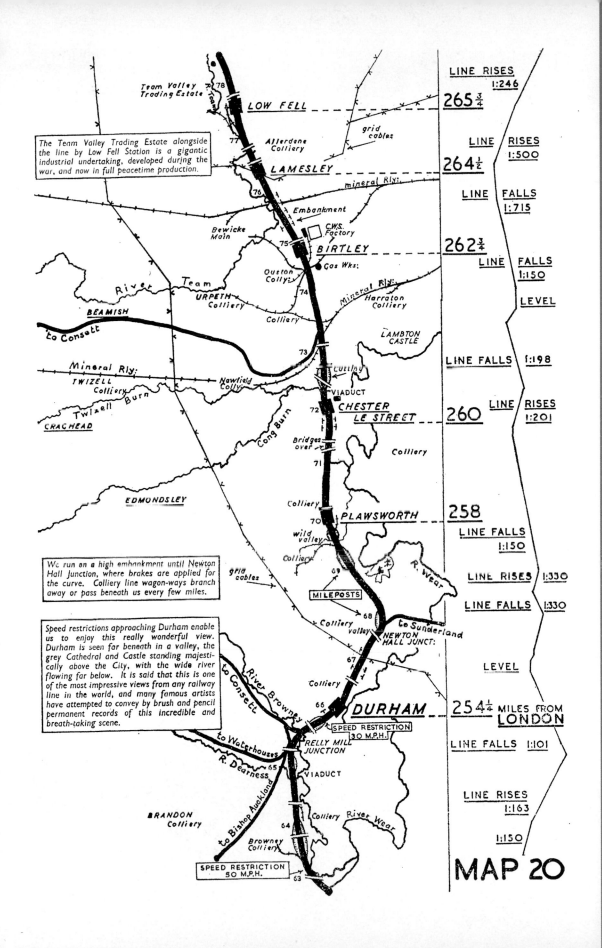

LINE RISES
1:246

265¾ LOW FELL

LINE RISES
1:500

264½ LAMESLEY

LINE FALLS
1:715

262¾ BIRTLEY

LINE FALLS
1:150

LEVEL

LINE FALLS 1:198

260 CHESTER LE STREET

LINE RISES
1:201

258 PLAWSWORTH

LINE FALLS
1:150

LINE RISES 1:330

LINE FALLS 1:330

LEVEL

254¼ MILES FROM
LONDON

LINE FALLS 1:101

LINE RISES
1:163

1:150

78
77
76
75
74
73
72
71
70
69
68
67
66
65
64
63

Team Valley Trading Estate

Allerdene Colliery

grid cables

mineral Rly.

Embankment

C.W.S. Factory

Bewicke Main

Ouston Colly.

Gas Wks.

URPETH COLLIERY

Colliery

Mineral Rly.

Harraton Colliery

LAMBTON CASTLE

River Team

BEAMISH

to Consett

Mineral Rly.
TWIZELL Colliery

Twizell Burn

CRAGHEAD

Nawfield Colly.

cutting

VIADUCT

Cong Burn

Bridges over

Colliery

EDMONDSLEY

Colliery

wild valley

Colliery

grid cables

MILEPOSTS

Colliery valley

to Sunderland

NEWTON HALL JUNCT.

Colliery

to Consett

River Browney

Colliery

DURHAM

to Waterhouses

R. Dearness

RELLY MILL JUNCTION

SPEED RESTRICTION 30 M.P.H.

VIADUCT

BRANDON Colliery

to Bishop Auckland

Colliery

River Wear

Browney Colliery

SPEED RESTRICTION 50 M.P.H.

The Team Valley Trading Estate alongside the line by Low Fell Station is a gigantic industrial undertaking, developed during the war, and now in full peacetime production.

We run on a high embankment until Newton Hall Junction, where brakes are applied for the curve. Colliery line wagon-ways branch away or pass beneath us every few miles.

Speed restrictions approaching Durham enable us to enjoy this really wonderful view. Durham is seen far beneath in a valley, the grey Cathedral and Castle standing majestically above the City, with the wide river flowing far below. It is said that this is one of the most impressive views from any railway line in the world, and many famous artists have attempted to convey by brush and pencil permanent records of this incredible and breath-taking scene.

MAP 20

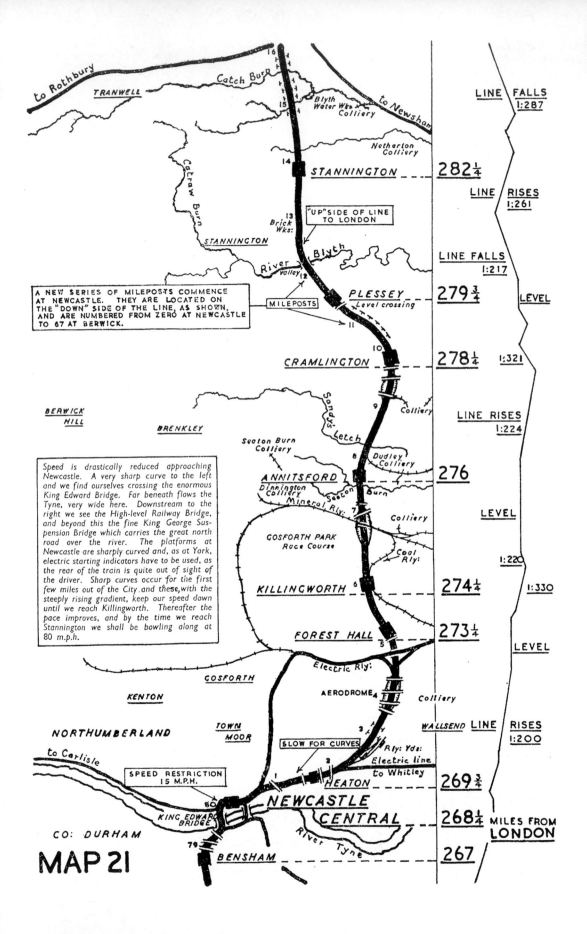

LINE FALLS
1:287

LINE RISES
1:261

to Rothbury

TRANWELL

Catch Burn

Blyth
Water Wks
Colliery

to Newsham

Netherton
Colliery

16

15

14

STANNINGTON — 282¼

Catraw Burn

13

Brick
Wks:

"UP" SIDE OF LINE
TO LONDON

STANNINGTON

River Blyth

valley 12

MILEPOSTS

A NEW SERIES OF MILEPOSTS COMMENCE
AT NEWCASTLE. THEY ARE LOCATED ON
THE "DOWN" SIDE OF THE LINE, AS SHOWN,
AND ARE NUMBERED FROM ZERO AT NEWCASTLE
TO 67 AT BERWICK.

PLESSEY — 279¾
Level crossing

LINE FALLS
1:217

LEVEL

11

10

CRAMLINGTON — 278¼

1:321

BERWICK
HILL

BRENKLEY

Seaton Burn
Colliery

Sandy's Letch

9

Colliery

LINE RISES
1:224

8

Dudley
Colliery

276

ANNITSFORD

Dinnington
Colliery

Mineral Rly.

Seaton Burn

7

LEVEL

Speed is drastically reduced approaching
Newcastle. A very sharp curve to the left
and we find ourselves crossing the enormous
King Edward Bridge. Far beneath flows the
Tyne, very wide here. Downstream to the
right we see the High-level Railway Bridge,
and beyond this the fine King George Sus-
pension Bridge which carries the great north
road over the river. The platforms at
Newcastle are sharply curved and, as at York,
electric starting indicators have to be used, as
the rear of the train is quite out of sight of
the driver. Sharp curves occur for the first
few miles out of the City, and these, with the
steeply rising gradient, keep our speed down
until we reach Killingworth. Thereafter the
pace improves, and by the time we reach
Stannington we shall be bowling along at
80 m.p.h.

Colliery

GOSFORTH PARK
Race Course

Coal
Rly.

1:220

KILLINGWORTH 6 — 274¼

1:330

FOREST HALL — 273¼

5

LEVEL

Electric Rly.

GOSFORTH

KENTON

TOWN
MOOR

AERODROME 4

Colliery

NORTHUMBERLAND

SLOW FOR CURVES

3

WALLSEND

LINE RISES
1:200

to Carlisle

2

Rly: Yds:
Electric line
to Whitley

SPEED RESTRICTION
15 M.P.H.

1

HEATON — 269¾

80

NEWCASTLE

KING EDWARD
BRIDGE

CENTRAL — 268¼ MILES FROM LONDON

CO: DURHAM

79

River Tyne

MAP 21

BENSHAM — 267

LONDON—EDINBURGH

EXACT DISTANCES BETWEEN STATIONS—EXPRESS TRAIN RUNNING TIMES

(1)	(2)		(3)	(4)			(5)
STATION	Distance Between Stations		Express Train Running Times	Actual Running Times			NOTES and Average Speeds over each Section
	Miles	Yards	Minutes	Minutes	Early	Late	
NEWCASTLE to MORPETH	16	1,100	28				From a standing start, we commence slowly, and for several miles our speed is restricted by curves. Rising gradients for 10 miles keep down our progress. High speeds are attained after Cramlington, but we must slow down for the curve at Morpeth. *Average 35.5 m.p.h.* (See Maps 21 and 22.)
MORPETH to ALNMOUTH	18	418	20				This is quite a fast section, particularly between Widdrington and Acklington, and on testing we shall find we are travelling at nearer 80 than 70 m.p.h. We average 54.7 m.p.h. over this 18¼ miles. (See Maps 22 and 23.)
ALNMOUTH to BELFORD	16	1,385	18				After climbing for 4 miles we make fine speed down the 1:150 gradient and pass over the Lucker Water-troughs at nearly 70 m.p.h., maintaining this speed to Belford. *Average speed 55.8 m.p.h.* (See Maps 23 and 24.)
BELFORD to BERWICK	15	616	18				The line falls all the way to Goswick and we make fine speed. The approach to Berwick through Tweedmouth and over the Royal Border Bridge is taken very slowly. (*Average speed 51.6 m.p.h.* (See Maps 24 and 25.)
BERWICK to RESTON	11	484	17				From a standing start we travel slowly up the 1:190 gradient past the border of England and Scotland. Once over the summit, near Ayton, we make fine progress. *Average speed only 39.7 m.p.h.* (See Map 25.)
RESTON to DUNBAR	17	—	21				Speed is not high for the first 5 miles of this section due to the rising gradients, but it is very high from Penmanshiel tunnel onwards. We approach Dunbar slowly. *Average speed 48.5 m.p.h.* (See Maps 25 and 26.)
DUNBAR to DREM	11	880	13				Although the gradients are not favourable, this is, nevertheless, a fast 11½ miles, and we average 53 m.p.h. (See Maps 26 and 27.)
DREM to WAVERLEY	17	1,320	30				Speed is high as far as Inveresk, but from here we slow down considerably as we approach Edinburgh. We climb a severe 1:98 gradient over the last 1¾ miles. *Average speed works out at 35.5 m.p.h.* (See Maps 27 and 28.)

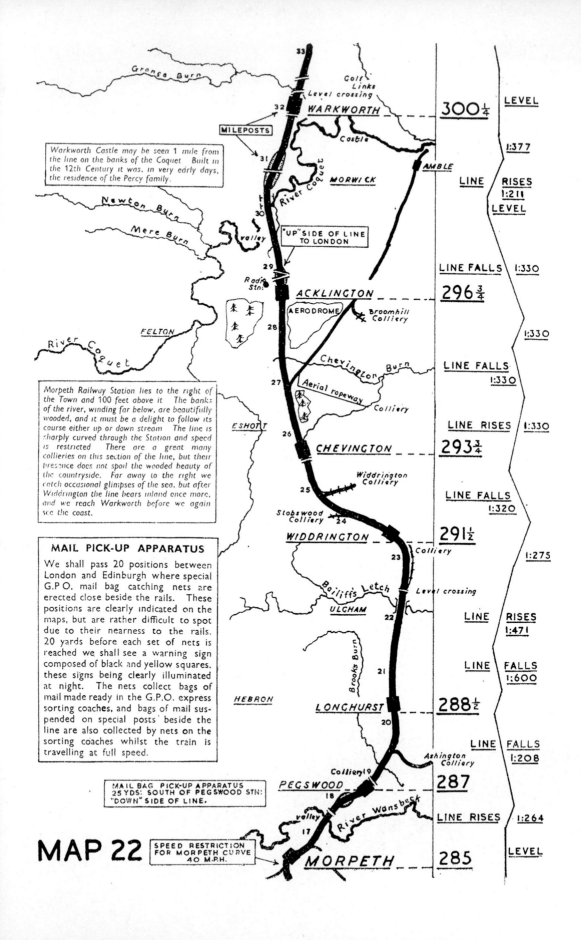

Grange Burn

33

Golf Links

Level crossing

WARKWORTH — 300¼ — LEVEL

32

MILEPOSTS

1:377

Warkworth Castle may be seen 1 mile from the line on the banks of the Coquet. Built in the 12th Century it was, in very early days, the residence of the Percy family.

Castle

31

Newton Burn

Mere Burn

MORWICK

AMBLE

LINE RISES 1:211

River Coquet

30

valley

LEVEL

"UP" SIDE OF LINE TO LONDON

29

Radio Stn.

LINE FALLS 1:330

ACKLINGTON — 296¾

FELTON

River Coquet

28

AERODROME

Broomhill Colliery

1:330

Chevington Burn

LINE FALLS 1:330

27

Aerial ropeway

Colliery

ESHOTT

26

LINE RISES 1:330

CHEVINGTON — 293¾

Morpeth Railway Station lies to the right of the Town and 100 feet above it. The banks of the river, winding far below, are beautifully wooded, and it must be a delight to follow its course either up or down stream. The line is sharply curved through the Station and speed is restricted. There are a great many collieries on this section of the line, but their presence does not spoil the wooded beauty of the countryside. Far away to the right we catch occasional glimpses of the sea, but after Widdrington the line bears inland once more, and we reach Warkworth before we again see the coast.

Widdrington Colliery

25

LINE FALLS 1:320

Stobswood Colliery

24

WIDDRINGTON — 291½

23

Colliery

1:275

MAIL PICK-UP APPARATUS

We shall pass 20 positions between London and Edinburgh where special G.P.O. mail bag catching nets are erected close beside the rails. These positions are clearly indicated on the maps, but are rather difficult to spot due to their nearness to the rails. 20 yards before each set of nets is reached we shall see a warning sign composed of black and yellow squares, these signs being clearly illuminated at night. The nets collect bags of mail made ready in the G.P.O. express sorting coaches, and bags of mail suspended on special posts beside the line are also collected by nets on the sorting coaches whilst the train is travelling at full speed.

Bailiffs Letch

Level crossing

ULGHAM

22

LINE RISES 1:471

Brooks Burn

21

LINE FALLS 1:600

HEBRON

LONGHURST — 288½

20

LINE FALLS 1:208

Ashington Colliery

MAIL BAG PICK-UP APPARATUS 25 YDS. SOUTH OF PEGSWOOD STN: "DOWN" SIDE OF LINE.

Colliery 19

PEGSWOOD — 287

18

valley

17

River Wansbeck

LINE RISES 1:264

MAP 22

SPEED RESTRICTION FOR MORPETH CURVE 40 M.P.H.

MORPETH — 285

LEVEL

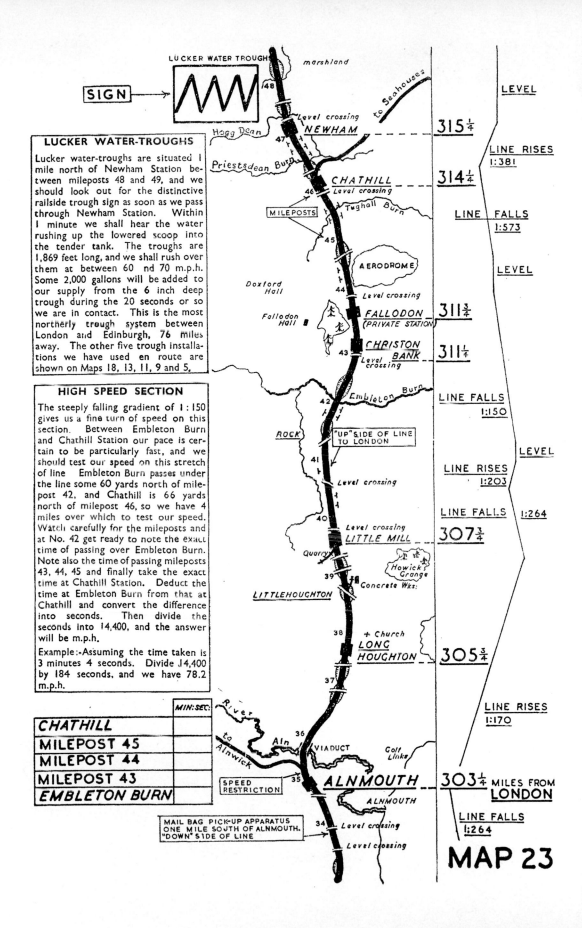

SIGN → LUCKER WATER TROUGHS

LUCKER WATER-TROUGHS

Lucker water-troughs are situated 1 mile north of Newham Station between mileposts 48 and 49, and we should look out for the distinctive railside trough sign as soon as we pass through Newham Station. Within 1 minute we shall hear the water rushing up the lowered scoop into the tender tank. The troughs are 1,869 feet long, and we shall rush over them at between 60 nd 70 m.p.h. Some 2,000 gallons will be added to our supply from the 6 inch deep trough during the 20 seconds or so we are in contact. This is the most northerly trough system between London and Edinburgh, 76 miles away. The other five trough installations we have used en route are shown on Maps 18, 13, 11, 9 and 5.

HIGH SPEED SECTION

The steeply falling gradient of 1 : 150 gives us a fine turn of speed on this section. Between Embleton Burn and Chathill Station our pace is certain to be particularly fast, and we should test our speed on this stretch of line. Embleton Burn passes under the line some 60 yards north of milepost 42, and Chathill is 66 yards north of milepost 46, so we have 4 miles over which to test our speed. Watch carefully for the mileposts and at No. 42 get ready to note the exact time of passing over Embleton Burn. Note also the time of passing mileposts 43, 44, 45 and finally take the exact time at Chathill Station. Deduct the time at Embleton Burn from that at Chathill and convert the difference into seconds. Then divide the seconds into 14,400, and the answer will be m.p.h.

Example:- Assuming the time taken is 3 minutes 4 seconds. Divide 14,400 by 184 seconds, and we have 78.2 m.p.h.

	MIN : SEC.
CHATHILL	
MILEPOST 45	
MILEPOST 44	
MILEPOST 43	
EMBLETON BURN	

MAP 23

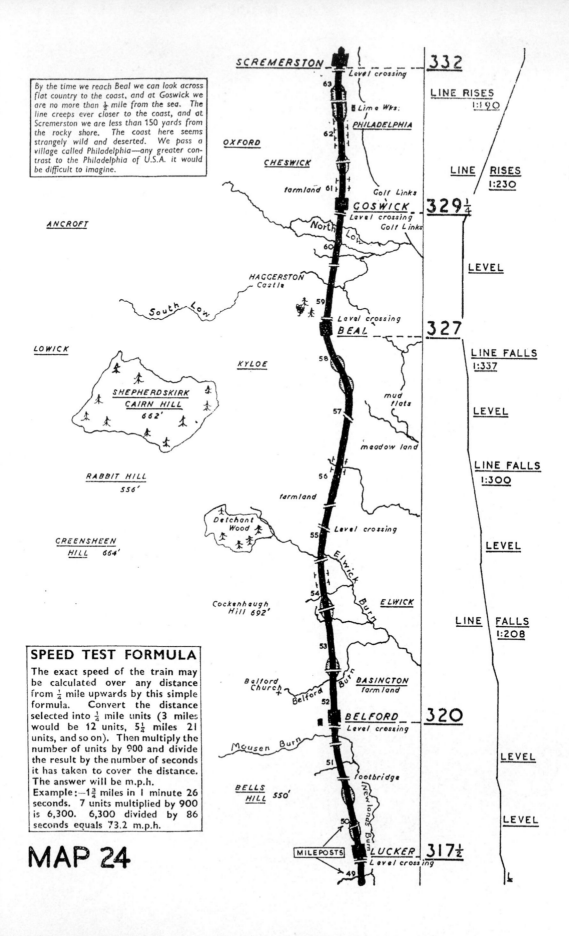

By the time we reach Beal we can look across flat country to the coast, and at Goswick we are no more than ½ mile from the sea. The line creeps ever closer to the coast, and at Scremerston we are less than 150 yards from the rocky shore. The coast here seems strangely wild and deserted. We pass a village called Philadelphia—any greater contrast to the Philadelphia of U.S.A. it would be difficult to imagine.

SCREMERSTON — 332
Level crossing
63
LINE RISES
1:190
Lime Wks.
PHILADELPHIA
62
OXFORD
CHESWICK
LINE RISES
1:230
farmland 61
Golf Links
GOSWICK — 329¼
Level crossing
Golf Links
ANCROFT
North Low
60
LEVEL
HAGGERSTON
Castle
South Low
59
Level crossing
BEAL — 327
58
LINE FALLS
1:337
LOWICK
KYLOE
57
mud flats
SHEPHERDSKIRK
CAIRN HILL
662'
LEVEL
meadow land
56
LINE FALLS
1:300
RABBIT HILL
556'
farmland
Detchant Wood
55
Level crossing
GREENSHEEN
HILL 664'
Elwick
LEVEL
54
Cockenheugh
Hill 692'
ELWICK
Elwick Burn
53
LINE FALLS
1:208

SPEED TEST FORMULA

The exact speed of the train may be calculated over any distance from ¼ mile upwards by this simple formula. Convert the distance selected into ¼ mile units (3 miles would be 12 units, 5¼ miles 21 units, and so on). Then multiply the number of units by 900 and divide the result by the number of seconds it has taken to cover the distance. The answer will be m.p.h.
Example:—1¾ miles in 1 minute 26 seconds. 7 units multiplied by 900 is 6,300. 6,300 divided by 86 seconds equals 73.2 m.p.h.

Belford Church
Belford Burn
BASINGTON
farmland
52
BELFORD — 320
Level crossing
Mousen Burn
51
LEVEL
footbridge
BELLS HILL 550'
Newlands Burn
50
LEVEL
MILEPOSTS
LUCKER — 317½
Level crossing
49

MAP 24

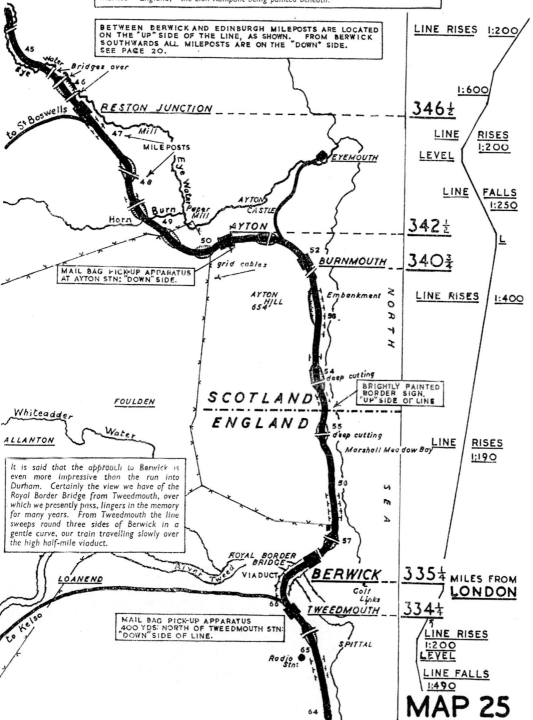

THE BORDER

Three miles north of Berwick, between mileposts 54 and 55, a brightly painted sign indicates the exact position of the boundary between England and Scotland. The sign is placed against a low stone wall on the "up" side of the line, and is easily visible from the train. Deep cuttings occur both to the north and south of the boundary, momentarily spoiling our view of the sea. On emerging into the clear from either cutting we should keep a sharp look out. On one side of the sign is painted the Scottish Unicorn, with above an arm marked "Scotland," pointing northwards. The other side shows a similar arm pointing southwards marked "England," the Lion Rampant being painted beneath.

BETWEEN BERWICK AND EDINBURGH MILEPOSTS ARE LOCATED ON THE "UP" SIDE OF THE LINE, AS SHOWN. FROM BERWICK SOUTHWARDS ALL MILEPOSTS ARE ON THE "DOWN" SIDE. SEE PAGE 20.

LINE RISES 1:200

1:600

RESTON JUNCTION — 346½

LINE RISES 1:200

LINE LEVEL

LINE FALLS 1:250

EYEMOUTH

AYTON CASTLE

Burn — Horn 49

Paper Mill

AYTON — 342½

52 — BURNMOUTH — 340¾

AYTON HILL 654

Embankment — LINE RISES 1:400

53

grid cables

MAIL BAG PICK-UP APPARATUS AT AYTON STN: "DOWN" SIDE.

NORTH

54 deep cutting

BRIGHTLY PAINTED BORDER SIGN. "UP" SIDE OF LINE

FOULDEN

SCOTLAND
ENGLAND

55 deep cutting

Marshall Meadow Bay — LINE RISES 1:190

Whiteadder

ALLANTON — Water

56

S E A

It is said that the approach to Berwick is even more impressive than the run into Durham. Certainly the view we have of the Royal Border Bridge from Tweedmouth, over which we presently pass, lingers in the memory for many years. From Tweedmouth the line sweeps round three sides of Berwick in a gentle curve, our train travelling slowly over the high half-mile viaduct.

57

ROYAL BORDER BRIDGE

LOANEND — River Tweed — VIADUCT

BERWICK — 335¼ MILES FROM LONDON

Golf Links

to Kelso

66 — TWEEDMOUTH — 334¼

LINE RISES 1:200

LEVEL

MAIL BAG PICK-UP APPARATUS 400 YDS. NORTH OF TWEEDMOUTH STN: "DOWN" SIDE OF LINE.

SPITTAL

65 — Radio Stn:

LINE FALLS 1:490

64

MAP 25

49

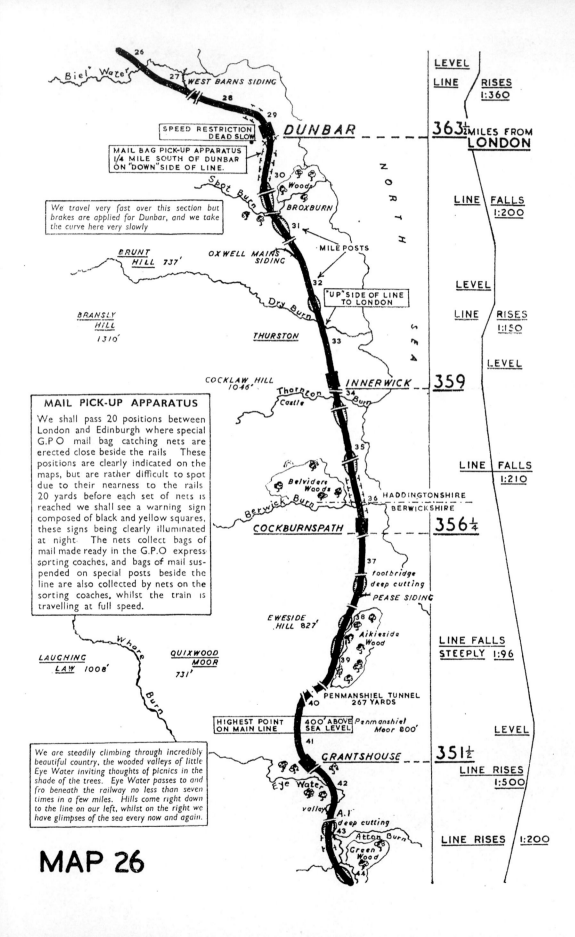

Biel' Water

26

27 WEST BARNS SIDING

28

29

DUNBAR

SPEED RESTRICTION
DEAD SLOW

MAIL BAG PICK-UP APPARATUS
1/4 MILE SOUTH OF DUNBAR
ON 'DOWN' SIDE OF LINE.

30

Woods

BROXBURN

Spot Burn

We travel very fast over this section but
brakes are applied for Dunbar, and we take
the curve here very slowly

31

BRUNT
HILL 737'

OXWELL MAINS
SIDING

MILE POSTS

32

BRANSLY
HILL
1310'

Dry Burn

THURSTON

33

'UP' SIDE OF LINE
TO LONDON

COCKLAW HILL
1046'

Thornton
Castle

INNERWICK

34

Burn

35

MAIL PICK-UP APPARATUS

We shall pass 20 positions between
London and Edinburgh where special
G.P.O mail bag catching nets are
erected close beside the rails These
positions are clearly indicated on the
maps, but are rather difficult to spot
due to their nearness to the rails
20 yards before each set of nets is
reached we shall see a warning sign
composed of black and yellow squares,
these signs being clearly illuminated
at night· The nets collect bags of
mail made ready in the G.P.O express
sorting coaches, and bags of mail suspended on special posts beside the
line are also collected by nets on the
sorting coaches, whilst the train is
travelling at full speed.

Belvidere
Woods

Berwick Burn

36

HADDINGTONSHIRE
BERWICKSHIRE

COCKBURNSPATH

37

footbridge

deep cutting

PEASE SIDING

EWESIDE
HILL 827'

38

Aikieside
Wood

39

LAUGHING
LAW 1008'

QUIXWOOD
MOOR
731'

Whare Burn

PENMANSHIEL TUNNEL
267 YARDS

40

HIGHEST POINT
ON MAIN LINE

400' ABOVE
SEA LEVEL

Penmanshiel
Moor 800'

41

We are steadily climbing through incredibly
beautiful country, the wooded valleys of little
Eye Water inviting thoughts of picnics in the
shade of the trees. Eye Water passes to and
fro beneath the railway no less than seven
times in a few miles. Hills come right down
to the line on our left, whilst on the right we
have glimpses of the sea every now and again.

GRANTSHOUSE

Eye Water

42

valley

A.1
deep cutting

43

Atton Burn

Green
Wood

44

MAP 26

LEVEL

LINE RISES
1:360

363¾ MILES FROM
LONDON

LINE FALLS
1:200

LEVEL

LINE RISES
1:150

LEVEL

359

LINE FALLS
1:210

356¼

LINE FALLS
STEEPLY 1:96

LEVEL

351½

LINE RISES
1:500

LINE RISES 1:200

N
O
R
T
H

S
E
A

50

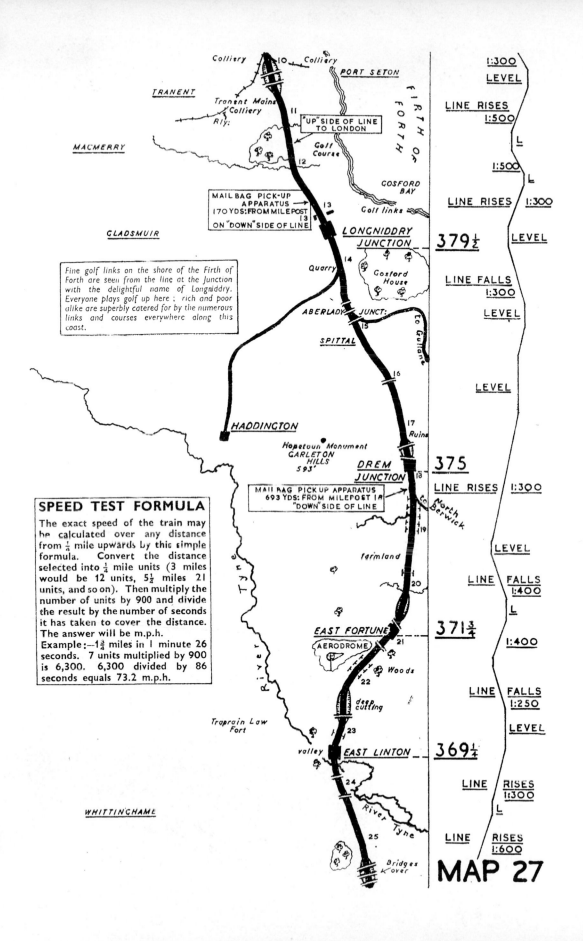

Colliery Colliery

TRANENT

PORT SETON

FIRTH OF FORTH

MACMERRY

Tranent Mains Colliery Rly.

"UP" SIDE OF LINE TO LONDON

Golf Course

GLADSMUIR

MAIL BAG PICK-UP APPARATUS
170 YDS: FROM MILE POST
ON "DOWN" SIDE OF LINE

GOSFORD BAY

Golf links

LONGNIDDRY JUNCTION

Fine golf links on the shore of the Firth of Forth are seen from the line at the Junction with the delightful name of Longniddry. Everyone plays golf up here; rich and poor alike are superbly catered for by the numerous links and courses everywhere along this coast.

Quarry

Gosford House

ABERLADY JUNCT:

to Gullane

SPITTAL

HADDINGTON

Hopetoun Monument
GARLETON HILLS
593'

DREM JUNCTION

Ruins

MAIL BAG PICK UP APPARATUS
693 YDS: FROM MILEPOST 18
"DOWN" SIDE OF LINE

to North Berwick

SPEED TEST FORMULA

The exact speed of the train may be calculated over any distance from $\frac{1}{4}$ mile upwards by this simple formula. Convert the distance selected into $\frac{1}{4}$ mile units (3 miles would be 12 units, $5\frac{1}{4}$ miles 21 units, and so on). Then multiply the number of units by 900 and divide the result by the number of seconds it has taken to cover the distance. The answer will be m.p.h.
Example:—$1\frac{3}{4}$ miles in 1 minute 26 seconds. 7 units multiplied by 900 is 6,300. 6,300 divided by 86 seconds equals 73.2 m.p.h.

River Tyne

farmland

EAST FORTUNE
AERODROME

Woods

deep cutting

Traprain Law Fort

valley EAST LINTON

River Tyne

WHITTINGHAME

Bridges over

MAP 27

1:300
LEVEL
LINE RISES 1:500
L
1:500
L
LINE RISES 1:300
LEVEL

379½

LINE FALLS 1:300
LEVEL

375

LINE RISES 1:300
LEVEL
LINE FALLS 1:400
L

371¾

1:400
LINE FALLS 1:250
LEVEL

369¼

LINE RISES 1:300
L
LINE RISES 1:600

EDINBURGH—When one arrives at Waverley Station one has arrived in Edinburgh—right in Edinburgh. No taxi rides are necessary through dingy streets from the Station to the centre; Waverley Station is the centre. It is as though Kings Cross were at Piccadilly Circus, or Bombay Terminus were on the waterfront. The only Terminus I know to be similarly placed is Central Station in New York; that also is right there. Waverley Station lies deep down in the earth, with Edinburgh rising above on all sides. Climb the granite steps from the platform and one stands in Princes Street in all its glory. Edinburgh is entirely different from any other British City; it is planned differently and built differently. It is incredibly beautiful and dignified, and its natural dignity and atmosphere is reflected right throughout the City and its inhabitants. It is reflected in what the people say and do; in how they dress their shop windows; in how one is received at one's hotel, and how one is served with a bus ticket. If anyone is ever rude or snappy to anyone else in Edinburgh I have yet to experience it. Stroll down the two miles of Princes Street, and note the quiet dignity and solid luxury of the famous shops. Take coffee at Crawford's or Mackie's, and let yourself go on the long low cakes studded with almonds. Note the Banks and Clubs on Princes Street where one ascends steps to gain admittance, and the bookshops off Princes Street with similar steps, except that here one goes down to arrive at the shop door. American visitors will find Edinburgh strangely reminiscent of Philadelphia, with the streets at right angles and the crescents behind with their tall, solid, stone houses. Edinburgh Hotels must be classed as the best in the world. The North British, the Royal British and the Caledonia, to mention only three, receive their visitors with a courtesy and efficiency that, for the moment, seems to be dying out in many cities. One's first visit to Edinburgh is unforgettable, and one always yearns to return. Perhaps it is the soft voices and kind faces of its people, or the feeling of well being one experiences there. Perhaps one gains something from the history steeped atmosphere of the place that so obviously controls the behaviour of its people. Perhaps it is just because it is Scotland.

EDINBURGH

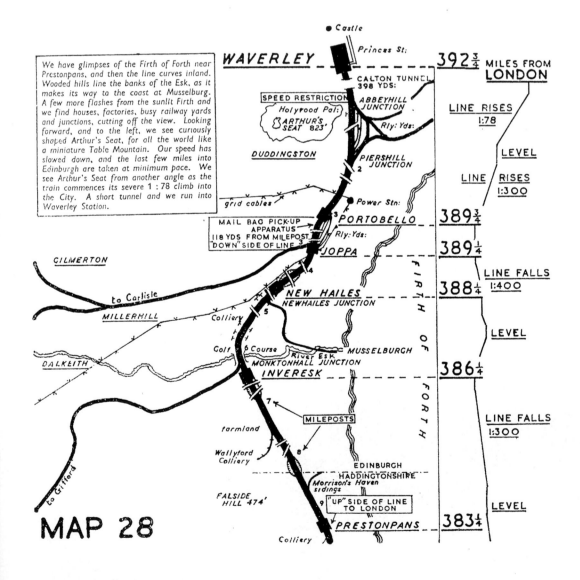

We have glimpses of the Firth of Forth near Prestonpans, and then the line curves inland. Wooded hills line the banks of the Esk, as it makes its way to the coast at Musselburg. A few more flashes from the sunlit Firth and we find houses, factories, busy railway yards and junctions, cutting off the view. Looking forward, and to the left, we see curiously shaped Arthur's Seat, for all the world like a miniature Table Mountain. Our speed has slowed down, and the last few miles into Edinburgh are taken at minimum pace. We see Arthur's Seat from another angle as the train commences its severe 1:78 climb into the City. A short tunnel and we run into Waverley Station.

MAP 28

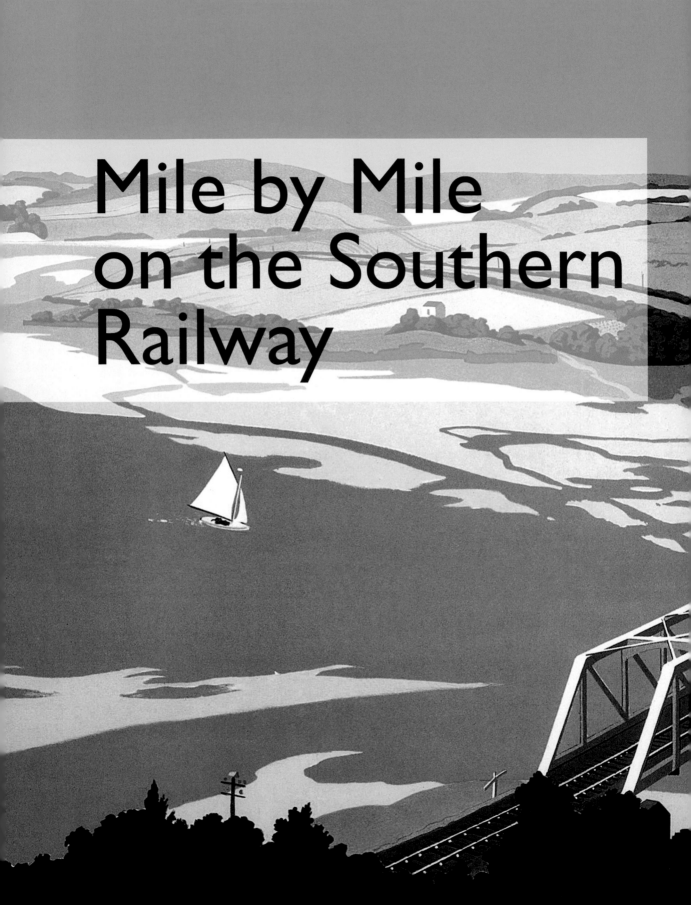

Mile by Mile on the Southern Railway

The Southern Railway Story

Home to the 'Golden Arrow', 'Night Ferry', 'Bournemouth Belle' and the trains that took holidaymakers to the seaside resorts of Kent, Sussex, Hampshire and Dorset, the Southern also carried many thousands to and from work each day, not by steam but by electric power.

Passengers were the principal business of the Southern Railway: tourists heading for the holiday destinations of the South Coast, Devon and Kent; travellers to and from the Channel ports; and a growing army of workers daily commuting into London. It was also an increasingly vociferous army, dissatisfied with unreliability, overcrowded trains and congested stations. For company chairman,

Sir Herbert Walker, the solution lay in two words: Southern Electric. It would be the most ambitious transformation undertaken by any of the 'Big Four' companies.

The smallest of those, both in area and mileage (2,186 route miles; 3,518km), the Southern was formed from three main constituents: the South Eastern & Chatham; the London, Brighton & South Coast; and the London & South Western Railway whose routes from London's Waterloo to south-west England are mapped out in *Mile by Mile*. Stretching from the Thames to the Tamar, the Southern served several major ports: Dover, Folkestone, Newhaven, Portsmouth, Southampton and Weymouth. It embraced the Victorian time capsule that was the railways of the Isle of Wight. At Basingstoke the ex-L&SWR main line divided, with a route to Salisbury and Exeter that threaded its way through the heart of Devon before descending into Plymouth and reaching into north Cornwall. The distinctive spheres of operation seamlessly led to the creation of three divisions within the company: Eastern, Central and Western.

◄ An upper quadrant signal being erected between Motspur Park and Leatherhead in Surrey in June 1936. The area, electrified in 1925, was served by 3SUB (Three-Car Suburban) multiple units like this one. With a centre trailer car flanked by two power cars, their maximum speed was 75mph (120.7kph).

Less seamless was the creation of a senior management. For its first twelve months the chiefs of the old companies rotated control, but by December 1923 the L&SWR's Sir Herbert Walker held primacy. By his retirement in 1937 he had proven himself one of the finest railway managers, not only for his bold venture into electrification but for his awareness of the value of publicity and promotion. In 1925, he made the key appointment of ex-newspaper editor John Elliot as Public Relations Assistant. Elliot would create the Southern's image as 'the holiday line', exploiting everything from colourful posters, evocative-sounding expresses (the 'Atlantic Coast Express', 'Bournemouth Belle') and boat trains (most famously the 'Golden Arrow') to locomotive names and observation cars. But his work was cut out convincing commuters of the qualities of the Southern's suburban services.

Around seventy per cent of the Southern's revenues came from carrying passengers, and increasingly the majority originated in the towns and suburbs south of London. On 27

▲ One of Oliver Bulleid's 'Battle of Britain' Pacifics, no.21C157 (later named *Biggin Hill*) brings the 'Golden Arrow' Pullman boat train out of London's Victoria station and heads for Dover. Following the ferry journey to Calais, SNCF's equivalent 'Flèche d'Or' will convey passengers to Paris Gare du Nord.

January 1925, the company took out newspaper advertisements to explain the problems this was creating and the means of solving them, chief of which was electrification. The system chosen was that introduced by the L&SWR, using a third (conductor) rail, but with the voltage increased from 660 volts to 750V DC. During the 1920s electrification went deep into Kent, Surrey and Sussex. By 1932, the Southern could boast 970 electrified route miles (1,561km) and, that decade, further extended to Brighton, Eastbourne and Portsmouth. It was the world's largest electrified main-line railway network, but the investment came at a price elsewhere.

At the Grouping, the Southern had inherited 2,281 locomotives. They were a mixed bag, with many once excellent engines now ageing and underpowered. This was Richard Maunsell's inheritance upon appointment as Chief Mechanical Engineer, and he would have known that wholesale renewals were out of the question. Maunsell looked at where best to spend his limited resources and, along with adding to a class of 2-6-0 'Moguls' that he had produced for the SE&CR, updated two of Robert Urie's 4-6-0 designs for the L&SWR: the 'S15' freight type and the larger-wheeled express passenger 'N15'. This last class caught the imagination of John Elliot. Recognising that the Southern served the majority of places associated with Arthurian legend, he branded the 'N15' 'King Arthurs.'

Maunsell, however, was determined to fulfil his scheme for a more powerful express passenger 4-6-0, one capable of hauling the heaviest boat trains. In August 1926, no.E850 *Lord Nelson* took the title of 'Britain's most powerful locomotive' (in terms of tractive effort), only for the Great Western to reclaim it within months with its 'King' class. There were two years of trials before the 'Lord Nelson' class was enlarged to sixteen, all named after admirals of the Royal Navy.

Peculiar to the line between Tunbridge Wells and Hastings were unusually narrow tunnels, a challenge that Maunsell met brilliantly. With its tapered profile and compact three cylinder layout, the 'Class V' of 1930 would become the last and most powerful 4-4-0 design to be built in Britain, and it inspired John Elliot to another stroke of public relations genius. He named the forty-strong class 'Schools', beginning with no.900 *Eton* and no.901 *Winchester*, and they proved Maunsell's masterpiece.

Its non-dependence on freight revenues and distance from the most depressed areas saw the Southern emerge from the economic crisis of the 1930s in relatively good health. War halted electrification, but it did lead to the recruitment of something of a maverick as the company's new Chief Mechanical

Engineer. Oliver Bulleid had been Sir Nigel Gresley's assistant on the LNER, and he seized the opportunity presented by the Southern to try out his radical ideas. Somehow bypassing wartime restrictions, he was able to construct two classes of streamlined (officially 'air-smoothed') express passenger Pacifics: the 'Merchant Navies' of 1941 and the lighter 'West Countries' and 'Battle of Britains' of 1945. With their chain-driven valve gear contained in an oil bath, among other innovations, they may have been a fitter's nightmare but they

were outstanding locomotives, still capable of speeds over 100 miles per hour (160.9kph) when finally withdrawn in 1967.

The Southern at War

In their names the 'Merchant Navy' and 'Battle of Britain' classes reflected the impact of war on the Southern Railway. Instead of carrying holidaymakers and Continental travellers to ports and resorts, it now handled troops and military equipment. Goods now accounted for sixty per cent of its traffic as the Southern

▲ Queueing to visit the footplate of 'Lord Nelson' class 4-6-0 no.860 *Lord Hawke* at a railway exhibition at Portsmouth Town Station on 21 October 1933. The 'SPL' headcode indicates that it would be departing later with a special train.

became crucial to the Normandy landings of 1944. Regular bombing attacks, especially on port installations, failed to halt the build-up to invasion, and the company's transformation from passenger carrier to freight hauler was as notable as that from steam to electric traction twenty years earlier.

THE ROUTE OF "MILE BY MILE"

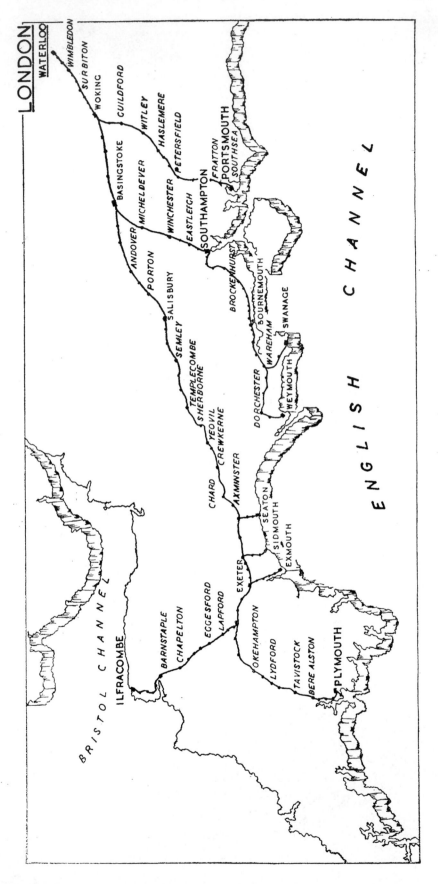

INDEX TO STATIONS & RIVERS PAGE 5.

The Journey

"MILE by MILE"
by
S. N. PIKE, M.B.E.

WATERLOO EDITION
SOUTHERN RAILWAY

A book of some 10,000 words and 27 maps, describing in detail the main line Railway between London and Towns of the South and South-West; showing :—

- GRADIENTS
- MILEAGES
- SPEEDS
- JUNCTIONS
- VIADUCTS
- TUNNELS
- RIVERS and
- ROADS

with an account of features of interest and beauty to be seen from the train.

The Author gratefully acknowledges the assistance received from Officials of the Southern Railway in the preparation of this book.

Published by
STUART N. PIKE,
Worthing, Sussex

SOLE DISTRIBUTORS
To whom all enquiries should be addressed :—
ATLAS PUBLISHING & DISTRIBUTING CO., LTD.,
18, BRIDE LANE, LONDON, E.C.4.

The
Best Railway Book
ever published

This book has been described as the " Best Railway Book ever published." Whether or no it deserves this description is left to the purchaser. Certainly the wealth of detail here collected must give it a high place amongst books about travelling by rail.

The route is through 149 Stations on the Southern Railway, covering the main line between London and the South and South-west. Each page contains a description of the countryside and what is to be seen of interest on that Section. On the right side of each page is data dear to the heart of the railway enthusiast. Gradients, bridges, viaducts and their height, tunnels and their length, junctions, cuttings, speeds, and approximate running times between Stations.

No less than 60 rivers and streams are encountered and named.

It is intended that the book be read whilst actually in the train. It may be commenced at any point of the journey. A glance at the name of the Station just passed, a reference to the Index, and what will be seen between there and the next Station is described. Not only what will be seen, but approximately how long it will take to reach that next Station and at what speed, and on what degree of gradient the train will be either climbing up, or coasting down at that moment.

Small figures indicate the height of the line and that of the surrounding country above sea level, enabling the traveller to anticipate his arrival at a valley, or otherwise. The position of all bridges—even foot bridges—over the line is indicated to enable features mentioned in the commentary to be the more easily pinpointed. For the same reason the position of grid cables near or crossing the line is given.

A gradient of 1 : 80 means that for every 80 yards or feet travelled the line has risen or fallen by one yard or one foot, as indicated on the right of each page.

To view the countryside as described by the Author, travellers towards the coast should sit facing the engine; those travelling towards London, with their backs to the engine.

Rivers we meet

Anton
Avon (Wilts.)
Avon (Hants.)
Axe

Basingstoke Canal
Batts Brook
Beaulieu
Blackwater
Bourne
Bray
Burn

Clyst
Corfe
Creedy
Culm
Culvery

Dalch

East Okement
Ems
Exe

Frome

Hogsmill

Itchen

Lew
Little Dart
Lodden
Loddon
Lumburn
Lyd
Lyde
Lymington
Lynher

Mole
Mude

Nadder

Okement
Otter

Parrett

Rother

Sem
Sid
Sherford
Stour (Dorset)
Stour (Hants.)

Tale
Tamar
Tavy
Taw
Test
Thames
Tilmore
Trent (Dorset)

Umborne

Walkham
Wandle
West Okement
Wey (Dorset)
Wey (Surrey)
Wylye

Yeo

Counties

London
Surrey
Sussex
Hampshire

Wiltshire
Dorsetshire
Somersetshire
Devonshire

Index to Stations

65

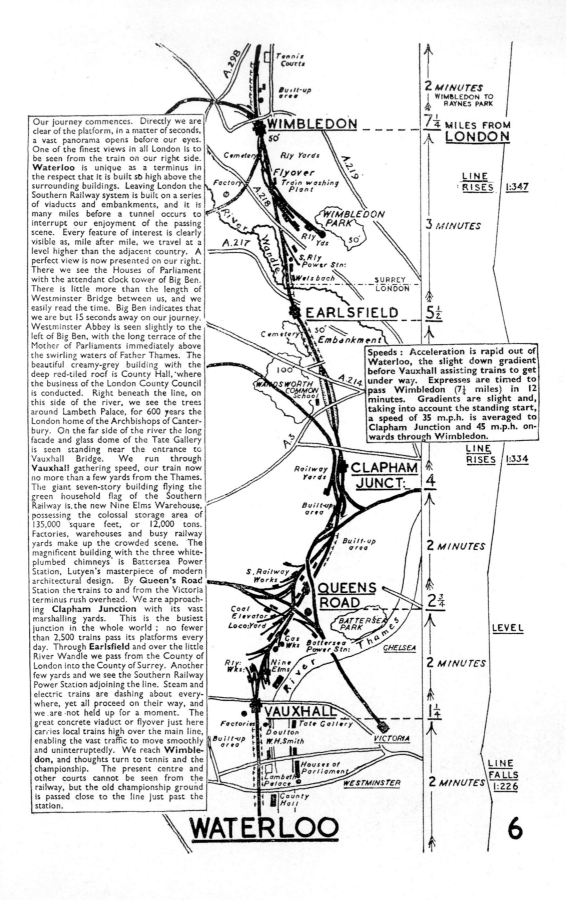

Our journey commences. Directly we are clear of the platform, in a matter of seconds, a vast panorama opens before our eyes. One of the finest views in all London is to be seen from the train on our right side. **Waterloo** is unique as a terminus in the respect that it is built so high above the surrounding buildings. Leaving London the Southern Railway system is built on a series of viaducts and embankments, and it is many miles before a tunnel occurs to interrupt our enjoyment of the passing scene. Every feature of interest is clearly visible as, mile after mile, we travel at a level higher than the adjacent country. A perfect view is now presented on our right. There we see the Houses of Parliament with the attendant clock tower of Big Ben. There is little more than the length of Westminster Bridge between us, and we easily read the time. Big Ben indicates that we are but 15 seconds away on our journey. Westminster Abbey is seen slightly to the left of Big Ben, with the long terrace of the Mother of Parliaments immediately above the swirling waters of Father Thames. The beautiful creamy-grey building with the deep red-tiled roof is County Hall, where the business of the London County Council is conducted. Right beneath the line, on this side of the river, we see the trees around Lambeth Palace, for 600 years the London home of the Archbishops of Canterbury. On the far side of the river the long facade and glass dome of the Tate Gallery is seen standing near the entrance to Vauxhall Bridge. We run through **Vauxhall** gathering speed, our train now no more than a few yards from the Thames. The giant seven-story building flying the green household flag of the Southern Railway is the new Nine Elms Warehouse, possessing the colossal storage area of 135,000 square feet, or 12,000 tons. Factories, warehouses and busy railway yards make up the crowded scene. The magnificent building with the three white-plumbed chimneys is Battersea Power Station, Lutyen's masterpiece of modern architectural design. By **Queen's Road** Station the trains to and from the Victoria terminus rush overhead. We are approaching **Clapham Junction** with its vast marshalling yards. This is the busiest junction in the whole world; no fewer than 2,500 trains pass its platforms every day. Through **Earlsfield** and over the little River Wandle we pass from the County of London into the County of Surrey. Another few yards and we see the Southern Railway Power Station adjoining the line. Steam and electric trains are dashing about everywhere, yet all proceed on their way, and we are not held up for a moment. The great concrete viaduct or flyover just here carries local trains high over the main line, enabling the vast traffic to move smoothly and uninterruptedly. We reach **Wimbledon**, and thoughts turn to tennis and the championship. The present centre and other courts cannot be seen from the railway, but the old championship ground is passed close to the line just past the station.

2 MINUTES WIMBLEDON TO RAYNES PARK

7¼ MILES FROM LONDON

LINE RISES 1:347

3 MINUTES

WIMBLEDON

EARLSFIELD 5½

Speeds : Acceleration is rapid out of Waterloo, the slight down gradient before Vauxhall assisting trains to get under way. Expresses are timed to pass Wimbledon (7¼ miles) in 12 minutes. Gradients are slight and, taking into account the standing start, a speed of 35 m.p.h. is averaged to Clapham Junction and 45 m.p.h. onwards through Wimbledon.

LINE RISES 1:334

CLAPHAM JUNCT. 4

2 MINUTES

QUEENS ROAD 2¾

LEVEL

2 MINUTES

1¼

VAUXHALL

LINE FALLS 1:226

2 MINUTES

WATERLOO

6

66

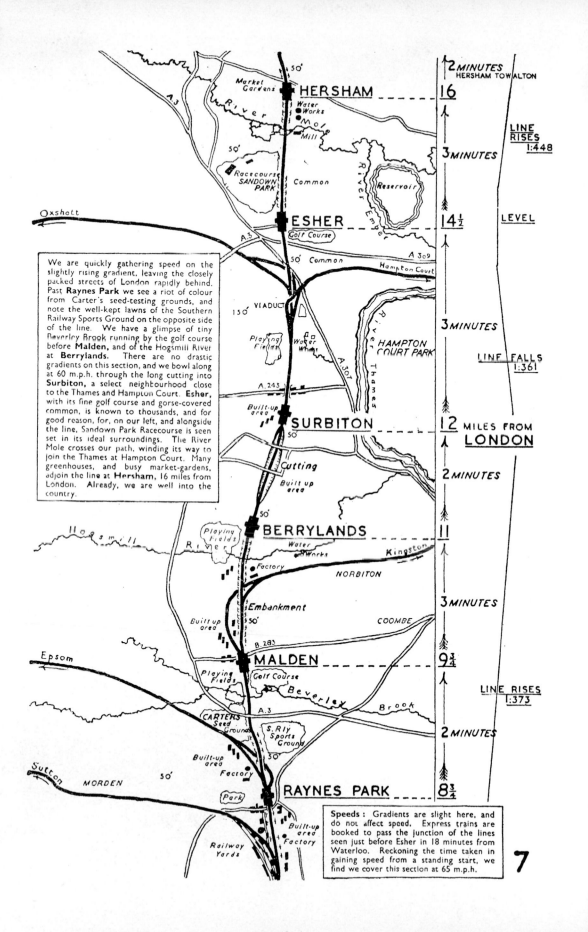

2 MINUTES
HERSHAM TO WALTON

HERSHAM — 16

50'

Market Gardens

Water Works

Mill

River Mole

3 MINUTES

LINE RISES 1:448

50'

Racecourse SANDOWN PARK

Common

River Ember

Reservoir

Oxshott

ESHER — 14½

LEVEL

A.3

Golf Course

50'   Common

A.309

Hampton Court

150'   VIADUCT

3 MINUTES

Playing Fields

Water Works

River Thames

HAMPTON COURT PARK

LINE FALLS 1:361

A.243

A.307

Built-up area

SURBITON — 12   MILES FROM **LONDON**

50'

Cutting

Built up area

2 MINUTES

We are quickly gathering speed on the slightly rising gradient, leaving the closely packed streets of London rapidly behind. Past **Raynes Park** we see a riot of colour from Carter's seed-testing grounds, and note the well-kept lawns of the Southern Railway Sports Ground on the opposite side of the line. We have a glimpse of tiny Beverley Brook running by the golf course before **Malden**, and of the Hogsmill River at **Berrylands**. There are no drastic gradients on this section, and we bowl along at 60 m.p.h. through the long cutting into **Surbiton**, a select neighbourhood close to the Thames and Hampton Court. **Esher**, with its fine golf course and gorse-covered common, is known to thousands, and for good reason, for, on our left, and alongside the line, Sandown Park Racecourse is seen set in its ideal surroundings. The River Mole crosses our path, winding its way to join the Thames at Hampton Court. Many greenhouses, and busy market-gardens, adjoin the line at **Hersham**, 16 miles from London. Already, we are well into the country.

50'

BERRYLANDS — 11

Hogsmill River

Playing Fields

Water Works

Kingston

Factory

NORBITON

Embankment

Built up area   50'

COOMBE

3 MINUTES

B.283

Epsom

MALDEN — 9¾

Playing Fields

Golf Course

Beverley   Brook

LINE RISES 1:373

A.3

CARTERS Seed Grounds

S. Rly Sports Ground

2 MINUTES

Built-up area   50'

Sutton

MORDEN   50'

Factory

Park

RAYNES PARK — 8¾

Built-up area   Factory

Railway Yards

Speeds : Gradients are slight here, and do not affect speed. Express trains are booked to pass the junction of the lines seen just before Esher in 18 minutes from Waterloo. Reckoning the time taken in gaining speed from a standing start, we find we cover this section at 65 m.p.h.

7

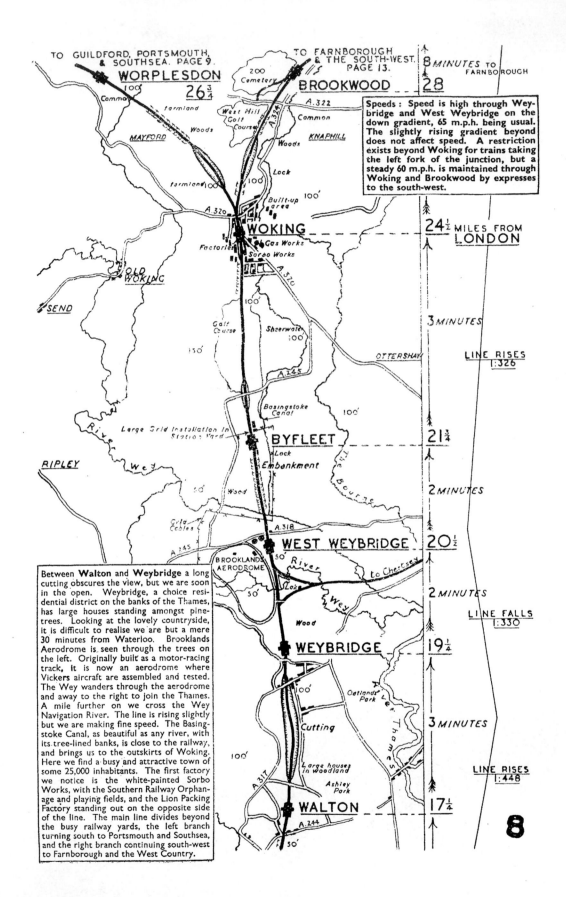

TO GUILDFORD, PORTSMOUTH & SOUTHSEA. PAGE 9.

TO FARNBOROUGH & THE SOUTH-WEST. PAGE 13.

8 MINUTES TO FARNBOROUGH

WORPLESDON 26¾

BROOKWOOD 28

200 Cemetery

A.322

A.324

Common

Common

West Hill Golf Course

KNAPHILL

farmland

MAYFORD

Woods

Woods

Lock

farmland 100'

100'

100'

Built-up area

A.320

WOKING

24½ MILES FROM LONDON

Factories

Gas Works

Sorbo Works

A.320

OLD WOKING

SEND

100'

3 MINUTES

Golf Course

Sheerwater 100'

OTTERSHAW

LINE RISES 1:326

150'

A.245

River

Basingstoke Canal

100'

21¾

Large Grid Installation in Station Yard

BYFLEET

Lock

2 MINUTES

RIPLEY

Wey

Embankment

Bourne

50'

Wood

A.318

WEST WEYBRIDGE 20½

Grid Cables

A.245

BROOKLANDS AERODROME

50' River

to Chertsey

2 MINUTES

50'

Lock

Wey

LINE FALLS 1:330

Wood

Between **Walton** and **Weybridge** a long cutting obscures the view, but we are soon in the open. Weybridge, a choice residential district on the banks of the Thames, has large houses standing amongst pine-trees. Looking at the lovely countryside, it is difficult to realise we are but a mere 30 minutes from Waterloo. Brooklands Aerodrome is seen through the trees on the left. Originally built as a motor-racing track, it is now an aerodrome where Vickers aircraft are assembled and tested. The Wey wanders through the aerodrome and away to the right to join the Thames. A mile further on we cross the Wey Navigation River. The line is rising slightly but we are making fine speed. The Basing-stoke Canal, as beautiful as any river, with its tree-lined banks, is close to the railway, and brings us to the outskirts of Woking. Here we find a busy and attractive town of some 25,000 inhabitants. The first factory we notice is the white-painted Sorbo Works, with the Southern Railway Orphanage and playing fields, and the Lion Packing Factory standing out on the opposite side of the line. The main line divides beyond the busy railway yards, the left branch turning south to Portsmouth and Southsea, and the right branch continuing south-west to Farnborough and the West Country.

WEYBRIDGE 19¼

100'

Oatlands Park

Thames

3 MINUTES

Cutting

100'

Large houses in woodland

LINE RISES 1:448

A.317

Ashley Park

WALTON 17¼

A.244

50'

8

Speeds : Speed is high through Wey-bridge and West Weybridge on the down gradient, 65 m.p.h. being usual. The slightly rising gradient beyond does not affect speed. A restriction exists beyond Woking for trains taking the left fork of the junction, but a steady 60 m.p.h. is maintained through Woking and Brookwood by expresses to the south-west.

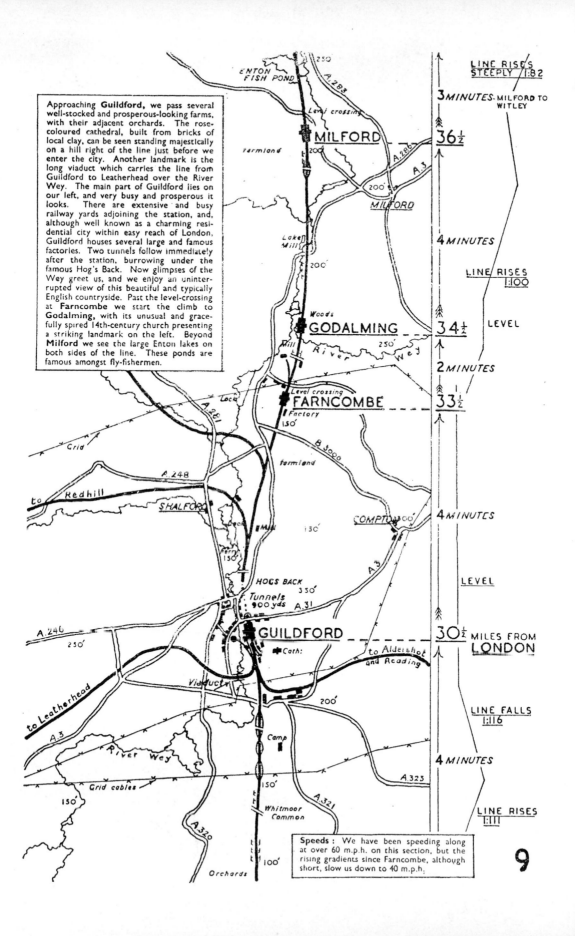

Approaching **Guildford,** we pass several well-stocked and prosperous-looking farms, with their adjacent orchards. The rose-coloured cathedral, built from bricks of local clay, can be seen standing majestically on a hill right of the line just before we enter the city. Another landmark is the long viaduct which carries the line from Guildford to Leatherhead over the River Wey. The main part of Guildford lies on our left, and very busy and prosperous it looks. There are extensive and busy railway yards adjoining the station, and, although well known as a charming residential city within easy reach of London, Guildford houses several large and famous factories. Two tunnels follow immediately after the station, burrowing under the famous Hog's Back. Now glimpses of the Wey greet us, and we enjoy an uninterrupted view of this beautiful and typically English countryside. Past the level-crossing at **Farncombe** we start the climb to **Godalming,** with its unusual and gracefully spired 14th-century church presenting a striking landmark on the left. Beyond **Milford** we see the large Enton lakes on both sides of the line. These ponds are famous amongst fly-fishermen.

LINE RISES STEEPLY 1:82

3 MINUTES—MILFORD TO WITLEY

36½ MILFORD

4 MINUTES

LINE RISES 1:100

LEVEL

34½ GODALMING

2 MINUTES

33½ FARNCOMBE

4 MINUTES

LEVEL

30½ MILES FROM LONDON GUILDFORD

LINE FALLS 1:116

4 MINUTES

LINE RISES 1:111

Speeds : We have been speeding along at over 60 m.p.h. on this section, but the rising gradients since Farncombe, although short, slow us down to 40 m.p.h.

9

ENTON FISH POND

Level crossing

farmland

MILFORD

Lake Mills

Woods

Mill River Wey

Level crossing

Factory

Grid

to Redhill

SHALFORD

COMPTON

HOGS BACK

Tunnels 900 yds

Cath:

to Aldershot and Reading

Viaduct

to Leatherhead

Camp

River Wey

Grid cables

Whitmoor Common

Orchards

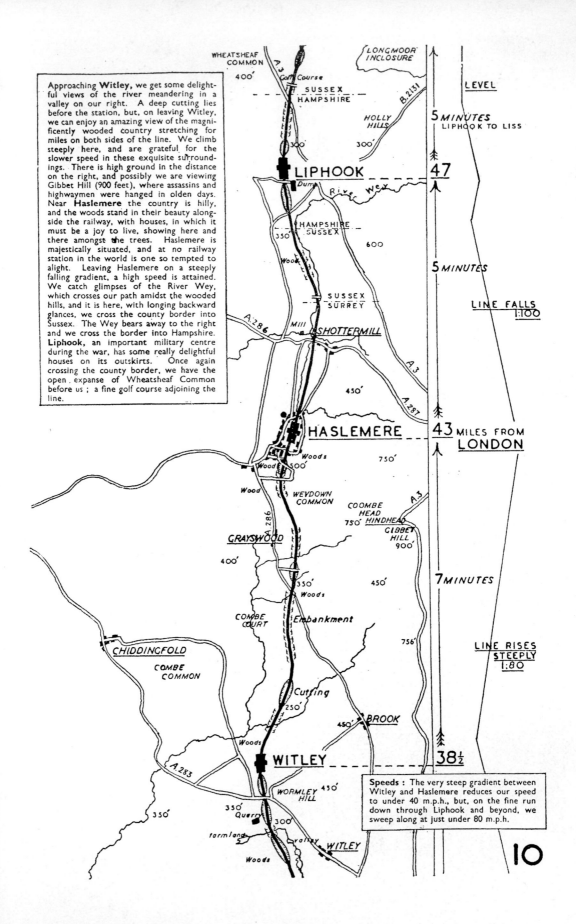

Approaching **Witley**, we get some delightful views of the river meandering in a valley on our right. A deep cutting lies before the station, but, on leaving Witley, we can enjoy an amazing view of the magnificently wooded country stretching for miles on both sides of the line. We climb steeply here, and are grateful for the slower speed in these exquisite surroundings. There is high ground in the distance on the right, and possibly we are viewing Gibbet Hill (900 feet), where assassins and highwaymen were hanged in olden days. Near **Haslemere** the country is hilly, and the woods stand in their beauty alongside the railway, with houses, in which it must be a joy to live, showing here and there amongst the trees. Haslemere is majestically situated, and at no railway station in the world is one so tempted to alight. Leaving Haslemere on a steeply falling gradient, a high speed is attained. We catch glimpses of the River Wey, which crosses our path amidst the wooded hills, and it is here, with longing backward glances, we cross the county border into Sussex. The Wey bears away to the right and we cross the border into Hampshire. **Liphook**, an important military centre during the war, has some really delightful houses on its outskirts. Once again crossing the county border, we have the open expanse of Wheatsheaf Common before us ; a fine golf course adjoining the line.

WHEATSHEAF COMMON

LONGMOOR INCLOSURE

Golf Course 400'

SUSSEX HAMPSHIRE

B.2131

LEVEL

HOLLY HILLS 300'

5 MINUTES LIPHOOK TO LISS

47

300'

LIPHOOK Dump

River Wey

HAMPSHIRE SUSSEX 600

350'

Woods

5 MINUTES

SUSSEX SURREY

LINE FALLS 1:100

A.286 Mill

SHOTTERMILL

A.3

450'

A.287

HASLEMERE

43 MILES FROM LONDON

Woods 500'

750'

Wood

Wood

WEYDOWN COMMON

COOMBE HEAD **HINDHEAD** 750'

A.3

GRAYSWOOD

A.286

GIBBET HILL 900'

400'

350'

450'

Woods

COMBE COURT

Embankment

756'

CHIDDINGFOLD

COMBE COMMON

7 MINUTES

LINE RISES STEEPLY 1:80

Cutting 250'

450' **BROOK**

Woods

38½

WITLEY

A.283

WORMLEY HILL 430'

350' Quarry

300'

350'

farmland valley **WITLEY**

Woods

Speeds : The very steep gradient between Witley and Haslemere reduces our speed to under 40 m.p.h., but, on the fine run down through Liphook and beyond, we sweep along at just under 80 m.p.h.

10

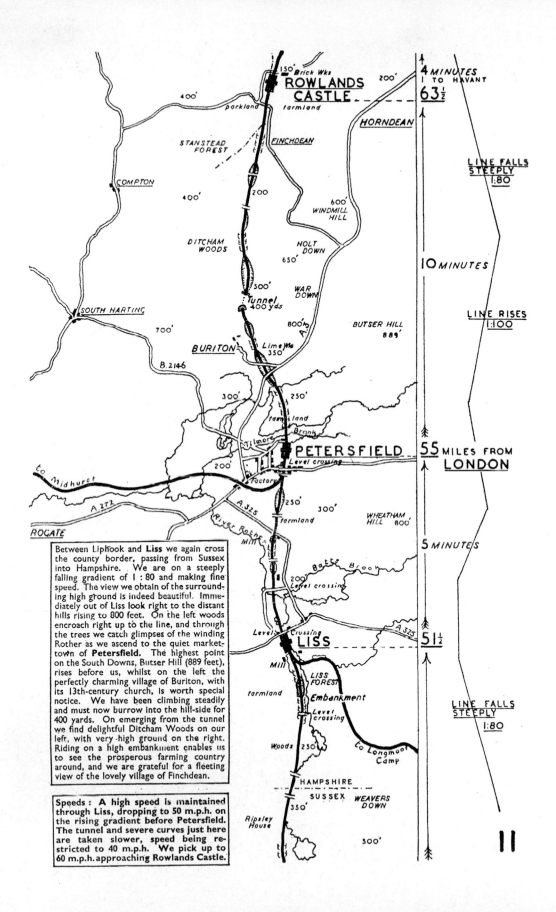

150' Brick Wks
ROWLANDS CASTLE
200'
parkland   farmland
400'
STANSTEAD FOREST   FINCHDEAN
HORNDEAN
COMPTON
400'
200'
600' WINDMILL HILL
DITCHAM WOODS
HOLT DOWN
650'
500'
WAR DOWN
Tunnel 400 yds
800'
BUTSER HILL 889'
SOUTH HARTING
700'
BURITON   Lime Wks 350'
B. 2146
300'   250'
farmland
Brook
Tilmore
PETERSFIELD
Level crossing
200'   Factory
To Midhurst   250'
A. 272   A. 325   farmland   300'
River Rother   WHEATHAM HILL 800'
ROGATE
Mill
Batts Brook
200'
Level crossing
To Longmoor Camp
Level Crossing
A. 325
LISS
Mill
LISS FOREST
farmland   Embankment
Level crossing
Woods 230'
HAMPSHIRE
SUSSEX   WEAVERS DOWN
350'
Ripsley House
300'

4 MINUTES TO HAVANT
63½
LINE FALLS STEEPLY 1:80
10 MINUTES
LINE RISES 1:100
55 MILES FROM **LONDON**
5 MINUTES
51½
LINE FALLS STEEPLY 1:80

Between Liphook and **Liss** we again cross the county border, passing from Sussex into Hampshire. We are on a steeply falling gradient of 1 : 80 and making fine speed. The view we obtain of the surrounding high ground is indeed beautiful. Immediately out of Liss look right to the distant hills rising to 800 feet. On the left woods encroach right up to the line, and through the trees we catch glimpses of the winding Rother as we ascend to the quiet market-town of **Petersfield**. The highest point on the South Downs, Butser Hill (889 feet), rises before us, whilst on the left the perfectly charming village of Buriton, with its 13th-century church, is worth special notice. We have been climbing steadily and must now burrow into the hill-side for 400 yards. On emerging from the tunnel we find delightful Ditcham Woods on our left, with very high ground on the right. Riding on a high embankment enables us to see the prosperous farming country around, and we are grateful for a fleeting view of the lovely village of Finchdean.

Speeds : A high speed is maintained through **Liss**, dropping to 50 m.p.h. on the rising gradient before Petersfield. The tunnel and severe curves just here are taken slower, speed being restricted to 40 m.p.h. We pick up to 60 m.p.h. approaching Rowlands Castle.

11

Within 15 minutes we shall have reached the sea. The hills are being left behind, and we are now running through flat farmland where numerous cattle peacefully graze. As we approach the old market town of **Havant**, we see the railway from Chichester approaching the junction. Our speed is now very slow as we take the curve into the station. The line turns sharply to the west here and we proceed slowly over the level crossings to Bedhampton Halt, where, looking left, we have our first view of the sea in Langstone Harbour, with Hayling Island in the distance. Looking right we see the line of disused forts on Ports Down, originally built to defend the harbour, with numerous well-sited houses on the lower slopes of the Downs. Through marshland we cross the junction of the line to Southampton, pass over the creek and on to **Hilsea Halt.** A large aerodrome is on the left and busy railway yards on the right. We notice the very large railway yards at **Fratton,** after which the train runs between rows of houses into **Portsmouth and Southsea** Station. The magnificent building with the tall clock tower is Portsmouth Guildhall. As we travel slowly on to the **Harbour** Station, looking right, we may just see the masts and rigging of Lord Nelson's flagship " Victory," Portsmouth's most famous monument.

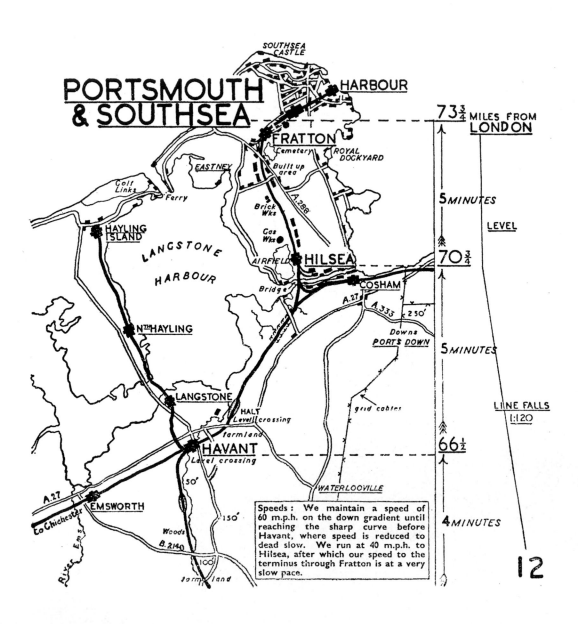

ENGLISH CHANNEL

72

PORTSMOUTH & SOUTHSEA

SOUTHSEA CASTLE

HARBOUR

FRATTON

Cemetery ROYAL DOCKYARD

Built up area

EASTNEY

Golf Links

Ferry

Brick Wks

A.288

Gas Wks

HAYLING ISLAND

LANGSTONE HARBOUR

AIRFIELD

HILSEA

Bridge

COSHAM

A.27

A.333

250'

Nᵀᴴ HAYLING

Downs
PORTS DOWN

grid cables

LANGSTONE

HALT
Level crossing

farmland

HAVANT

Level crossing

WATERLOOVILLE

50'

A.27

To Chichester

EMSWORTH

River Ems

Woods

150'

B.2140

100'

farmland

73¾ MILES FROM LONDON

5 MINUTES

LEVEL

70¾

5 MINUTES

LINE FALLS 1:120

66½

4 MINUTES

Speeds : We maintain a speed of 60 m.p.h. on the down gradient until reaching the sharp curve before Havant, where speed is reduced to dead slow. We run at 40 m.p.h. to Hilsea, after which our speed to the terminus through Fratton is at a very slow pace.

12

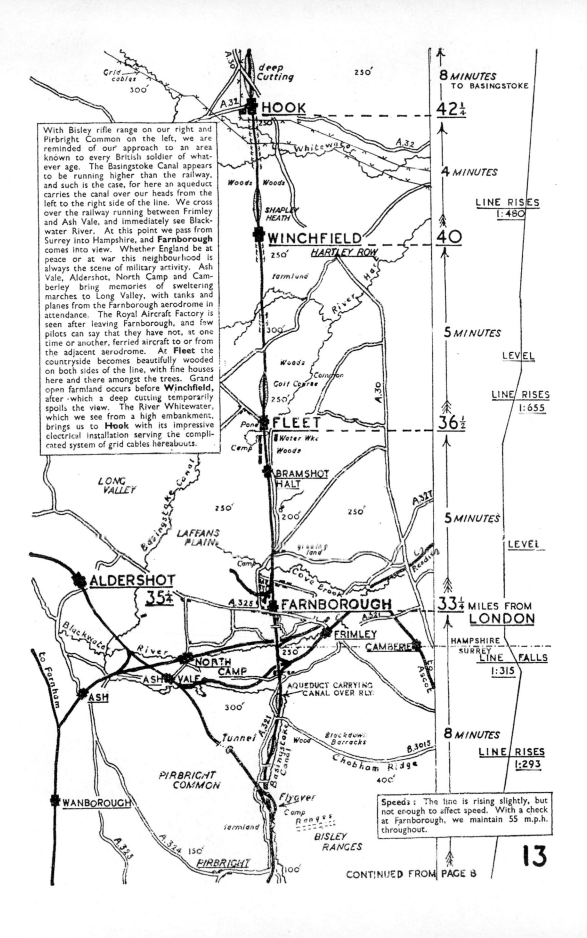

With Bisley rifle range on our right and Pirbright Common on the left, we are reminded of our approach to an area known to every British soldier of whatever age. The Basingstoke Canal appears to be running higher than the railway, and such is the case, for here an aqueduct carries the canal over our heads from the left to the right side of the line. We cross over the railway running between Frimley and Ash Vale, and immediately see Blackwater River. At this point we pass from Surrey into Hampshire, and **Farnborough** comes into view. Whether England be at peace or at war this neighbourhood is always the scene of military activity. Ash Vale, Aldershot, North Camp and Camberley bring memories of sweltering marches to Long Valley, with tanks and planes from the Farnborough aerodrome in attendance. The Royal Aircraft Factory is seen after leaving Farnborough, and few pilots can say that they have not, at one time or another, ferried aircraft to or from the adjacent aerodrome. At **Fleet** the countryside becomes beautifully wooded on both sides of the line, with fine houses here and there amongst the trees. Grand open farmland occurs before **Winchfield**, after which a deep cutting temporarily spoils the view. The River Whitewater, which we see from a high embankment, brings us to **Hook** with its impressive electrical installation serving the complicated system of grid cables hereabouts.

Grid cables 300'
250'
A.30
deep Cutting
A.31
HOOK
8 MINUTES TO BASINGSTOKE
42¼
Whitewater
A.32
250'
4 MINUTES
Woods Woods
LINE RISES 1:480
SHAPLEY HEATH
WINCHFIELD
40
HARTLEY ROW
250'
farmland
River Hart
300'
A.30
5 MINUTES
Woods
LEVEL
Common
Golf Course
LINE RISES 1:655
250'
Pond
FLEET
36½
Camp
Water Wks
Woods
BRAMSHOT HALT
A.327
5 MINUTES
LONG VALLEY
250'
250'
200'
LAFFANS PLAIN
grazing land
Crook
LEVEL
Basingstoke Canal
Camp
Cove Brook
ALDERSHOT
35¾
A.325
FARNBOROUGH
33¼ MILES FROM **LONDON**
Blackwater River
250'
A.321
FRIMLEY
CAMBERLEY
to Farnham
NORTH CAMP
HAMPSHIRE SURREY
LINE FALLS 1:315
ASH VALE
300'
to Ascot
ASH
AQUEDUCT CARRYING CANAL OVER RLY.
A.321
Tunnel
Blackdown Barracks
Wood
B.3015
8 MINUTES
PIRBRIGHT COMMON
Basingstoke Canal
Chobham Ridge
400'
LINE RISES 1:293
WANBOROUGH
Flyover
Camp
Ranges
A.323
A.324
150'
farmland
BISLEY RANGES
Speeds: The line is rising slightly, but not enough to affect speed. With a check at Farnborough, we maintain 55 m.p.h. throughout.
PIRBRIGHT
100'
13

CONTINUED FROM PAGE 8

73

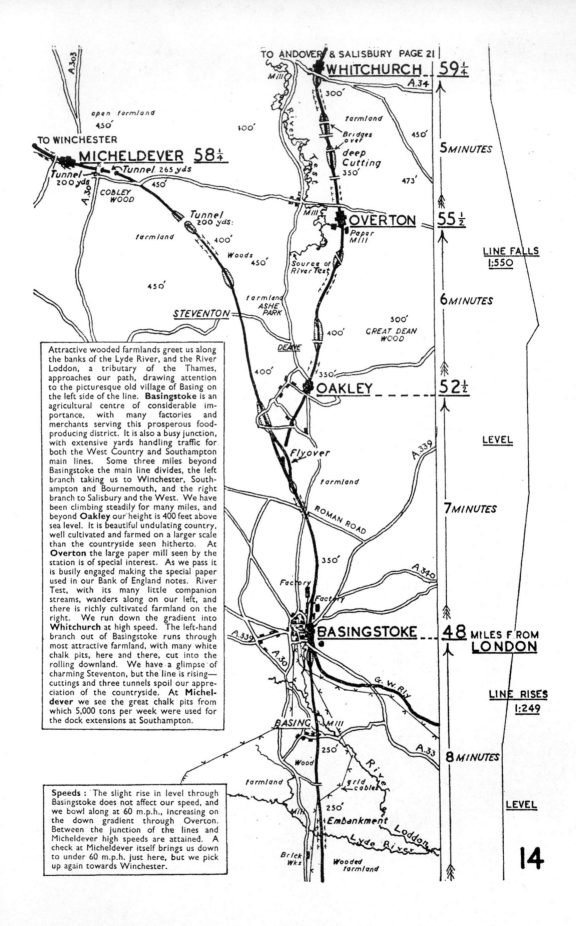

TO ANDOVER & SALISBURY PAGE 21

A.303

open farmland
450'

TO WINCHESTER

MICHELDEVER 58¼

Tunnel 200 yds   Tunnel 265 yds

A.30   COBLEY WOOD   450'

Tunnel 200 yds

farmland   400'

Woods 450'

450'

450'

STEVENTON

400'

DEANE

400'

Mill
River Test
300'

farmland

450'

473'

Bridges over
deep Cutting
350'

Mill

OVERTON 55½

Paper Mill

Source of River Test

farmland ASHE PARK

350'

400'   GREAT DEAN WOOD
500'

350'

OAKLEY 52½

Flyover

farmland

ROMAN ROAD

350'

A.339

A.340

Factory

Factory

A.339   **BASINGSTOKE**   48

A.30   G.W.Rly

BASING   MILL

250'   Wood

grid cables

250'

A.33

Brick Wks   Wooded farmland

Embankment   River Loddon

Lyde River

WHITCHURCH 59¼
A.34

5 MINUTES

LINE FALLS 1:550

6 MINUTES

LEVEL

7 MINUTES

MILES FROM **LONDON**

LINE RISES 1:249

8 MINUTES

LEVEL

14

Attractive wooded farmlands greet us along the banks of the Lyde River, and the River Loddon, a tributary of the Thames, approaches our path, drawing attention to the picturesque old village of Basing on the left side of the line. **Basingstoke** is an agricultural centre of considerable importance, with many factories and merchants serving this prosperous food-producing district. It is also a busy junction, with extensive yards handling traffic for both the West Country and Southampton main lines. Some three miles beyond Basingstoke the main line divides, the left branch taking us to Winchester, Southampton and Bournemouth, and the right branch to Salisbury and the West. We have been climbing steadily for many miles, and beyond **Oakley** our height is 400 feet above sea level. It is beautiful undulating country, well cultivated and farmed on a larger scale than the countryside seen hitherto. At **Overton** the large paper mill seen by the station is of special interest. As we pass it is busily engaged making the special paper used in our Bank of England notes. River Test, with its many little companion streams, wanders along on our left, and there is richly cultivated farmland on the right. We run down the gradient into **Whitchurch** at high speed. The left-hand branch out of Basingstoke runs through most attractive farmland, with many white chalk pits, here and there, cut into the rolling downland. We have a glimpse of charming Steventon, but the line is rising—cuttings and three tunnels spoil our appreciation of the countryside. At **Micheldever** we see the great chalk pits from which 5,000 tons per week were used for the dock extensions at Southampton.

Speeds : The slight rise in level through Basingstoke does not affect our speed, and we bowl along at 60 m.p.h., increasing on the down gradient through Overton. Between the junction of the lines and Micheldever high speeds are attained. A check at Micheldever itself brings us down to under 60 m.p.h. just here, but we pick up again towards Winchester.

74

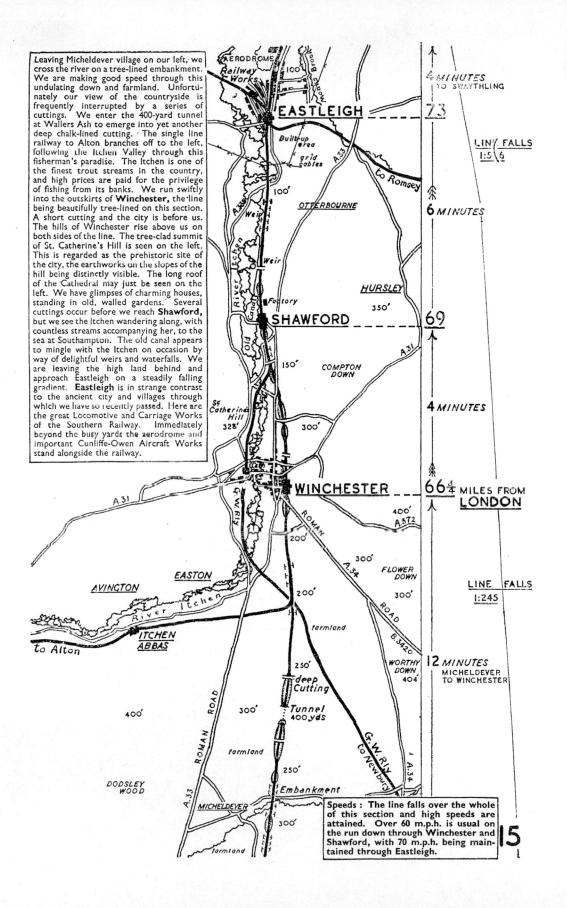

Leaving Micheldever village on our left, we cross the river on a tree-lined embankment. We are making good speed through this undulating down and farmland. Unfortunately our view of the countryside is frequently interrupted by a series of cuttings. We enter the 400-yard tunnel at Wallers Ash to emerge into yet another deep chalk-lined cutting. The single line railway to Alton branches off to the left, following the Itchen Valley through this fisherman's paradise. The Itchen is one of the finest trout streams in the country, and high prices are paid for the privilege of fishing from its banks. We run swiftly into the outskirts of **Winchester**, the line being beautifully tree-lined on this section. A short cutting and the city is before us. The hills of Winchester rise above us on both sides of the line. The tree-clad summit of St. Catherine's Hill is seen on the left. This is regarded as the prehistoric site of the city, the earthworks on the slopes of the hill being distinctly visible. The long roof of the Cathedral may just be seen on the left. We have glimpses of charming houses, standing in old, walled gardens. Several cuttings occur before we reach **Shawford**, but we see the Itchen wandering along, with countless streams accompanying her, to the sea at Southampton. The old canal appears to mingle with the Itchen on occasion by way of delightful weirs and waterfalls. We are leaving the high land behind and approach Eastleigh on a steadily falling gradient. **Eastleigh** is in strange contrast to the ancient city and villages through which we have so recently passed. Here are the great Locomotive and Carriage Works of the Southern Railway. Immediately beyond the busy yards the aerodrome and important Cunliffe-Owen Aircraft Works stand alongside the railway.

Speeds : The line falls over the whole of this section and high speeds are attained. Over 60 m.p.h. is usual on the run down through Winchester and Shawford, with 70 m.p.h. being maintained through Eastleigh.

We approach the built-up area of **Sway-thling.** Shortly after passing the water works on the left, we have our last view of the Itchen, now about to become tidal and flow into the sea at Southampton Water. There is a connection between the next station, **St. Denys,** and Paris. It derives its name from the priory founded there, the convent being subject to the Royal Abbey of St. Denys, near Paris. The great timber yards we see on the left mark the site of Clausentum, the Roman Southampton. Enormous gas holders at **Northam** dwarf all buildings around, and we are now in a highly industrialised and built-up area. We proceed slowly through the tunnel to **Southampton Central.** The enormous Solent Flour Mill on the left was build on land reclaimed from the estuary of the River Test. Up to a few years ago the river ran quite close to the railway—now it is half a mile away. We see the line of giant cranes lining the docks and almost immediately we travel alongside the wonderful " King George V " Graving Dock. This dock, 1,200 feet long, is the largest in the world, 750,000 tons of concrete being used in its construction. Leaving **Totton,** with its numerous oil tanks and busy factories, we very soon reach open country. By the time we reach **Lyndhurst Road** we are well into the New Forest, where William Rufus met his death. For hundreds of years most of the forest has remained untouched and un-spoiled. From our train it seems there are parts where no foot has ever stepped, the only sign of life amongst the ancient trees and clearings being the wild New Forest ponies, grazing timidly close to the line. We reach **Beaulieu Road,** the same wild forest land stretching for miles around us.

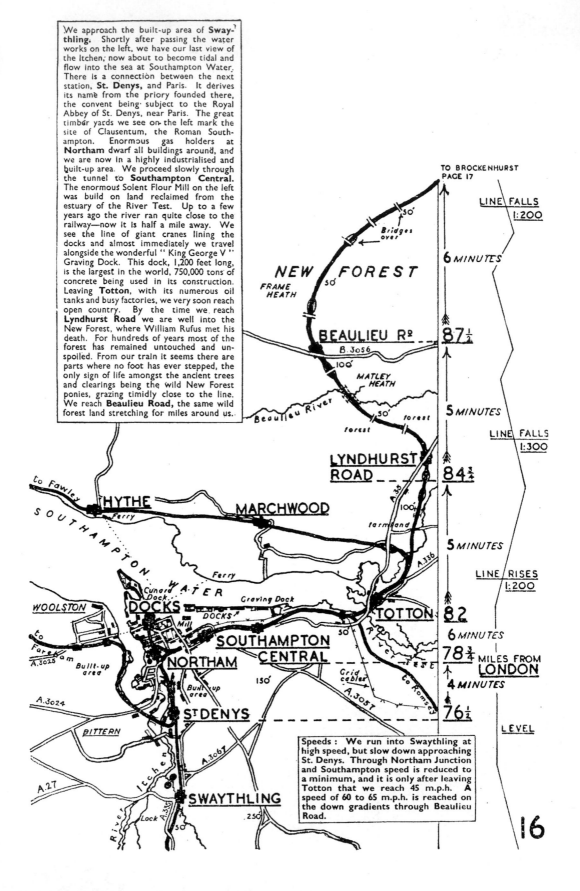

TO BROCKENHURST
PAGE 17

LINE FALLS
1:200

6 MINUTES

NEW FOREST

FRAME HEATH

Bridges over

50'

BEAULIEU R?   87½
B. 3056

100'

MATLEY HEATH

5 MINUTES

LINE FALLS
1:300

Beaulieu River

forest   50'   forest

forest

LYNDHURST
ROAD   84¾

A.35   100'

farmland

5 MINUTES

LINE RISES
1:200

A.336

to Fawley

HYTHE   MARCHWOOD
Ferry

SOUTHAMPTON   WATER

WOOLSTON

Cunard Dock

DOCKS   Graving Dock

DOCKS   Mill

TOTTON   82

6 MINUTES

78¾   MILES FROM LONDON

4 MINUTES

76½

LEVEL

to Fareham
A.3025   Built-up area

A.3024

NORTHAM

SOUTHAMPTON
CENTRAL

150'

Built up area

St DENYS

BITTERN

A.3057

Grid cables

to Romsey

River TEST

50'

A.27   A.3057

River Itchen

Lock   A.335
50'   250'

SWAYTHLING

Speeds : We run into Swaythling at high speed, but slow down approaching St. Denys. Through Northam Junction and Southampton speed is reduced to a minimum, and it is only after leaving Totton that we reach 45 m.p.h. A speed of 60 to 65 m.p.h. is reached on the down gradients through Beaulieu Road.

16

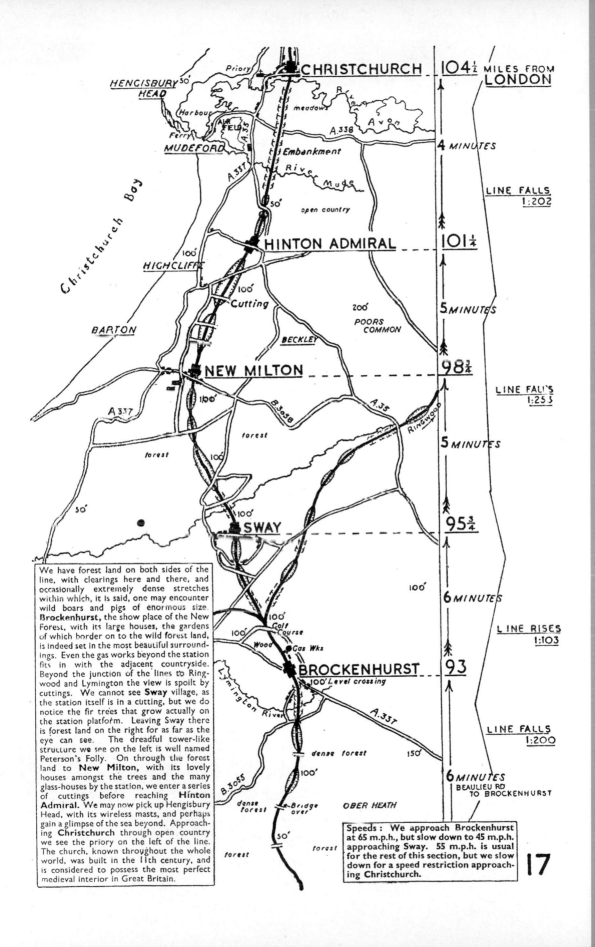

HENGISBURY HEAD
50'

Priory

CHRISTCHURCH 104½ MILES FROM LONDON

meadows

R. Avon

A.338

4 MINUTES

LINE FALLS 1:202

Harbour

AIR FIELDS

A.35

Ferry

MUDEFORD

A.337

Embankment

River Mude

50'

open country

Christchurch Bay

HINTON ADMIRAL 101¼

HIGHCLIFF

100'

100'

Cutting

5 MINUTES

200'

POORS COMMON

BECKLEY

BARTON

NEW MILTON 98¾

A.337

100'

B.3058

A.35

Ringwood

LINE FALLS 1:253

forest

forest

100'

5 MINUTES

50'

100'

SWAY 95¾

100'

6 MINUTES

LINE RISES 1:103

100'

Golf Course

100'

Wood

Gas Wks

BROCKENHURST 93

100' Level crossing

Lymington River

A.337

dense forest

150'

LINE FALLS 1:200

B.3055

100'

dense forest

Bridge over

OBER HEATH

6 MINUTES
BEAULIEU RD TO BROCKENHURST

50'

forest

forest

We have forest land on both sides of the line, with clearings here and there, and occasionally extremely dense stretches within which, it is said, one may encounter wild boars and pigs of enormous size. **Brockenhurst**, the show place of the New Forest, with its large houses, the gardens of which border on to the wild forest land, is indeed set in the most beautiful surroundings. Even the gas works beyond the station fits in with the adjacent countryside. Beyond the junction of the lines to Ringwood and Lymington the view is spoilt by cuttings. We cannot see **Sway** village, as the station itself is in a cutting, but we do notice the fir trees that grow actually on the station platform. Leaving Sway there is forest land on the right for as far as the eye can see. The dreadful tower-like structure we see on the left is well named Peterson's Folly. On through the forest land to **New Milton**, with its lovely houses amongst the trees and the many glass-houses by the station, we enter a series of cuttings before reaching **Hinton Admiral**. We may now pick up Hengisbury Head, with its wireless masts, and perhaps gain a glimpse of the sea beyond. Approaching **Christchurch** through open country we see the priory on the left of the line. The church, known throughout the whole world, was built in the 11th century, and is considered to possess the most perfect medieval interior in Great Britain.

Speeds : We approach Brockenhurst at 65 m.p.h., but slow down to 45 m.p.h. approaching Sway. 55 m.p.h. is usual for the rest of this section, but we slow down for a speed restriction approaching Christchurch.

17

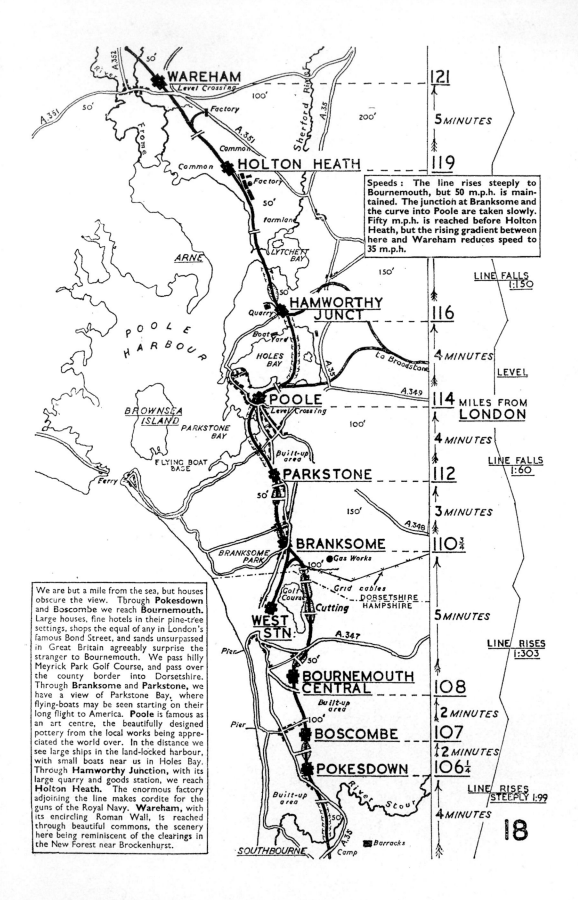

WAREHAM
Level Crossing

River A.352

50'

A.351

50'

Factory

100'

A.351

Common

Common

Sherford River

A.35

200'

HOLTON HEATH

Factory

50'

farmland

ARNE

LYTCHETT BAY

150'

50'

Quarry

HAMWORTHY JUNCT

Boat Yard

HOLES BAY

A.35

to Broadstone

POOLE
HARBOUR

A.349

BROWNSEA ISLAND

PARKSTONE BAY

Built-up area

POOLE
Level Crossing

100'

FLYING BOAT BASE

Ferry

50'

PARKSTONE

150'

A.348

BRANKSOME PARK

BRANKSOME

Gas Works

100'

Grid cables

DORSETSHIRE
HAMPSHIRE

Golf Course

Cutting

WEST STN.

Pier

A.347

50'

BOURNEMOUTH CENTRAL

Built-up area

Pier

100'

BOSCOMBE

POKESDOWN

Built-up area

River Stour

50'

SOUTHBOURNE

Camp

Barracks

121
5 MINUTES
119

Speeds: The line rises steeply to Bournemouth, but 50 m.p.h. is maintained. The junction at Branksome and the curve into Poole are taken slowly. Fifty m.p.h. is reached before Holton Heath, but the rising gradient between here and Wareham reduces speed to 35 m.p.h.

LINE FALLS 1:150

116
4 MINUTES

LEVEL

114 MILES FROM LONDON

4 MINUTES

LINE FALLS 1:60

112
3 MINUTES

110¾
5 MINUTES

LINE RISES 1:303

108
2 MINUTES

107
2 MINUTES

106¼

LINE RISES STEEPLY 1:99

4 MINUTES

18

We are but a mile from the sea, but houses obscure the view. Through **Pokesdown** and **Boscombe** we reach **Bournemouth**. Large houses, fine hotels in their pine-tree settings, shops the equal of any in London's famous Bond Street, and sands unsurpassed in Great Britain agreeably surprise the stranger to Bournemouth. We pass hilly Meyrick Park Golf Course, and pass over the county border into Dorsetshire. Through **Branksome** and **Parkstone**, we have a view of Parkstone Bay, where flying-boats may be seen starting on their long flight to America. **Poole** is famous as an art centre, the beautifully designed pottery from the local works being appreciated the world over. In the distance we see large ships in the land-locked harbour, with small boats near us in Holes Bay. Through **Hamworthy Junction**, with its large quarry and goods station, we reach **Holton Heath**. The enormous factory adjoining the line makes cordite for the guns of the Royal Navy. **Wareham**, with its encircling Roman Wall, is reached through beautiful commons, the scenery here being reminiscent of the clearings in the New Forest near Brockenhurst.

78

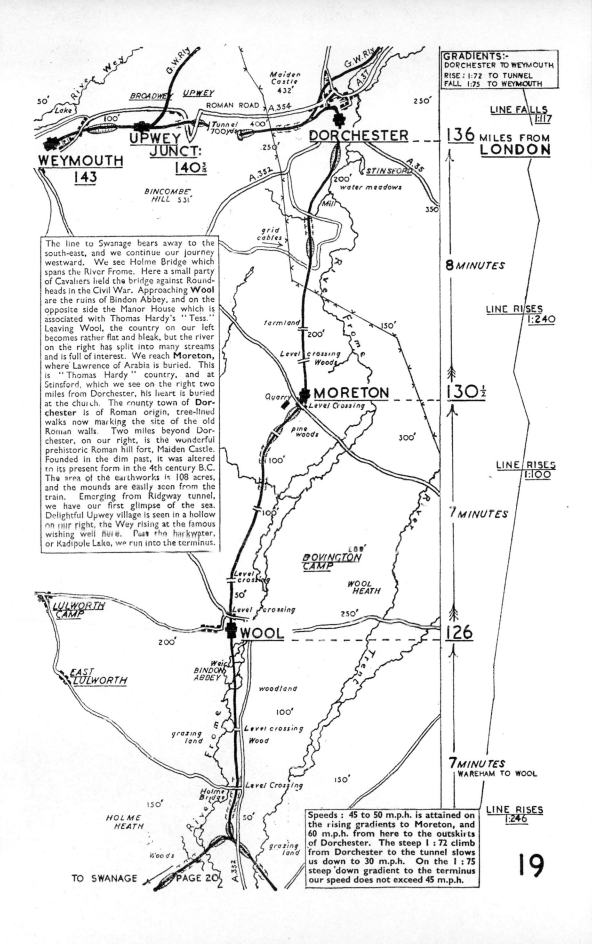

The line to Swanage bears away to the south-east, and we continue our journey westward. We see Holme Bridge which spans the River Frome. Here a small party of Cavaliers held the bridge against Roundheads in the Civil War. Approaching **Wool** are the ruins of Bindon Abbey, and on the opposite side the Manor House which is associated with Thomas Hardy's "Tess." Leaving Wool, the country on our left becomes rather flat and bleak, but the river on the right has split into many streams and is full of interest. We reach **Moreton**, where Lawrence of Arabia is buried. This is "Thomas Hardy" country, and at Stinsford, which we see on the right two miles from Dorchester, his heart is buried at the church. The county town of **Dorchester** is of Roman origin, tree-lined walks now marking the site of the old Roman walls. Two miles beyond Dorchester, on our right, is the wonderful prehistoric Roman hill fort, Maiden Castle. Founded in the dim past, it was altered to its present form in the 4th century B.C. The area of the earthworks is 108 acres, and the mounds are easily seen from the train. Emerging from Ridgway tunnel, we have our first glimpse of the sea. Delightful Upwey village is seen in a hollow on our right, the Wey rising at the famous wishing well here. Past the backwater, or Radipole Lake, we run into the terminus.

GRADIENTS:—
DORCHESTER TO WEYMOUTH
RISE : 1:72 TO TUNNEL
FALL 1:75 TO WEYMOUTH

LINE FALLS 1:117

136 MILES FROM **LONDON**

8 MINUTES

LINE RISES 1:240

130½

LINE RISES 1:100

7 MINUTES

126

7 MINUTES
WAREHAM TO WOOL

LINE RISES 1:246

Speeds : 45 to 50 m.p.h. is attained on the rising gradients to Moreton, and 60 m.p.h. from here to the outskirts of Dorchester. The steep 1 : 72 climb from Dorchester to the tunnel slows us down to 30 m.p.h. On the 1 : 75 steep down gradient to the terminus our speed does not exceed 45 m.p.h.

19

TO SWANAGE PAGE 20

WEYMOUTH 143

UPWEY JUNCT: 140¾

DORCHESTER

MORETON

WOOL

This is lovely moorland country with woods bordering the line. High ground towers above us on the right, whilst on the left we look across the moorland to Arne and Poole Bay. **Corfe Castle** lies in a gap in the Purbeck Hills. The ruins of the castle stand on a hillock just before the station, completely dominating the quaint and picturesque grey stone village grouped beneath. The origin of the castle is obscure, but, according to tradition, it was the scene of the murder of King Edward in A.D. 978. A busy creamery stands in the station yard, with a hill rising 200 feet sheer behind it. Woods alongside the line intermingle with stretches of gorse-covered common. We are nearly at the seaside. Hills shelter **Swanage** from all but the soft winds from the south, and bathing between Peveril Point and Ballard Point is a delight for those who demand that their swimming and beach idling shall not be spoilt by unkind winds. The population of Swanage is given as 6,000. By the presence of the several fine hotels, and the number of modern shops ready to greet the visitor, it is apparent that a large number of holiday-makers must swell the population both in and out of the season. The reason is not far to seek. A few hours spent in Swanage determines one to come again ; to come again soon, and next time to stay just as long as one's circumstances permit.

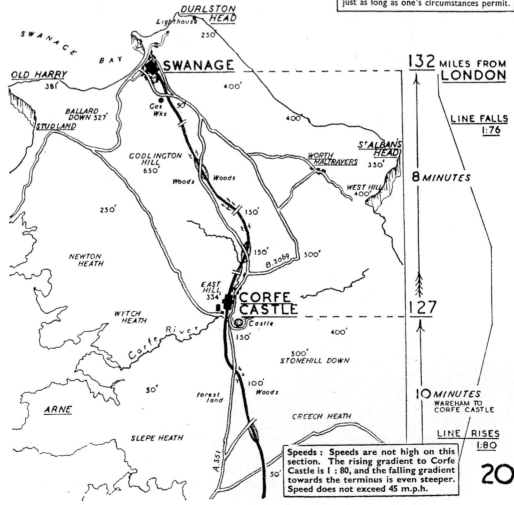

132 MILES FROM **LONDON**

LINE FALLS 1:76

8 MINUTES

127

10 MINUTES
WAREHAM TO
CORFE CASTLE

LINE RISES 1:80

20

Speeds : Speeds are not high on this section. The rising gradient to Corfe Castle is 1 : 80, and the falling gradient towards the terminus is even steeper. Speed does not exceed 45 m.p.h.

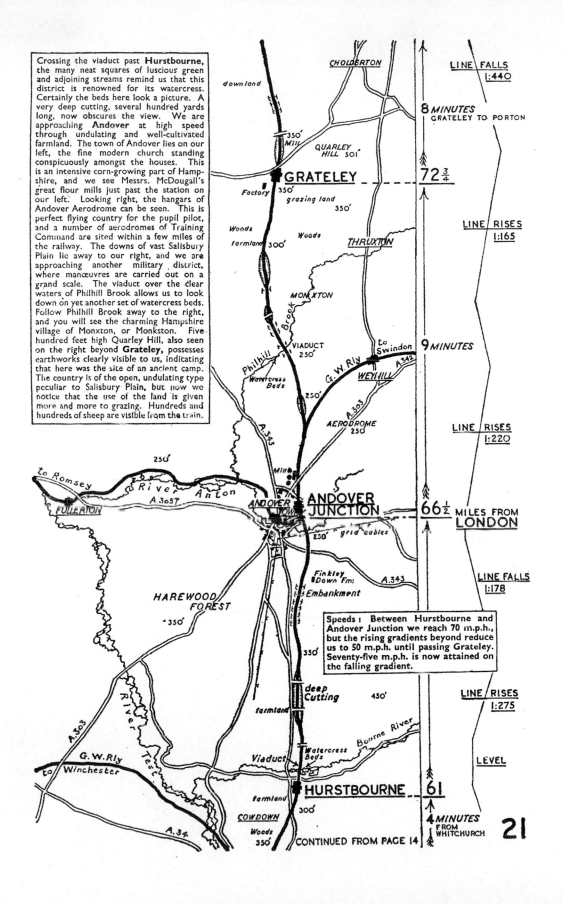

Crossing the viaduct past **Hurstbourne**, the many neat squares of luscious green and adjoining streams remind us that this district is renowned for its watercress. Certainly the beds here look a picture. A very deep cutting, several hundred yards long, now obscures the view. We are approaching **Andover** at high speed through undulating and well-cultivated farmland. The town of Andover lies on our left, the fine modern church standing conspicuously amongst the houses. This is an intensive corn-growing part of Hampshire, and we see Messrs. McDougall's great flour mills just past the station on our left. Looking right, the hangars of Andover Aerodrome can be seen. This is perfect flying country for the pupil pilot, and a number of aerodromes of Training Command are sited within a few miles of the railway. The downs of vast Salisbury Plain lie away to our right, and we are approaching another military district, where manœuvres are carried out on a grand scale. The viaduct over the clear waters of Philhill Brook allows us to look down on yet another set of watercress beds. Follow Philhill Brook away to the right, and you will see the charming Hampshire village of Monxton, or Monkston. Five hundred feet high Quarley Hill, also seen on the right beyond **Grateley**, possesses earthworks clearly visible to us, indicating that here was the site of an ancient camp. The country is of the open, undulating type peculiar to Salisbury Plain, but now we notice that the use of the land is given more and more to grazing. Hundreds and hundreds of sheep are visible from the train.

CHOLDERTON

downland

LINE FALLS 1:440

8 MINUTES
GRATELEY TO PORTON

350' MILL

QUARLEY HILL 501'

GRATELEY 72¾

Factory 350'

grazing land 350'

LINE RISES 1:165

Woods

farmland 300' Woods

THRUXTON

MONXTON

Brook

VIADUCT 250'

to Swindon

9 MINUTES

Philhill

Watercress Beds

G.W.Rly A.342

WEYHILL

250' A.303

LINE RISES 1:220

A.343

AERODROME 250'

to Romsey

250'

River Anton

A.3057

Mill

FULLERTON

ANDOVER JUNCTION 66½ MILES FROM LONDON

250' grid cables

Finkley Down Fm. A.343

LINE FALLS 1:178

Embankment

HAREWOOD FOREST

350'

Speeds : Between Hurstbourne and Andover Junction we reach 70 m.p.h., but the rising gradients beyond reduce us to 50 m.p.h. until passing Grateley. Seventy-five m.p.h. is now attained on the falling gradient.

350'

450'

LINE RISES 1:275

deep Cutting

farmland

Bourne River

River Test

A.303

G.W.Rly to Winchester

Viaduct

Watercress Beds

LEVEL

farmland

HURSTBOURNE 61

COWDOWN 300'

4 MINUTES FROM WHITCHURCH

Woods 350' CONTINUED FROM PAGE 14

21

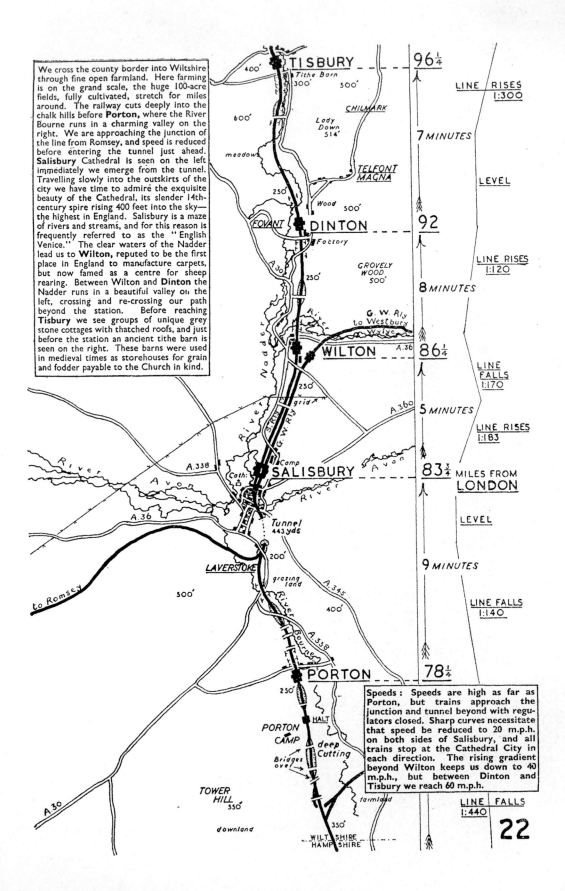

We cross the county border into Wiltshire through fine open farmland. Here farming is on the grand scale, the huge 100-acre fields, fully cultivated, stretch for miles around. The railway cuts deeply into the chalk hills before **Porton**, where the River Bourne runs in a charming valley on the right. We are approaching the junction of the line from Romsey, and speed is reduced before entering the tunnel just ahead. **Salisbury** Cathedral is seen on the left immediately we emerge from the tunnel. Travelling slowly into the outskirts of the city we have time to admire the exquisite beauty of the Cathedral, its slender 14th-century spire rising 400 feet into the sky—the highest in England. Salisbury is a maze of rivers and streams, and for this reason is frequently referred to as the "English Venice." The clear waters of the Nadder lead us to **Wilton**, reputed to be the first place in England to manufacture carpets, but now famed as a centre for sheep rearing. Between Wilton and **Dinton** the Nadder runs in a beautiful valley on the left, crossing and re-crossing our path beyond the station. Before reaching **Tisbury** we see groups of unique grey stone cottages with thatched roofs, and just before the station an ancient tithe barn is seen on the right. These barns were used in medieval times as storehouses for grain and fodder payable to the Church in kind.

82

TISBURY — — — 96¼

LINE RISES 1:300

7 MINUTES

LEVEL

DINTON 92

LINE RISES 1:120

8 MINUTES

WILTON — — — 86¼

LINE FALLS 1:170

5 MINUTES

LINE RISES 1:183

SALISBURY 83¾ MILES FROM **LONDON**

LEVEL

9 MINUTES

LINE FALLS 1:140

PORTON 78¼

Speeds : Speeds are high as far as Porton, but trains approach the junction and tunnel beyond with regulators closed. Sharp curves necessitate that speed be reduced to 20 m.p.h. on both sides of Salisbury, and all trains stop at the Cathedral City in each direction. The rising gradient beyond Wilton keeps us down to 40 m.p.h., but between Dinton and Tisbury we reach 60 m.p.h.

LINE FALLS 1:440

22

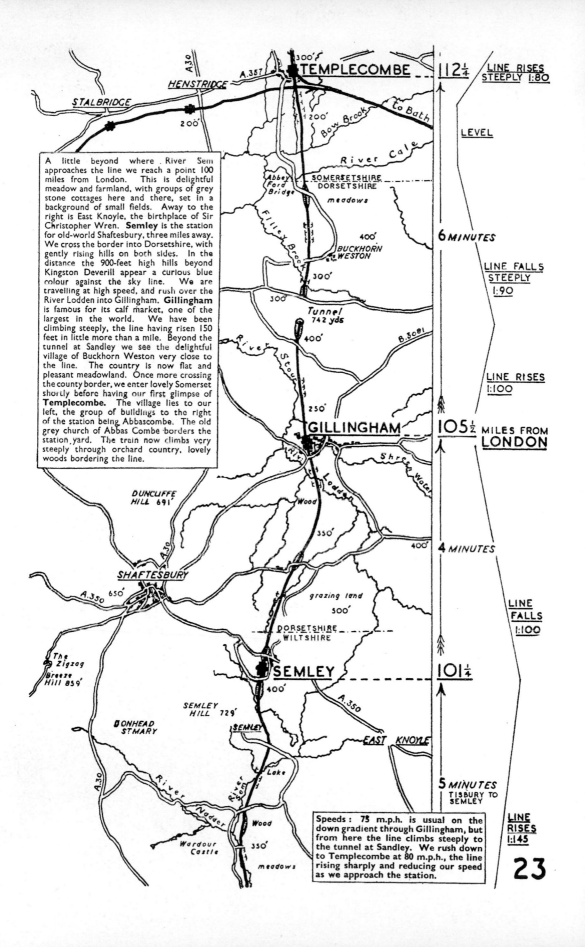

A little beyond where River Sem approaches the line we reach a point 100 miles from London. This is delightful meadow and farmland, with groups of grey stone cottages here and there, set in a background of small fields. Away to the right is East Knoyle, the birthplace of Sir Christopher Wren. **Semley** is the station for old-world Shaftesbury, three miles away. We cross the border into Dorsetshire, with gently rising hills on both sides. In the distance the 900-feet high hills beyond Kingston Deverill appear a curious blue colour against the sky line. We are travelling at high speed, and rush over the River Lodden into Gillingham. **Gillingham** is famous for its calf market, one of the largest in the world. We have been climbing steeply, the line having risen 150 feet in little more than a mile. Beyond the tunnel at Sandley we see the delightful village of Buckhorn Weston very close to the line. The country is now flat and pleasant meadowland. Once more crossing the county border, we enter lovely Somerset shortly before having our first glimpse of **Templecombe.** The village lies to our left, the group of buildings to the right of the station being Abbascombe. The old grey church of Abbas Combe borders the station yard. The train now climbs very steeply through orchard country, lovely woods bordering the line.

TEMPLECOMBE — 112¼ — LINE RISES STEEPLY 1:80

LEVEL

6 MINUTES

LINE FALLS STEEPLY 1:90

LINE RISES 1:100

GILLINGHAM — 105½ — MILES FROM LONDON

4 MINUTES

LINE FALLS 1:100

SEMLEY — 101¼

5 MINUTES TISBURY TO SEMLEY

LINE RISES 1:145

Speeds : 75 m.p.h. is usual on the down gradient through Gillingham, but from here the line climbs steeply to the tunnel at Sandley. We rush down to Templecombe at 80 m.p.h., the line rising sharply and reducing our speed as we approach the station.

23

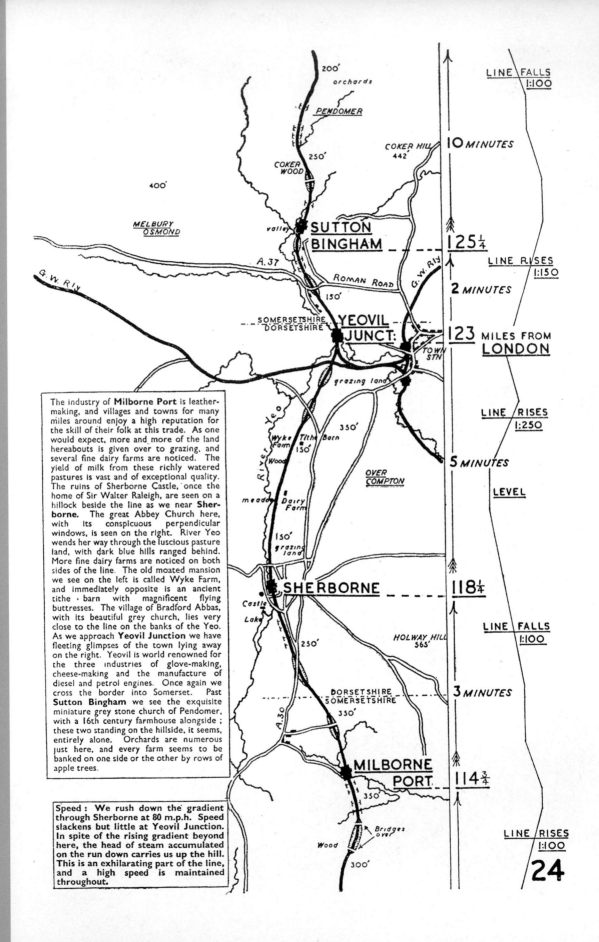

The industry of **Milborne Port** is leather-making, and villages and towns for many miles around enjoy a high reputation for the skill of their folk at this trade. As one would expect, more and more of the land hereabouts is given over to grazing, and several fine dairy farms are noticed. The yield of milk from these richly watered pastures is vast and of exceptional quality. The ruins of Sherborne Castle, once the home of Sir Walter Raleigh, are seen on a hillock beside the line as we near **Sherborne**. The great Abbey Church here, with its conspicuous perpendicular windows, is seen on the right. River Yeo wends her way through the luscious pasture land, with dark blue hills ranged behind. More fine dairy farms are noticed on both sides of the line. The old moated mansion we see on the left is called Wyke Farm, and immediately opposite is an ancient tithe · barn with magnificent flying buttresses. The village of Bradford Abbas, with its beautiful grey church, lies very close to the line on the banks of the Yeo. As we approach **Yeovil Junction** we have fleeting glimpses of the town lying away on the right. Yeovil is world renowned for the three industries of glove-making, cheese-making and the manufacture of diesel and petrol engines. Once again we cross the border into Somerset. Past **Sutton Bingham** we see the exquisite miniature grey stone church of Pendomer, with a 16th century farmhouse alongside ; these two standing on the hillside, it seems, entirely alone. Orchards are numerous just here, and every farm seems to be banked on one side or the other by rows of apple trees.

Speed : We rush down the gradient through Sherborne at 80 m.p.h. Speed slackens but little at Yeovil Junction. In spite of the rising gradient beyond here, the head of steam accumulated on the run down carries us up the hill. This is an exhilarating part of the line, and a high speed is maintained throughout.

84

24

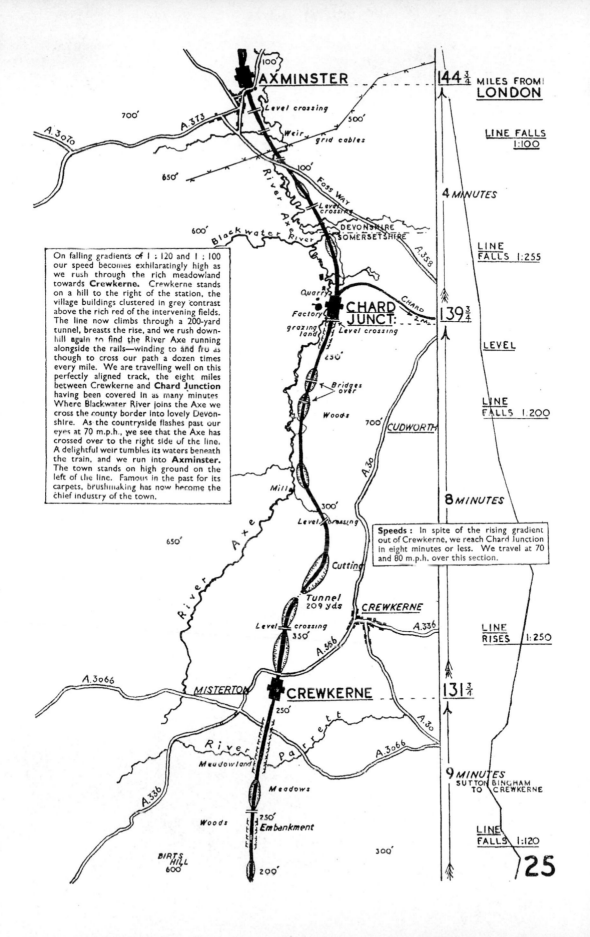

On falling gradients of 1 : 120 and 1 : 100 our speed becomes exhilaratingly high as we rush through the rich meadowland towards **Crewkerne.** Crewkerne stands on a hill to the right of the station, the village buildings clustered in grey contrast above the rich red of the intervening fields. The line now climbs through a 200-yard tunnel, breasts the rise, and we rush downhill again to find the River Axe running alongside the rails—winding to and fro as though to cross our path a dozen times every mile. We are travelling well on this perfectly aligned track, the eight miles between Crewkerne and **Chard Junction** having been covered in as many minutes Where Blackwater River joins the Axe we cross the county border into lovely Devonshire. As the countryside flashes past our eyes at 70 m.p.h., we see that the Axe has crossed over to the right side of the line. A delightful weir tumbles its waters beneath the train, and we run into **Axminster.** The town stands on high ground on the left of the line. Famous in the past for its carpets, brushmaking has now become the chief industry of the town.

Speeds : In spite of the rising gradient out of Crewkerne, we reach Chard Junction in eight minutes or less. We travel at 70 and 80 m.p.h. over this section.

AXMINSTER — 144¾ MILES FROM LONDON

LINE FALLS 1:100

4 MINUTES

LINE FALLS 1:255

CHARD JUNCT: — 139¾

LEVEL

LINE FALLS 1:200

8 MINUTES

CREWKERNE

LINE RISES 1:250

131¾

9 MINUTES SUTTON BINGHAM TO CREWKERNE

LINE FALLS 1:120

25

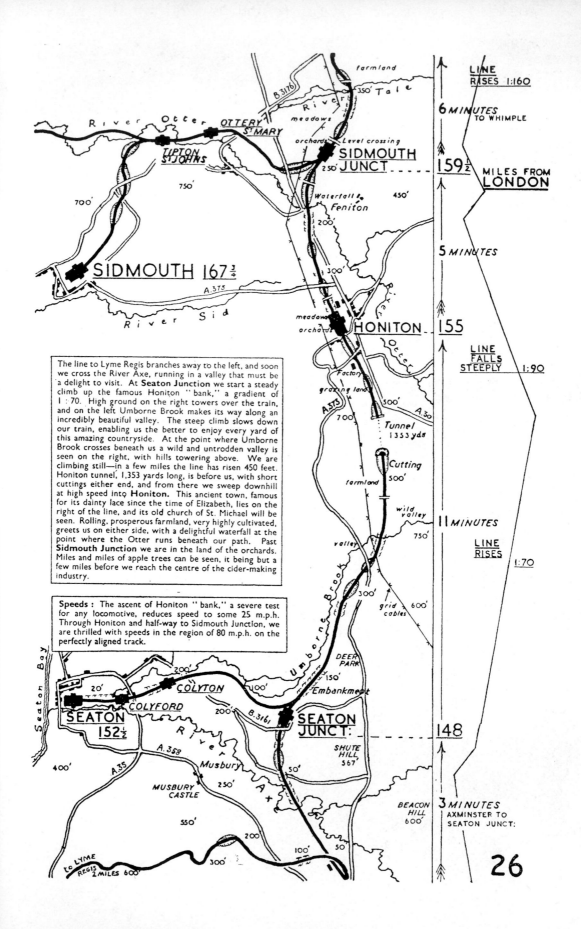

The line to Lyme Regis branches away to the left, and soon we cross the River Axe, running in a valley that must be a delight to visit. At **Seaton Junction** we start a steady climb up the famous Honiton "bank," a gradient of 1 : 70. High ground on the right towers over the train, and on the left Umborne Brook makes its way along an incredibly beautiful valley. The steep climb slows down our train, enabling us the better to enjoy every yard of this amazing countryside. At the point where Umborne Brook crosses beneath us a wild and untrodden valley is seen on the right, with hills towering above. We are climbing still—in a few miles the line has risen 450 feet. Honiton tunnel, 1,353 yards long, is before us, with short cuttings either end, and from there we sweep downhill at high speed into **Honiton**. This ancient town, famous for its dainty lace since the time of Elizabeth, lies on the right of the line, and its old church of St. Michael will be seen. Rolling, prosperous farmland, very highly cultivated, greets us on either side, with a delightful waterfall at the point where the Otter runs beneath our path. Past **Sidmouth Junction** we are in the land of the orchards. Miles and miles of apple trees can be seen, it being but a few miles before we reach the centre of the cider-making industry.

Speeds : The ascent of Honiton "bank," a severe test for any locomotive, reduces speed to some 25 m.p.h. Through Honiton and half-way to Sidmouth Junction, we are thrilled with speeds in the region of 80 m.p.h. on the perfectly aligned track.

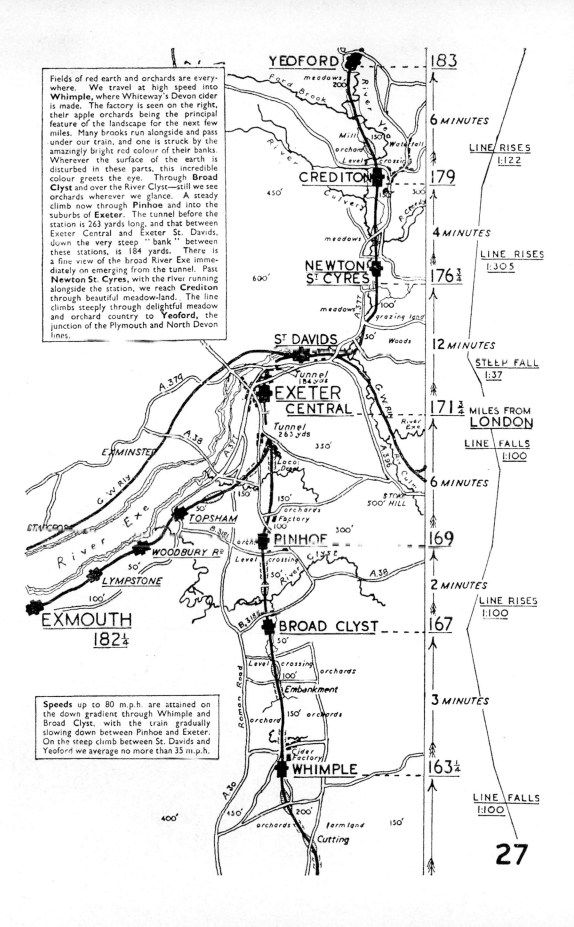

Fields of red earth and orchards are everywhere. We travel at high speed into **Whimple**, where Whiteway's Devon cider is made. The factory is seen on the right, their apple orchards being the principal feature of the landscape for the next few miles. Many brooks run alongside and pass under our train, and one is struck by the amazingly bright red colour of their banks. Wherever the surface of the earth is disturbed in these parts, this incredible colour greets the eye. Through **Broad Clyst** and over the River Clyst—still we see orchards wherever we glance. A steady climb now through **Pinhoe** and into the suburbs of **Exeter**. The tunnel before the station is 263 yards long, and that between Exeter Central and Exeter St. Davids, down the very steep "bank" between these stations, is 184 yards. There is a fine view of the broad River Exe immediately on emerging from the tunnel. Past **Newton St. Cyres**, with the river running alongside the station, we reach **Crediton** through beautiful meadow-land. The line climbs steeply through delightful meadow and orchard country to **Yeoford**, the junction of the Plymouth and North Devon lines.

Speeds up to 80 m.p.h. are attained on the down gradient through Whimple and Broad Clyst, with the train gradually slowing down between Pinhoe and Exeter. On the steep climb between St. Davids and Yeoford we average no more than 35 m.p.h.

YEOFORD — 183
6 MINUTES
LINE RISES 1:122
CREDITON — 179
4 MINUTES
LINE RISES 1:305
NEWTON ST CYRES — 176¾
12 MINUTES
STEEP FALL 1:37
ST DAVIDS
EXETER CENTRAL — 171¾ MILES FROM LONDON
LINE FALLS 1:100
6 MINUTES
PINHOE — 169
2 MINUTES
LINE RISES 1:100
BROAD CLYST — 167
3 MINUTES
WHIMPLE — 163¼
LINE FALLS 1:100

EXMOUTH 182¼

27

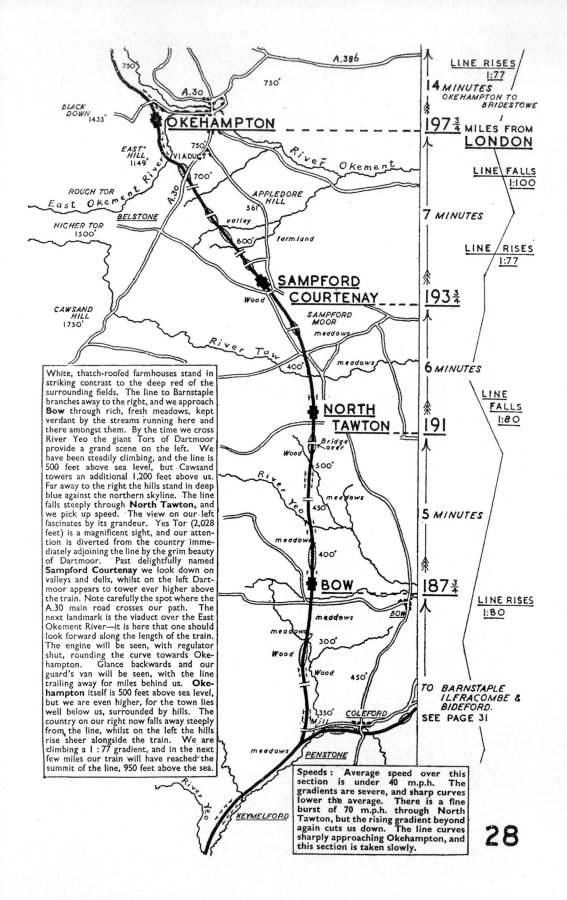

LINE RISES 1:77

14 MINUTES OKEHAMPTON TO BRIDESTOWE

197¾ MILES FROM **LONDON**

LINE FALLS 1:100

7 MINUTES

LINE RISES 1:77

193¾

6 MINUTES

LINE FALLS 1:80

191

5 MINUTES

187¾

LINE RISES 1:80

TO BARNSTAPLE ILFRACOMBE & BIDEFORD. SEE PAGE 31

A.386

750'

750'

BLACK DOWN 1433'

OKEHAMPTON

A.30

EAST HILL 1149'

VIADUCT

750'

ROUGH TOR

700'

East Okement River

APPLEDORE HILL 561'

River Okement

BELSTONE

valley

HIGHER TOR 1500'

600'

farmland

SAMPFORD COURTENAY

Wood

CAWSAND HILL 1750'

SAMPFORD MOOR

meadows

River Taw

400'

meadows

NORTH TAWTON

Wood

Bridge over

500'

River Yeo

meadows

450'

meadows

400'

BOW

BOW

meadows

meadows

300'

Wood

Wood

450'

350' Mill

COLEFORD

meadows

PENSTONE

River Yeo

KEYMELFORD

White, thatch-roofed farmhouses stand in striking contrast to the deep red of the surrounding fields. The line to Barnstaple branches away to the right, and we approach **Bow** through rich, fresh meadows, kept verdant by the streams running here and there amongst them. By the time we cross River Yeo the giant Tors of Dartmoor provide a grand scene on the left. We have been steadily climbing, and the line is 500 feet above sea level, but Cawsand towers an additional 1,200 feet above us. Far away to the right the hills stand in deep blue against the northern skyline. The line falls steeply through **North Tawton**, and we pick up speed. The view on our left fascinates by its grandeur. Yes Tor (2,028 feet) is a magnificent sight, and our attention is diverted from the country immediately adjoining the line by the grim beauty of Dartmoor. Past delightfully named **Sampford Courtenay** we look down on valleys and dells, whilst on the left Dartmoor appears to tower ever higher above the train. Note carefully the spot where the A.30 main road crosses our path. The next landmark is the viaduct over the East Okement River—it is here that one should look forward along the length of the train. The engine will be seen, with regulator shut, rounding the curve towards Okehampton. Glance backwards and our guard's van will be seen, with the line trailing away for miles behind us. **Okehampton** itself is 500 feet above sea level, but we are even higher, for the town lies well below us, surrounded by hills. The country on our right now falls away steeply from the line, whilst on the left the hills rise sheer alongside the train. We are climbing a 1:77 gradient, and in the next few miles our train will have reached the summit of the line, 950 feet above the sea.

Speeds : Average speed over this section is under 40 m.p.h. The gradients are severe, and sharp curves lower the average. There is a fine burst of 70 m.p.h. through North Tawton, but the rising gradient beyond again cuts us down. The line curves sharply approaching Okehampton, and this section is taken slowly.

28

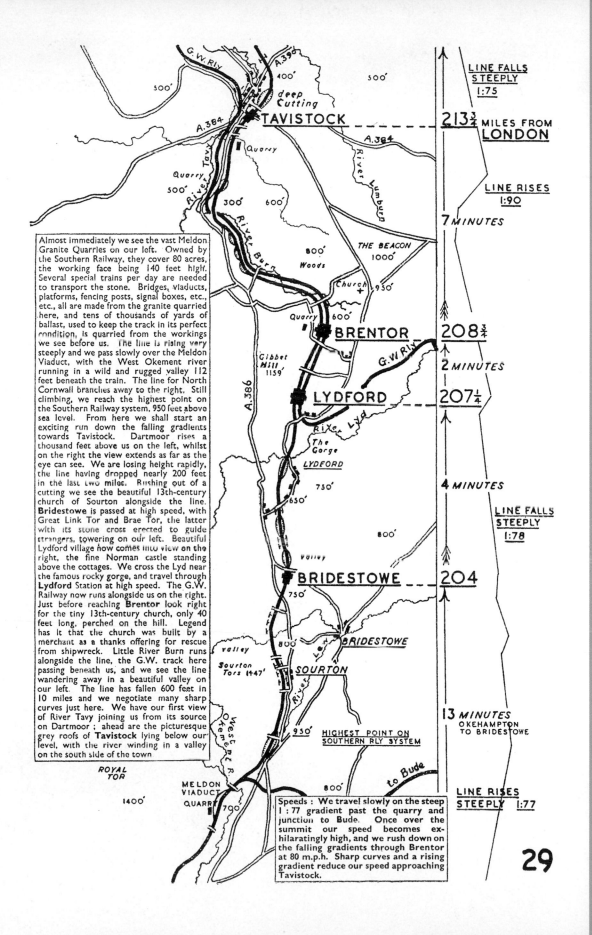

Almost immediately we see the vast Meldon Granite Quarries on our left. Owned by the Southern Railway, they cover 80 acres, the working face being 140 feet high. Several special trains per day are needed to transport the stone. Bridges, viaducts, platforms, fencing posts, signal boxes, etc., etc., all are made from the granite quarried here, and tens of thousands of yards of ballast, used to keep the track in its perfect condition, is quarried from the workings we see before us. The line is rising very steeply and we pass slowly over the Meldon Viaduct, with the West Okement river running in a wild and rugged valley 112 feet beneath the train. The line for North Cornwall branches away to the right. Still climbing, we reach the highest point on the Southern Railway system, 950 feet above sea level. From here we shall start an exciting run down the falling gradients towards Tavistock. Dartmoor rises a thousand feet above us on the left, whilst on the right the view extends as far as the eye can see. We are losing height rapidly, the line having dropped nearly 200 feet in the last two miles. Rushing out of a cutting we see the beautiful 13th-century church of Sourton alongside the line. **Bridestowe** is passed at high speed, with Great Link Tor and Brae Tor, the latter with its stone cross erected to guide strangers, towering on our left. Beautiful Lydford village now comes into view on the right, the fine Norman castle standing above the cottages. We cross the Lyd near the famous rocky gorge, and travel through **Lydford** Station at high speed. The G.W. Railway now runs alongside us on the right. Just before reaching **Brentor** look right for the tiny 13th-century church, only 40 feet long, perched on the hill. Legend has it that the church was built by a merchant as a thanks offering for rescue from shipwreck. Little River Burn runs alongside the line, the G.W. track here passing beneath us, and we see the line wandering away in a beautiful valley on our left. The line has fallen 600 feet in 10 miles and we negotiate many sharp curves just here. We have our first view of River Tavy joining us from its source on Dartmoor; ahead are the picturesque grey roofs of **Tavistock** lying below our level, with the river winding in a valley on the south side of the town.

Speeds : We travel slowly on the steep 1 : 77 gradient past the quarry and junction to Bude. Once over the summit our speed becomes exhilaratingly high, and we rush down on the falling gradients through Brentor at 80 m.p.h. Sharp curves and a rising gradient reduce our speed approaching Tavistock.

29

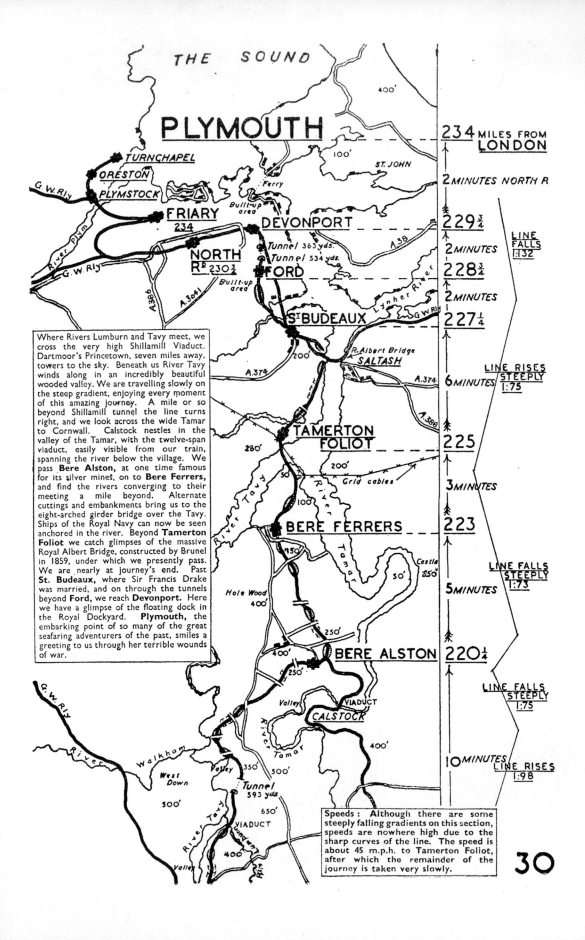

THE SOUND

PLYMOUTH

TURNCHAPEL

ORESTON

PLYMSTOCK

G.W.Rly

Ferry

Built-up area

ST. JOHN

100'

400'

FRIARY
234

DEVONPORT

A.38

River Plym

G.W. Rly

NORTH
Rd 230¾

A.386

A.3041

Built-up area

FORD

Tunnel 363 yds.

Tunnel 534 yds.

St BUDEAUX

200'

A.374

R. Albert Bridge
SALTASH

Lynher River

A.374

G.W.Rly

A.388

TAMERTON
FOLIOT

280'

200'

Grid cables

River Tavy

50'

100'

BERE FERRERS

150'

River Tamar

Castle
250'

50'

Hole Wood
400'

250'

400'

250'

BERE ALSTON

250'

River Walkham

Valley

VIADUCT

CALSTOCK

West
Down

500'

Valley

350'

500'

Tunnel
593 yds

650'

VIADUCT

River Tavy

400'

Valley

River Tamar

400'

---

234 MILES FROM **LONDON**

2 MINUTES NORTH Rd

229¾

LINE
FALLS
1:132

2 MINUTES

228¾

2 MINUTES

227¼

LINE RISES
STEEPLY
1:75

6 MINUTES

225

3 MINUTES

223

LINE FALLS
STEEPLY
1:73

5 MINUTES

220¼

LINE FALLS
STEEPLY
1:75

10 MINUTES LINE RISES
1:98

Where Rivers Lumburn and Tavy meet, we cross the very high Shillamill Viaduct. Dartmoor's Princetown, seven miles away, towers to the sky. Beneath us River Tavy winds along in an incredibly beautiful wooded valley. We are travelling slowly on the steep gradient, enjoying every moment of this amazing journey. A mile or so beyond Shillamill tunnel the line turns right, and we look across the wide Tamar to Cornwall. Calstock nestles in the valley of the Tamar, with the twelve-span viaduct, easily visible from our train, spanning the river below the village. We pass **Bere Alston,** at one time famous for its silver mines, on to **Bere Ferrers,** and find the rivers converging to their meeting a mile beyond. Alternate cuttings and embankments bring us to the eight-arched girder bridge over the Tavy. Ships of the Royal Navy can now be seen anchored in the river. Beyond **Tamerton Foliot** we catch glimpses of the massive Royal Albert Bridge, constructed by Brunel in 1859, under which we presently pass. We are nearly at journey's end. Past **St. Budeaux,** where Sir Francis Drake was married, and on through the tunnels beyond **Ford,** we reach **Devonport.** Here we have a glimpse of the floating dock in the Royal Dockyard. **Plymouth,** the embarking point of so many of the great seafaring adventurers of the past, smiles a greeting to us through her terrible wounds of war.

Speeds : Although there are some steeply falling gradients on this section, speeds are nowhere high due to the sharp curves of the line. The speed is about 45 m.p.h. to Tamerton Foliot, after which the remainder of the journey is taken very slowly.

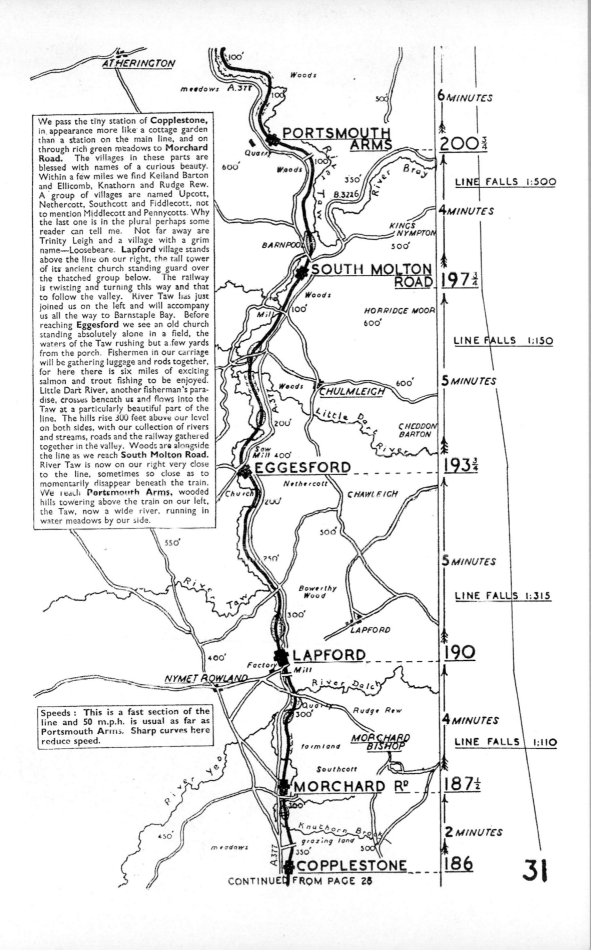

ATHERINGTON

We pass the tiny station of **Copplestone**, in appearance more like a cottage garden than a station on the main line, and on through rich green meadows to **Morchard Road**. The villages in these parts are blessed with names of a curious beauty. Within a few miles we find Keiland Barton and Ellicomb, Knathorn and Rudge Rew. A group of villages are named Upcott, Nethercott, Southcott and Fiddlecott, not to mention Middlecott and Pennycotts. Why the last one is in the plural perhaps some reader can tell me. Not far away are Trinity Leigh and a village with a grim name—Loosebeare. **Lapford** village stands above the line on our right, the tall tower of its ancient church standing guard over the thatched group below. The railway is twisting and turning this way and that to follow the valley. River Taw has just joined us on the left and will accompany us all the way to Barnstaple Bay. Before reaching **Eggesford** we see an old church standing absolutely alone in a field, the waters of the Taw rushing but a few yards from the porch. Fishermen in our carriage will be gathering luggage and rods together, for here there is six miles of exciting salmon and trout fishing to be enjoyed. Little Dart River, another fisherman's paradise, crosses beneath us and flows into the Taw at a particularly beautiful part of the line. The hills rise 300 feet above our level on both sides, with our collection of rivers and streams, roads and the railway gathered together in the valley. Woods are alongside the line as we reach **South Molton Road**. River Taw is now on our right very close to the line, sometimes so close as to momentarily disappear beneath the train. We reach **Portsmouth Arms**, wooded hills towering above the train on our left, the Taw, now a wide river, running in water meadows by our side.

Speeds: This is a fast section of the line and 50 m.p.h. is usual as far as Portsmouth Arms. Sharp curves here reduce speed.

PORTSMOUTH ARMS 200¾
6 MINUTES
LINE FALLS 1:500
4 MINUTES

KINGS NYMPTON 500'

SOUTH MOLTON ROAD 197¾

HORRIDGE MOOR 600'

LINE FALLS 1:150
5 MINUTES

CHULMLEIGH

Little Dart River

CHEDDON BARTON

EGGESFORD 193¾

Nethercott
CHAWLEIGH

5 MINUTES

Bowerthy Wood

LINE FALLS 1:315

LAPFORD

LAPFORD 190

River Dalch

Rudge Rew

4 MINUTES
LINE FALLS 1:110

MORCHARD BISHOP

Southcott

MORCHARD Rᴰ 187½

Knathorn Brook
grazing land
2 MINUTES

COPPLESTONE 186

CONTINUED FROM PAGE 28

31

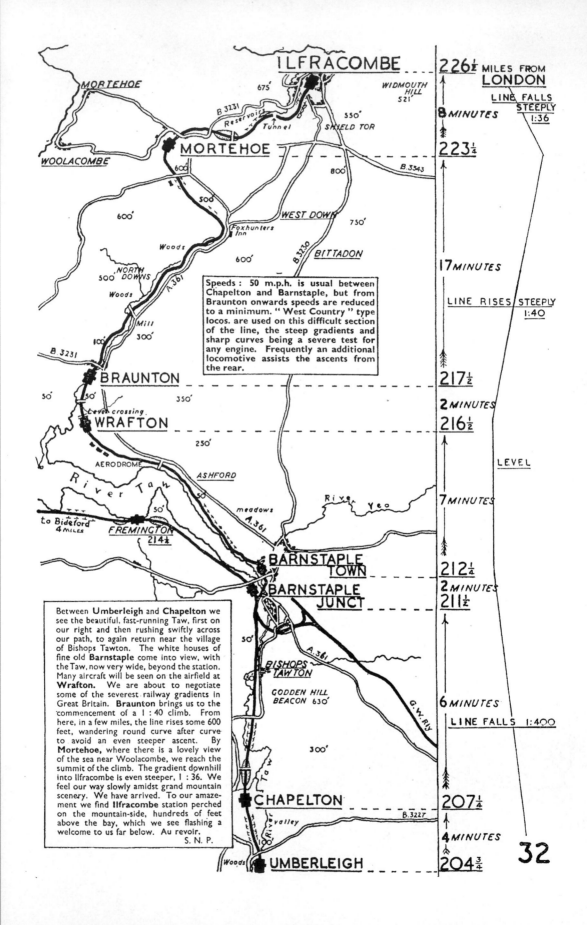

MILES FROM LONDON

ILFRACOMBE — 226½

LINE FALLS STEEPLY 1:36

8 MINUTES

MORTEHOE — 223¼

17 MINUTES

LINE RISES STEEPLY 1:40

Speeds : 50 m.p.h. is usual between Chapelton and Barnstaple, but from Braunton onwards speeds are reduced to a minimum. "West Country" type locos. are used on this difficult section of the line, the steep gradients and sharp curves being a severe test for any engine. Frequently an additional locomotive assists the ascents from the rear.

BRAUNTON — 217½

2 MINUTES

WRAFTON — 216½

LEVEL

7 MINUTES

FREMINGTON — 214¼

BARNSTAPLE TOWN — 212¼

2 MINUTES

BARNSTAPLE JUNCT — 211½

Between **Umberleigh** and **Chapelton** we see the beautiful, fast-running Taw, first on our right and then rushing swiftly across our path, to again return near the village of Bishops Tawton. The white houses of fine old **Barnstaple** come into view, with the Taw, now very wide, beyond the station. Many aircraft will be seen on the airfield at **Wrafton.** We are about to negotiate some of the severest railway gradients in Great Britain. **Braunton** brings us to the commencement of a 1 : 40 climb. From here, in a few miles, the line rises some 600 feet, wandering round curve after curve to avoid an even steeper ascent. By **Mortehoe,** where there is a lovely view of the sea near Woolacombe, we reach the summit of the climb. The gradient downhill into Ilfracombe is even steeper, 1 : 36. We feel our way slowly amidst grand mountain scenery. We have arrived. To our amazement we find **Ilfracombe** station perched on the mountain-side, hundreds of feet above the bay, which we see flashing a welcome to us far below. Au revoir.
S. N. P.

6 MINUTES

LINE FALLS 1:400

CHAPELTON — 207¼

4 MINUTES

UMBERLEIGH — 204¾

32

LONDON über OSTENDE-DOVER

WINTER 1937/38

Budapest k. p. u. (Ostbhf.) ab	10⁰⁵[o] L	—	23⁵⁰	8¹⁰(p)	8⁰⁰(p)
Wien Westbhf.	15¹⁴ L		10³⁵	14²⁰(p)	14²⁰(p)
München Hbf.	—	13⁰⁶(a):14⁰³	17¹⁶	23³⁰	22³⁵(a):23²⁰
Nürnberg Hbf.	22³⁵ L	15¹⁴[m]	19¹⁹	19¹²(g)	2⁰⁰
Stuttgart Hbf.		16³⁶:17⁰⁵	20³¹(k)	23¹⁰	2¹²
Basel D.R.B.		15¹⁰	19²⁵(r)	23¹⁰	0³³[b]
Freiburg i. Br. Hbf.		16⁰⁴	20¹⁸(r)	23⁵⁹	1²⁴(b)
Baden-Baden		17¹⁸	21²⁷	0²⁶(f)	1⁵⁶(f)(b)
Karlsruhe Hbf.		18⁰⁴(h):18⁰⁶	22⁰⁶(r)	1³⁴	3⁴¹(b)
Heidelberg Hbf.		18⁴³	22⁵⁸[m]	1⁰⁵	4¹⁶
Mannheim Hbf.		19¹⁰	23³¹[m]	2¹³	4³⁹
Ludwigshafen Hbf.		19³¹[j]	23³⁵(e)	1⁴⁵	5¹⁰
Frankfurt a. M. Hbf.	2¹¹ L	20⁰⁴	0¹³	4⁴⁶	7¹⁹
Mainz Hbf.	2³⁸[o]	20³⁵	0³⁷(e)	5¹⁹	7⁵⁶(e)
Wiesbaden Hbf.	2⁵³ L	20¹⁷[j]	1¹⁰	4³³[j]	8¹⁶
Köln Hbf.	5²⁵ L	1⁰¹	4²¹	9⁰⁰(d)	11¹⁰(d)
Ostende		11⁰⁰		15²⁰	
London (Victoria) an		16²⁰		20⁴⁵(f)	

(L) = Schlafwagenzug 1. und 2. Klasse, verkehrt nur Dienstags, Donnerstags, Samstags von Budapest.   (b) = Umsteigen in Ludwigshafen (an 4⁰⁰, ab 5²⁵).
(d) = Pullmanzug 1. und 2. Klasse Köln–Ostende.   (e) = Umsteigen in Wiesbaden.   (f) = ab mit Städt. Straßenbahn.   (g) = Umsteigen in Stuttgart.   (h) = Sonntags 21⁰⁰.
(j) = Umsteigen in Mainz Hbf.   (k) = Umsteigen in Karlsruhe o. Frankfurt a. M.   (m) = Umsteigen in Frankfurt Hbf.   (o) = ab Budapest Westbhf.   (p) = über Salzburg–München.
(r) = in Berliner Kurswagen, Umsteigen in Frankfurt a. M. Hbf.

Verkehr nur Di, Mi, Do, Fr, Sa, So

FAHRKARTEN und **AUSKUNFT** auf allen größeren Bahnhöfen durch **MER-BUROS** und die
General-Vertretung der **SOUTHERN RAILWAY**, Köln, Domhof 6

SOUTHERN RAILWAY OF ENGLAND

Mile by Mile
on the LMSR

- Norman Wilkinson -

The LMSR Story

From Gloucester to Glasgow, Wolverhampton to Wick, the LMSR was largest of the 'Big Four.' It was initially divided by rivalries but later united by the awe-inspiring sight of Stanier Pacifics conquering the northern fells and connecting London with the north-west and Scotland.

Forming the London Midland & Scottish Railway called for a grudging alliance between two bitter rivals. The London & North Western relished its nickname of the 'Premier Line.' Superiority came from being, in the form of the London & Birmingham Railway, the first main line into the capital. The Midland Railway was a comparative upstart that had dared to challenge the L&NWR on its home ground. With 2,186 (3,518km) and 2,835 route miles (4,562.49km) respectively, these were easily the largest of the constituent companies. Of the others, the Lancashire & Yorkshire had merged with the L&NWR in January 1922, which left the North Staffordshire and Furness Railways to join the fold. Three major Scottish concerns were absorbed: the Caledonian, Glasgow & South Western, and Highland.

The North London Railway had been under L&NWR control since 1909, and in 1912 the Midland had acquired the London, Tilbury & Southend Railway. Adding these saw the LMSR's tentacles extend from London's docks and the Thames Estuary to Holyhead, through central Wales to Swansea, and to Wick and Thurso in northernmost Scotland. Its trains reached Bristol and Gloucester and (through a joint operation with the Southern Railway over the Somerset & Dorset line) Bath and Bournemouth. Another joint line, the Midland & Great Northern, linked the East Midlands with the Norfolk coast. However, the bulk of the LMSR's revenue (sixty per cent of it from freight) originated in the industrial heartlands of the Midlands, Potteries, Greater Manchester, West Yorkshire, Merseyside, Furness and southern Scotland. Through them ran the two routes illustrated in *Mile by Mile*.

▲ Following William Stanier's introduction of heavier locomotives and trains, many structures had to be strengthened. Here, a crane lowers cross-sections to be laid over girders during bridge reconstruction (probably on the River Derwent between Derby and Ambergate) in May 1934.

▲ Stanier needed a locomotive capable of hauling heavier trains over the northern hills, and his 'Princess Royal' Pacifics broke records in doing so. In November 1936, during out-and-back trials between Euston and Glasgow, no.6201 *Princess Elizabeth* took only 5 hours 37 minutes on its 401-mile (645.3-km) return trip, averaging 71.4mph (114.9kph).

North-West Passage

Leaving Euston, the L&NWR threaded through Hertfordshire and Buckinghamshire before reaching Rugby, where lines left for Birmingham, Coventry and Northampton. Crewe, 158 miles (254.2km) from London, had become a major railway hub with links to Shrewsbury, Chester, the North Wales coast, Liverpool, Manchester and Stoke-on-Trent. From Crewe the West Coast main line extended northwards to Preston, Carlisle and onwards to Glasgow.

In 1868, the Midland opened its Gothic-style terminus of St Pancras a quarter of a mile from Euston. From here it took a path through Bedford, Leicester and Loughborough before dividing to serve Nottingham, Derby (the headquarters of the company), Chesterfield, Manchester, Sheffield and Leeds. The Midland's ambitions did not end there. The construction of the Leeds-Settle-Carlisle line was costly in both human and financial terms but, when opened in 1875, it gave the Midland its long sought-after route into Scotland, ending dependence on the L&NWR for access north of the border.

Today, the LMSR would have entered the record books. It was the world's largest privately run transport enterprise, and the biggest commercial concern within the British Empire. It employed 274,000 people, owned 10,385 locomotives, ruled over 7,909 route miles (12,728.3km) and had a presence in thirty-two out of forty English counties. It was, though, an unwieldy organisation, something not helped by continuing rivalry between Midland and L&NWR factions. Generally the Midland prevailed. The selection of its 'crimson lake' livery for passenger locomotives and rolling stock over the L&NWR's 'blackberry black' may have been inconsequential, but persistence with the Midland's 'small engine' policy had severe repercussions.

Company chairman Sir Guy Granet, an ex-Midland man, ensured that in 1925 Derby's Henry Fowler, who was more metallurgist than mechanic, became Chief Mechanical Engineer. Despite the arrival of heavier rolling stock – the LMSR pioneered all-steel carriages – and longer trains, Fowler continued with the passenger 4-4-0s and goods 0-6-0s that

filled the Midland ranks. Greater power was urgently needed, and it came in the shape of the 'Royal Scot' 4-6-0. Though credited to Fowler, the design – based (with its blessing) on the Southern Railway's 'Lord Nelson' – was attributable to the Chief Draughtsman of Glasgow's North British Locomotive Company, Herbert Chambers. His employers were rewarded with a contract for fifty engines, delivered in record time during 1927. Though they transformed Anglo-Scottish services, the impact of the 'Scots' was inevitably limited.

Company head Sir Josiah Stamp recognised that updating the LMSR's motive power cried out for fresh ideas, and, on Fowler's retirement, recruited William Stanier from the GWR. Stanier, tutored in the Churchward school, restocked the fleet with modern designs. He introduced a 2-8-0 freighter, a mixed traffic 4-6-0 (the 'Black 5'), the 'Jubilee' 4-6-0 for passenger services, and classes of 2-6-2 and 2-6-4 tank engines. Stanier's most celebrated designs were the 'Princess Royal' and streamlined 'Princess Coronation' 4-6-2s whose principal role was to compete with the LNER Pacifics on the London to Scotland run. This they did, covering the 401 miles (645,3km) from Euston to Glasgow in six-and-a-half hours, an average speed of 62mph (99.7kph).

In twelve years up to 1944, Stanier transformed front-line LMSR motive power and created an impressive template for the future. Construction of no fewer than 842 'Black 5s' continued up to 1951, while the '8F' 2-8-0 was selected for wartime use until its requirement for scarce metals led to a more basic design.

Given the size and scope of its operations, the LMSR's profitability had been disappointing. In 1927 an American-style management system had been brought in with vice-presidents reporting to a company president (Josiah Stamp was the first). It gave the organisation a fresh impetus. Operating departments no longer dictated matters; instead, commercial managers told them what they required. The effect was soon felt as the LMSR introduced bargain fares, excursion trains and special deals for freight customers. Passenger journeys rose dramatically from 6,500 million in 1932 to 8,500 million in 1937; and, during 1938, the LMSR ran no fewer than 22,000 special trains.

Given its earlier reluctance to change, it was remarkable that, in 1947, the LMSR, working in conjunction with English Electric, unveiled Britain's first two main-line diesel-electric locomotives, nos.10000 and 10001. But it would be Stanier's engines that had the last word, with both '8F' 2-8-0s and 'Black 5s' operating up to British Railways' final day of steam working, 11 August 1968.

◀ No.6225 *Duchess of Gloucester* was the first of a batch of 'Coronation' Pacifics painted 'crimson lake' to match standard LMSR rolling stock. Outshopped from Crewe in May 1938, it leaves Euston on 8 June, taking a group of railway experts to an Institute of Locomotive Engineers' meeting in Glasgow.

▶ 'Royal Scot' no.6130 *West Yorkshire Regiment* accelerates through the rock cuttings and tunnels on the exit from Liverpool Lime Street with a train for Euston. It is in original, parallel-boiler condition; under Stanier the entire class was rebuilt with taper boilers to improve performance. Two 'Royal Scots' have survived: no.46100 *Royal Scot* and no.46115 *Scots Guardsman*.

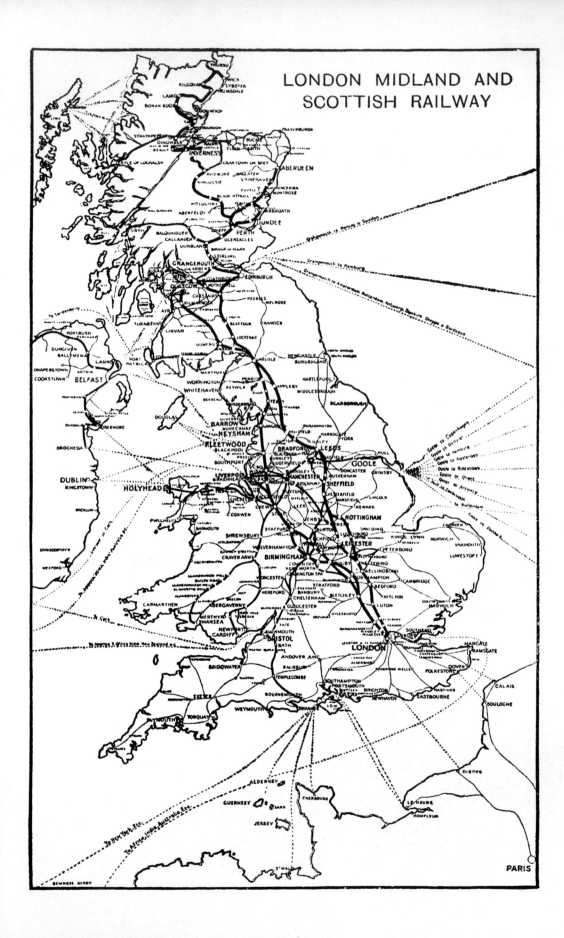

LONDON MIDLAND AND SCOTTISH RAILWAY

Mile by Mile

ON THE L.M.S.

by

S. N. PIKE, M.B.E.

MIDLAND REGION EDITION
BRITISH RAILWAYS

The journey between Euston and St. Pancras and the North and North-West described in detail :—

- GRADIENTS OF THE LINE
- SPEED TESTS AND MILEAGES
- VIADUCTS, BRIDGES AND EMBANKMENTS
- TUNNELS, CUTTINGS AND CROSSOVERS
- STREAMS, RIVERS AND ROADS
- MINES, FACTORIES AND WORKS

with an account of features of interest and beauty to be seen from the train.

Published by
STUART N. PIKE,
3, Canterbury House,
Worthing, Sussex

Sole Distributors to the Trade :—
Atlas Publishing and Distributing Co., Ltd.,
18, Bride Lane, London, E.C.4.

PRINCIPAL STATIONS

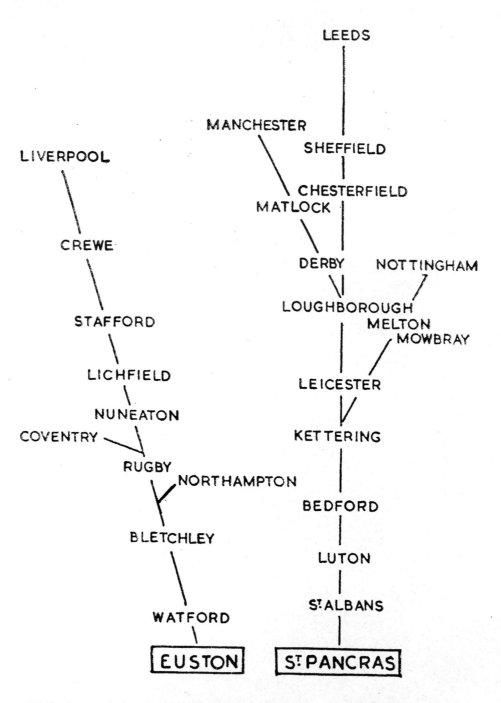

FOR INDEX TO ALL STATIONS
SEE PAGE 4

Author's Note

In this, my third railway book, I have to again acknowledge, with grateful thanks, the valuable assistance I have received from all grades of railway officials. Those whose daily work it is to ensure speedy and comfortable travel on the Midland Region of British Railways have thrown themselves enthusiastically into the task of helping me with the construction of this little book.

Embodied in this edition are many helpful suggestions received from readers of my previous books " Mile by Mile on the Southern Railway " and " Mile by Mile on the L.N.E.R."   To these correspondents I am extremely grateful, and if I have not adopted all the ideas put forward it is because I wished to keep all three booklets in line as to style, size and price, so that they all may be considered as companion editions and, with the forthcoming Western Region edition (G.W. Railway), form a set covering the most used main railway lines in the country.

I am indebted to the Railway Publishing Co. Ltd. for their kind permission to reproduce certain of the diagrams from their publication " Gradients of British Main Line Railways."

To save correspondence I would say here that I will advise all old and new post customers for my books when the G.W. Railway (Western Region) edition is ready for sale, and as other railway books by me become available.

3 Canterbury House,
       Worthing, Sussex.

S. N. P.

Index to Stations

Rivers we meet

Canals

For index of Tunnels and Water-Troughs en route see page 6

Tunnels en Route

Water-Trough Installations en Route

106

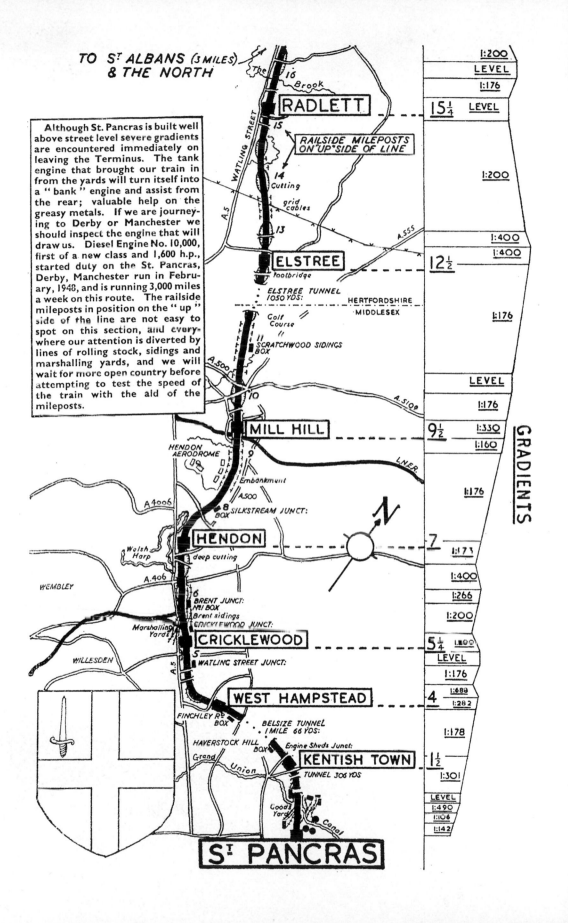

TO S^T ALBANS (3 MILES) & THE NORTH

The Brook

16

RADLETT

15

RAILSIDE MILEPOSTS ON "UP" SIDE OF LINE

14 Cutting

grid cables

A.555

13

ELSTREE

footbridge

ELSTREE TUNNEL 1050 YDS.

HERTFORDSHIRE
MIDDLESEX

Golf Course

11 SCRATCHWOOD SIDINGS BOX

A.500

A.5109

10

MILL HILL

HENDON AERODROME

9

Embankment

A.500

L.N.E.R.

8 BOX SILKSTREAM JUNCT:

HENDON

Welsh Harp

deep cutting

A.406

WEMBLEY

6 BRENT JUNCT: Nº1 BOX
Brent sidings
CRICKLEWOOD JUNCT:

Marshalling Yards

CRICKLEWOOD

5

WILLESDEN

WATLING STREET JUNCT:

WEST HAMPSTEAD

FINCHLEY Rº BOX

BELSIZE TUNNEL
1 MILE 66 YDS.

HAVERSTOCK HILL BOX

Grand Union

Engine Sheds Junct:

KENTISH TOWN

TUNNEL 306 YDS.

Goods Yard

Canal

S^T PANCRAS

Although St. Pancras is built well above street level severe gradients are encountered immediately on leaving the Terminus. The tank engine that brought our train in from the yards will turn itself into a "bank" engine and assist from the rear; valuable help on the greasy metals. If we are journeying to Derby or Manchester we should inspect the engine that will draw us. Diesel Engine No. 10,000, first of a new class and 1,600 h.p., started duty on the St. Pancras, Derby, Manchester run in February, 1948, and is running 3,000 miles a week on this route. The railside mileposts in position on the "up" side of the line are not easy to spot on this section, and everywhere our attention is diverted by lines of rolling stock, sidings and marshalling yards, and we will wait for more open country before attempting to test the speed of the train with the aid of the mileposts.

GRADIENTS

1:200	LEVEL
	LEVEL
1:176	
15¼	LEVEL
	1:200
	1:400
	1:400
12½	
	1:176
	LEVEL
	1:176
9½	1:330
	1:160
	1:176
7	1:173
	1:400
	1:266
	1:200
5¼	1:200
	LEVEL
	1:176
4	1:688
	1:282
	1:178
1½	1:301
	LEVEL
	1:490
	1:106
	1:142

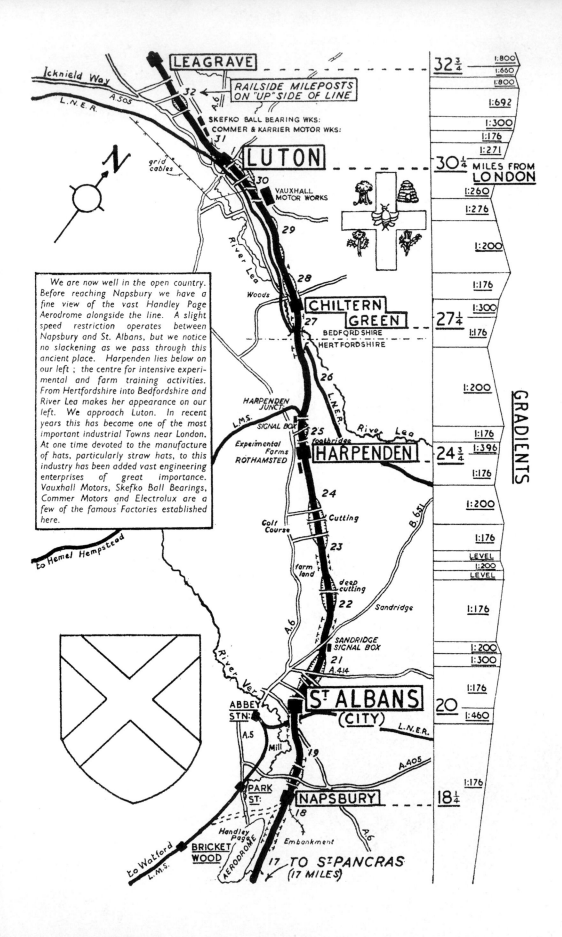

We are now well in the open country. Before reaching Napsbury we have a fine view of the vast Handley Page Aerodrome alongside the line. A slight speed restriction operates between Napsbury and St. Albans, but we notice no slackening as we pass through this ancient place. Harpenden lies below on our left ; the centre for intensive experimental and farm training activities. From Hertfordshire into Bedfordshire and River Lea makes her appearance on our left. We approach Luton. In recent years this has become one of the most important industrial Towns near London. At one time devoted to the manufacture of hats, particularly straw hats, to this industry has been added vast engineering enterprises of great importance. Vauxhall Motors, Skefko Ball Bearings, Commer Motors and Electrolux are a few of the famous Factories established here.

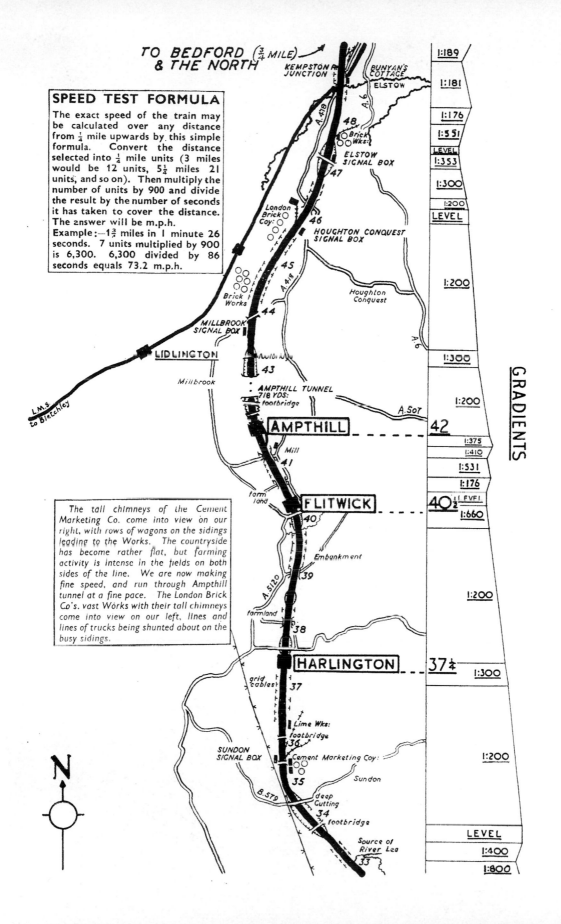

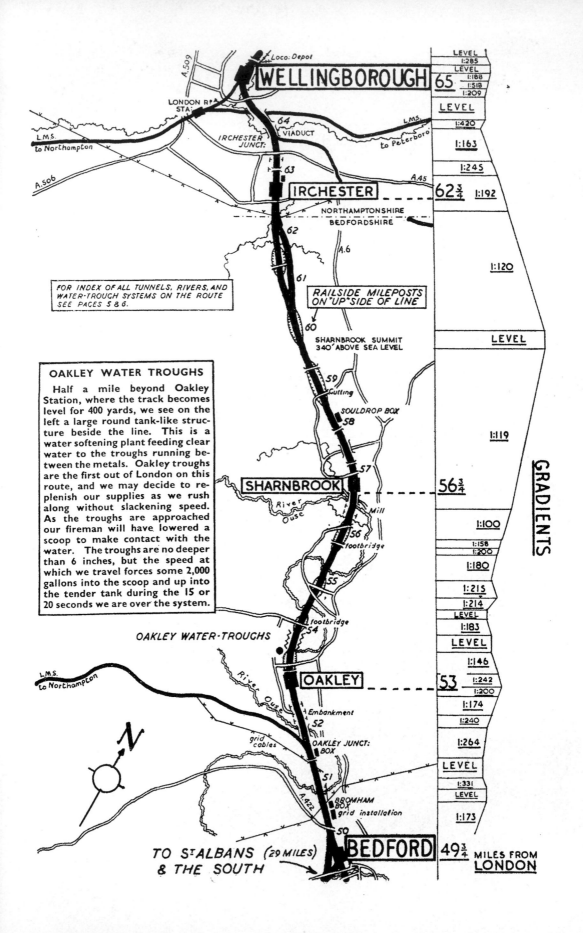

OAKLEY WATER TROUGHS

Half a mile beyond Oakley Station, where the track becomes level for 400 yards, we see on the left a large round tank-like structure beside the line. This is a water softening plant feeding clear water to the troughs running between the metals. Oakley troughs are the first out of London on this route, and we may decide to replenish our supplies as we rush along without slackening speed. As the troughs are approached our fireman will have lowered a scoop to make contact with the water. The troughs are no deeper than 6 inches, but the speed at which we travel forces some 2,000 gallons into the scoop and up into the tender tank during the 15 or 20 seconds we are over the system.

FOR INDEX OF ALL TUNNELS, RIVERS, AND WATER-TROUGH SYSTEMS ON THE ROUTE SEE PAGES 5 & 6.

RAILSIDE MILEPOSTS ON "UP" SIDE OF LINE

WELLINGBOROUGH 65

Loco: Depot
LONDON R⁰ STA:
IRCHESTER JUNCT:
VIADUCT
to Peterboro
to Northampton
IRCHESTER 62¾
NORTHAMPTONSHIRE
BEDFORDSHIRE
SHARNBROOK SUMMIT 340' ABOVE SEA LEVEL
Cutting
SOULDROP BOX
SHARNBROOK 56¾
River Ouse
Mill
footbridge
footbridge
OAKLEY WATER-TROUGHS
to Northampton
River Ouse
OAKLEY 53
Embankment
grid cables
OAKLEY JUNCT: BOX
BROMHAM BOX
grid installation
TO St ALBANS (29 MILES) & THE SOUTH
BEDFORD 49¾

GRADIENTS

Gradient
LEVEL 1:285
LEVEL 1:188
1:518
1:209
LEVEL
1:420
1:163
1:245
1:192
1:120
LEVEL
1:119
1:100
1:158
1:200
1:180
1:215
1:214
LEVEL
1:183
LEVEL
1:146
1:242
1:200
1:174
1:240
1:264
LEVEL
1:331
LEVEL
1:173

MILES FROM LONDON

110

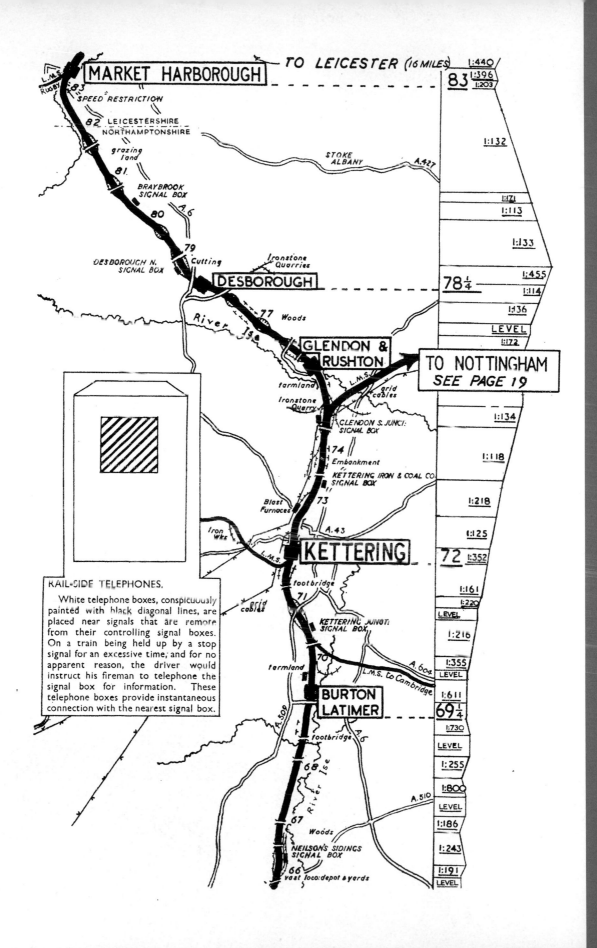

TO LEICESTER (16 MILES)

1:440

MARKET HARBOROUGH

83 1:396
    1:203

L.M.S. RUGBY

SPEED RESTRICTION

82 LEICESTERSHIRE
    NORTHAMPTONSHIRE

1:132

grazing land

81

STOKE ALBANY   A.427

BRAYBROOK SIGNAL BOX

80   A.6

1:171
1:113

79   *Cutting*

DESBOROUGH N. SIGNAL BOX

1:133

Ironstone Quarries

DESBOROUGH

78¼ 1:455
     1:114

77 *Woods*

1:136

River Ise

LEVEL
1:172

GLENDON & RUSHTON

L.M.S.

TO NOTTINGHAM
SEE PAGE 19

farmland   *grid cables*

Ironstone Quarry

GLENDON S. JUNCT. SIGNAL BOX

1:134

74 *Embankment*

1:118

KETTERING IRON & COAL CO. SIGNAL BOX

73

1:218

Blast Furnaces

Iron Wks   A.43

1:125

L.M.S.

KETTERING

72 1:352

footbridge

1:161
1:220

71   *grid cables*

LEVEL

KETTERING JUNCT. SIGNAL BOX

1:216

70

L.M.S. to Cambridge   A.604

1:355
LEVEL

farmland

BURTON LATIMER

69¼ 1:611

A.509

A.6

1:730

footbridge

LEVEL

68

1:255

River Ise

A.510

1:800
LEVEL

67 *Woods*

1:186

NEILSON'S SIDINGS SIGNAL BOX

1:243

66 *vast loco: depot & yards*

1:191
LEVEL

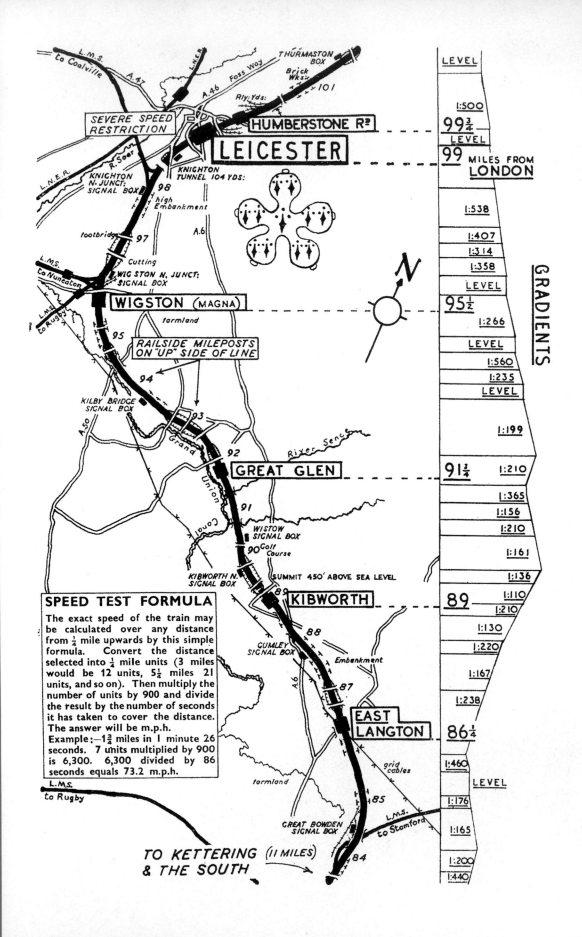

LEVEL

1:500

99¾ LEVEL

99 MILES FROM **LONDON**

1:538

1:407

1:314

1:358

LEVEL

95½

1:266

LEVEL

1:560

1:235

LEVEL

1:199

91¼ 1:210

1:365

1:156

1:210

1:161

1:136

89 1:110

1:210

1:130

1:220

1:167

1:238

86¼

1:460

LEVEL

1:176

1:165

1:200

1:440

GRADIENTS

L.M.S. to Coalville

A.47

L.N.E.R.

Foss Way

THURMASTON BOX

Brick Wks.

Rly. Yds.

A.46

101

SEVERE SPEED RESTRICTION

HUMBERSTONE R^D

LEICESTER

R. Soar

L.N.E.R.

KNIGHTON N. JUNCT: SIGNAL BOX

KNIGHTON TUNNEL 104 YDS:

98

high Embankment

A.6

footbridge

97

L.M.S. to Nuneaton

Cutting

WIGSTON N. JUNCT: SIGNAL BOX

L.M.S. to Rugby

WIGSTON (MAGNA)

farmland

95

RAILSIDE MILEPOSTS ON "UP" SIDE OF LINE

94

A.50

KILBY BRIDGE SIGNAL BOX

93

Grand

92

River Sence

GREAT GLEN

Union

91

Canal

WISTOW SIGNAL BOX

90 Golf Course

KIBWORTH N. SIGNAL BOX

SUMMIT 450' ABOVE SEA LEVEL

89

KIBWORTH

88

SPEED TEST FORMULA

The exact speed of the train may be calculated over any distance from ¼ mile upwards by this simple formula. Convert the distance selected into ¼ mile units (3 miles would be 12 units, 5¼ miles 21 units, and so on). Then multiply the number of units by 900 and divide the result by the number of seconds it has taken to cover the distance. The answer will be m.p.h. Example:—1¾ miles in 1 minute 26 seconds. 7 units multiplied by 900 is 6,300. 6,300 divided by 86 seconds equals 73.2 m.p.h.

GUMLEY SIGNAL BOX

A.6

Embankment

87

EAST LANGTON

grid cables

L.M.S. to Rugby

farmland

85

GREAT BOWDEN SIGNAL BOX

L.M.S. to Stamford

TO KETTERING (11 MILES) & THE SOUTH

84

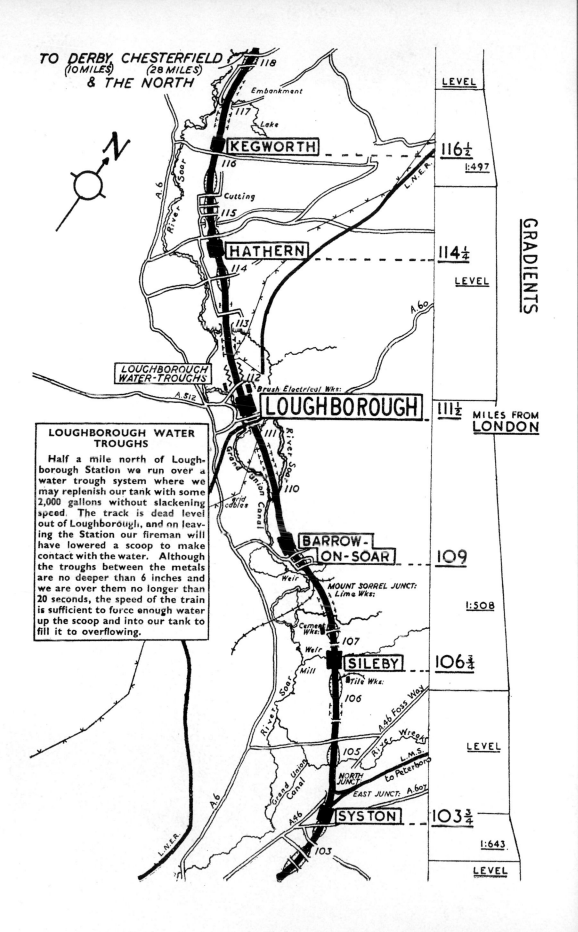

TO DERBY, CHESTERFIELD (10 MILES) (28 MILES) & THE NORTH

Embankment

Lake

KEGWORTH 116

River Soar

A.6

Cutting 115

HATHERN 114

113

L.N.E.R.

A.60

LOUGHBOROUGH WATER-TROUGHS

A.512 112

Brush Electrical Wks:

LOUGHBOROUGH

111

River Soar

LOUGHBOROUGH WATER TROUGHS

Half a mile north of Loughborough Station we run over a water trough system where we may replenish our tank with some 2,000 gallons without slackening speed. The track is dead level out of Loughborough, and on leaving the Station our fireman will have lowered a scoop to make contact with the water. Although the troughs between the metals are no deeper than 6 inches and we are over them no longer than 20 seconds, the speed of the train is sufficient to force enough water up the scoop and into our tank to fill it to overflowing.

Grid cables

Grand Union Canal

110

BARROW-ON-SOAR 109

Weir

MOUNT SORREL JUNCT: Lime Wks:

Cement Wks: 107

Weir

Mill

SILEBY

Tile Wks: 106

River Soar

A.46 Foss Way

River Wreak 105

L.M.S. to Peterboro

Grand Union Canal

NORTH JUNCT:

EAST JUNCT: A.607

A.6

SYSTON 103

A.46

L.N.E.R.

GRADIENTS

LEVEL

116½ 1:497

114¼ LEVEL

111½ MILES FROM LONDON

109

1:508

106¾

LEVEL

103¾ 1:643

LEVEL

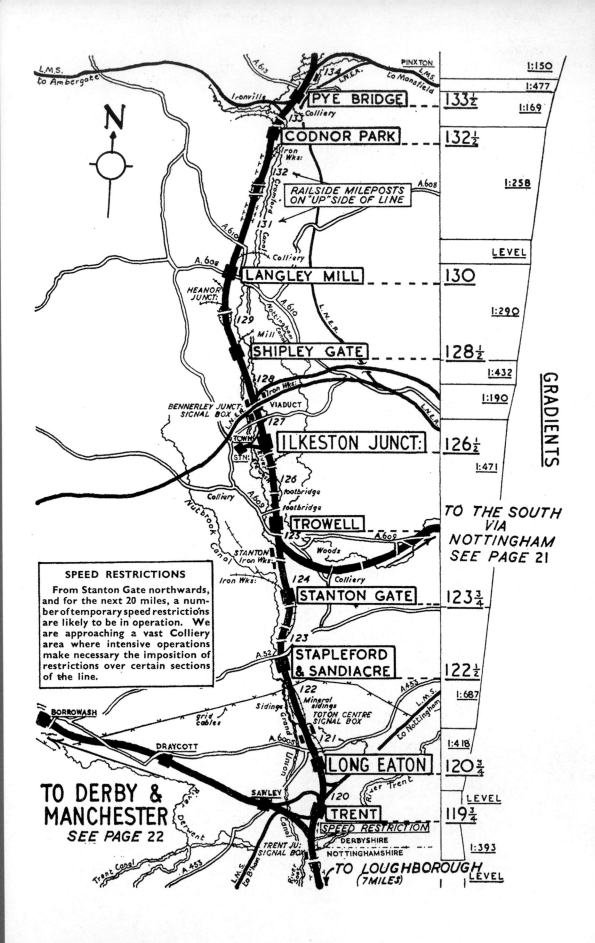

114

N

LMS. to Ambergate

A.613

134   L.N.E.R.   PINXTON   LMS. to Mansfield

1:150

1:477

Ironville

135   Colliery

PYE BRIDGE — — 133½   1:169

CODNOR PARK — — 132½

132   Iron Wks.

A.608   1:258

RAILSIDE MILEPOSTS ON "UP" SIDE OF LINE

131   Cromford Canal   A.610

A.608

Colliery   LEVEL

A.609   **LANGLEY MILL** — — 130

HEANOR JUNCT: A.610   L.N.E.R.   1:290

129   Nottingham Canal

Mill

SHIPLEY GATE — — 128½   1:432

128   Iron Wks.   1:190

BENNERLEY JUNCT: SIGNAL BOX   VIADUCT   L.N.E.R.

127

TOWN   **ILKESTON JUNCT:** — 126½   1:471

STN.

126   footbridge

footbridge

Colliery   A.609

Nutbrook Canal   **TROWELL** — —

125   Woods   A.609

TO THE SOUTH VIA NOTTINGHAM SEE PAGE 21

STANTON Iron Wks:

Iron Wks: 124   Colliery

STANTON GATE — 123¾

SPEED RESTRICTIONS

From Stanton Gate northwards, and for the next 20 miles, a number of temporary speed restrictions are likely to be in operation. We are approaching a vast Colliery area where intensive operations make necessary the imposition of restrictions over certain sections of the line.

123

A.52   **STAPLEFORD & SANDIACRE** — 122½

122   A.453   LMS.   1:687

Mineral sidings   to Nottingham

TOTON CENTRE SIGNAL BOX

BORROWASH   grid cables   Sidings   Grand Union Canal

A.6005   121   1:418

DRAYCOTT   **LONG EATON** — 120¾

SAWLEY   River Trent   LEVEL

120   **TRENT** — 119¾

TO DERBY & MANCHESTER *SEE PAGE 22*   River Derwent   Trent Canal   **SPEED RESTRICTION**   DERBYSHIRE NOTTINGHAMSHIRE   1:393

TRENT JU: SIGNAL BOX

Trent Canal   A.453   LMS. to B'ham   River Soar

TO LOUGHBOROUGH (7 MILES)   LEVEL

GRADIENTS

TO THE SOUTH VIA NOTTINGHAM SEE PAGE 21

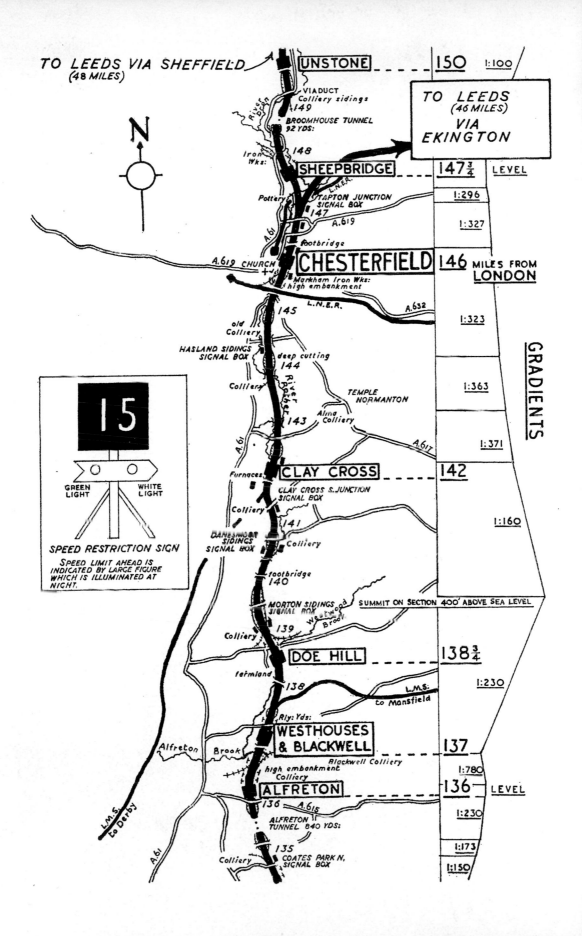

TO LEEDS VIA SHEFFIELD
(48 MILES)

N

UNSTONE — — — 150   1:100

VIADUCT
Colliery sidings
149
BROOMHOUSE TUNNEL
92 YDS:
148

TO LEEDS
(46 MILES)
VIA
EKINGTON

Iron
Wks:

SHEEPBRIDGE — — — 147¾   LEVEL

Pottery   L.N.E.R.
TAPTON JUNCTION
SIGNAL BOX
147   1:296

A.61   A.619   1:327

footbridge

A.619 CHURCH

CHESTERFIELD   146   MILES FROM LONDON

Markham Iron Wks:
high embankment
145
L.N.E.R.   A.632

1:323

old
Colliery

HASLAND SIDINGS
SIGNAL BOX
144   deep cutting

Colliery   River Rother

TEMPLE
NORMANTON
Alma
Colliery
143

1:363

A.61   A.617   1:371

15

GREEN   WHITE
LIGHT   LIGHT

SPEED RESTRICTION SIGN

SPEED LIMIT AHEAD IS
INDICATED BY LARGE FIGURE
WHICH IS ILLUMINATED AT
NIGHT.

Furnaces   CLAY CROSS — — — 142
CLAY CROSS S.JUNCTION
SIGNAL BOX

Colliery   1:160

141

DANESMOOR
SIDINGS
SIGNAL BOX   Colliery

footbridge
140

MORTON SIDINGS
SIGNAL BOX
Westwood
Brook   SUMMIT ON SECTION 400' ABOVE SEA LEVEL

Colliery   139

DOE HILL — — — 138¾

farmland
138   L.M.S.   1:230
to Mansfield

Rly:Yds:

Alfreton   Brook   WESTHOUSES
& BLACKWELL   137
Blackwell Colliery

high embankment   1:780
Colliery

ALFRETON — — — 136   LEVEL

136   A.615   1:230
ALFRETON
TUNNEL 840 YDS:

L.M.S.
to Derby   1:173

A.61   135

Colliery   COATES PARK N,
SIGNAL BOX   1:150

GRADIENTS

115

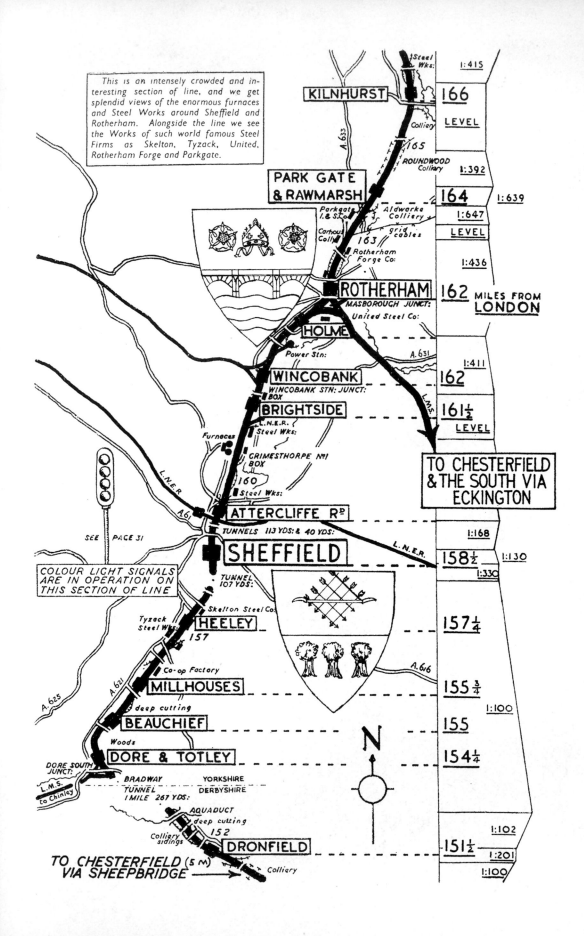

This is an intensely crowded and interesting section of line, and we get splendid views of the enormous furnaces and Steel Works around Sheffield and Rotherham. Alongside the line we see the Works of such world famous Steel Firms as Skelton, Tyzack, United, Rotherham Forge and Parkgate.

Steel Wks:

KILNHURST

1:415

166

LEVEL

A.633

Colliery

165

ROUNDWOOD Colliery

1:392

PARK GATE & RAWMARSH

164

1:639

Parkgate I. & S. Co.

Aldwarke Colliery

1:647

grid cables

LEVEL

Carhouse Colly.

163

1:436

Rotherham Forge Co:

ROTHERHAM

162

MILES FROM LONDON

MASBOROUGH JUNCT:

United Steel Co:

HOLME

Power Stn:

A.631

WINCOBANK

1:411

162

WINCOBANK STN: JUNCT: BOX

BRIGHTSIDE

161½

LEVEL

L.N.E.R. Steel Wks:

Furnaces

GRIMESTHORPE Nº1 BOX

TO CHESTERFIELD & THE SOUTH VIA ECKINGTON

L.N.E.R

160

Steel Wks:

ATTERCLIFFE Rᴰ

A.61

1:168

SEE PAGE 31

TUNNELS 113 YDS: & 40 YDS:

L.N.E.R.

SHEFFIELD

158½

1:130

1:330

COLOUR LIGHT SIGNALS ARE IN OPERATION ON THIS SECTION OF LINE

TUNNEL 107 YDS:

Skelton Steel Co:

157¼

Tyzack Steel Wks:

HEELEY

157

A.616

A.621

Co-op Factory

MILLHOUSES

155¾

A.625

deep cutting

1:100

BEAUCHIEF

155

Woods

N

DORE & TOTLEY

154¼

DORE SOUTH JUNCT:

BRADWAY TUNNEL 1 MILE 267 YDS:

YORKSHIRE DERBYSHIRE

L.M.S. to Chinley

AQUADUCT deep cutting

1:102

152

Colliery sidings

DRONFIELD

151½

1:201

TO CHESTERFIELD (5 M) VIA SHEEPBRIDGE

Colliery

1:100

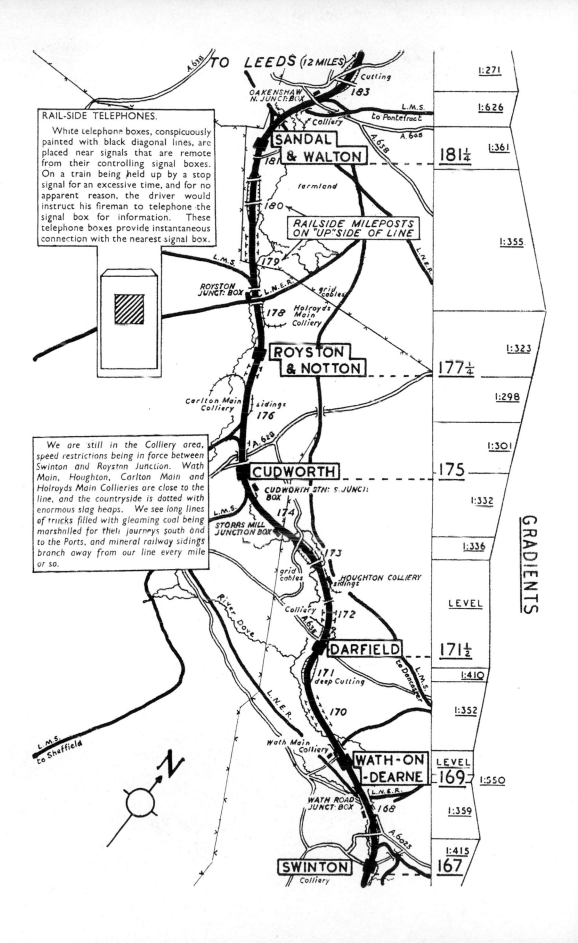

TO LEEDS (12 MILES)

Cutting
183

OAKENSHAW
N. JUNCT: BOX

L.M.S.
to Pontefract

A.658
A.645

Colliery

SANDAL & WALTON

181

farmland

180

RAILSIDE MILEPOSTS ON "UP" SIDE OF LINE

RAIL-SIDE TELEPHONES.

White telephone boxes, conspicuously painted with black diagonal lines, are placed near signals that are remote from their controlling signal boxes. On a train being held up by a stop signal for an excessive time, and for no apparent reason, the driver would instruct his fireman to telephone the signal box for information. These telephone boxes provide instantaneous connection with the nearest signal box.

L.M.S.
179

ROYSTON
JUNCT: BOX
L.N.E.R.

grid cables

Holroyd's Main Colliery

178

ROYSTON & NOTTON

Carlton Main Colliery

sidings
176

A.628

CUDWORTH

CUDWORTH STN: S. JUNCT: BOX

We are still in the Colliery area, speed restrictions being in force between Swinton and Royston Junction. Wath Main, Houghton, Carlton Main and Holroyds Main Collieries are close to the line, and the countryside is dotted with enormous slag heaps. We see long lines of trucks filled with gleaming coal being marshalled for their journeys south and to the Ports, and mineral railway sidings branch away from our line every mile or so.

L.M.S.
174

STORRS MILL
JUNCTION BOX

173

grid cables

HOUGHTON COLLIERY
sidings

Colliery
172

River Dove

A.659

DARFIELD

171
deep Cutting

L.N.E.R.

170

L.M.S.
to Sheffield

N

Wath Main Colliery

WATH-ON-DEARNE

WATH ROAD
JUNCT: BOX

L.N.E.R.

168

A.6023

SWINTON
Colliery

GRADIENTS

1:271

1:626

181¼ 1:361

1:355

1:323

177¼

1:298

1:301

175

1:332

1:336

LEVEL

171½

1:410

1:352

LEVEL
169 1:550

1:359

1:415
167

LEEDS

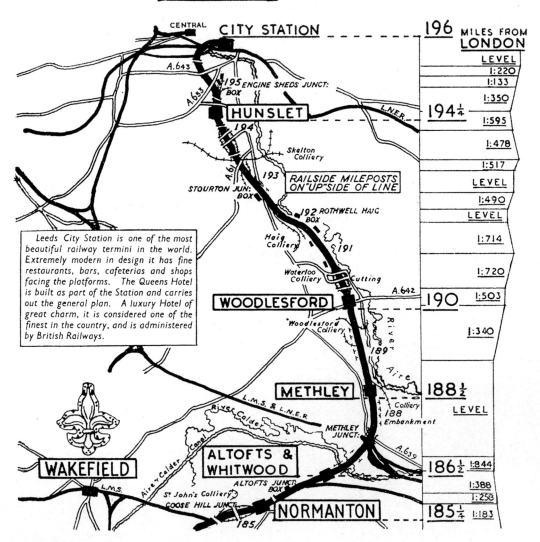

Leeds City Station is one of the most beautiful railway termini in the world. Extremely modern in design it has fine restaurants, bars, cafeterias and shops facing the platforms. The Queens Hotel is built as part of the Station and carries out the general plan. A luxury Hotel of great charm, it is considered one of the finest in the country, and is administered by British Railways.

CITY STATION — 196 MILES FROM LONDON

195 ENGINE SHEDS JUNCT: BOX

HUNSLET — 194¼

194

Skelton Colliery

STOURTON JUN: BOX — 193

RAILSIDE MILEPOSTS ON "UP" SIDE OF LINE

192 ROTHWELL HAIG BOX

Haig Colliery — 191

Waterloo Colliery — Cutting

WOODLESFORD — 190 — A.642

Woodlesford Colliery — 189

METHLEY — 188½ LEVEL

Colliery — 188 Embankment

METHLEY JUNCT:

L.M.S. & L.N.E.R.

River Calder

A.639

ALTOFTS & WHITWOOD — 186½ — 1:844

WAKEFIELD

Aire & Calder Canal

ALTOFTS JUNCT: BOX — 1:388

St John's Colliery — 1:258

GOOSE HILL JUNCT:

NORMANTON — 185¼ — 1:183

185

Gradient profile (right-hand scale)

LEVEL
1:220
1:133
1:350
1:595
1:478
1:517
LEVEL
1:490
LEVEL
1:714
1:720
1:503
1:340

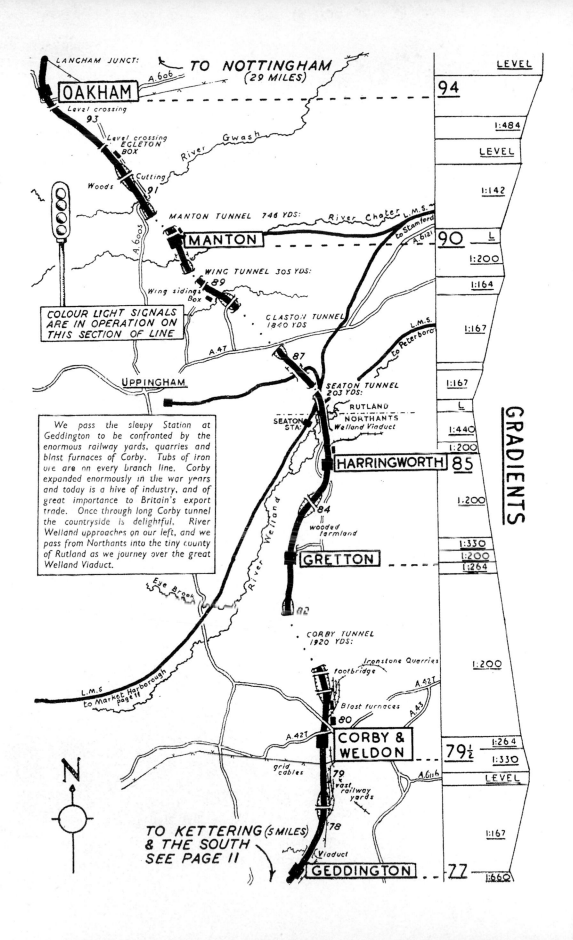

LANGHAM JUNCT:

TO NOTTINGHAM
(29 MILES)

A.606

OAKHAM

Level crossing
93

Level crossing
EGLETON
BOX

A.6003

Cutting
91

Woods

River Gwash

MANTON TUNNEL 746 YDS: River Chater   L.M.S.
to Stamford

MANTON   A.6121   **90**

WING TUNNEL 305 YDS:
89

Wing sidings
Box

GLASTON TUNNEL
1840 YDS:

L.M.S.
to Peterboro'

87

A.47

**COLOUR LIGHT SIGNALS
ARE IN OPERATION ON
THIS SECTION OF LINE**

UPPINGHAM

SEATON TUNNEL
203 YDS:

RUTLAND
NORTHANTS
Welland Viaduct

SEATON
STA:

We pass the sleepy Station at
Geddington to be confronted by the
enormous railway yards, quarries and
blast furnaces of Corby. Tubs of iron
ore are on every branch line. Corby
expanded enormously in the war years
and today is a hive of industry, and of
great importance to Britain's export
trade. Once through long Corby tunnel
the countryside is delightful. River
Welland approaches on our left, and we
pass from Northants into the tiny county
of Rutland as we journey over the great
Welland Viaduct.

HARRINGWORTH   **85**

84

wooded farmland

River Welland

Eye Brook

GRETTON

82

CORBY TUNNEL
1920 YDS:

Ironstone Quarries
footbridge
A.427

L.M.S
to Market Harborough
page 11

Blast furnaces   A.43

80

A.427

**CORBY &
WELDON**   **79½**

grid cables

A.6116

79
vast railway yards

N

78

TO KETTERING (5 MILES)
**& THE SOUTH
SEE PAGE 11**

Viaduct

GEDDINGTON   **77**

GRADIENTS

LEVEL
94
1:484
LEVEL
1:142
L
1:200
1:164
1:167
1:167
L
1:440
1:200
1:200
1:330
1:200
1:264
1:200
1:264
1:330
LEVEL
1:167
1:660

119

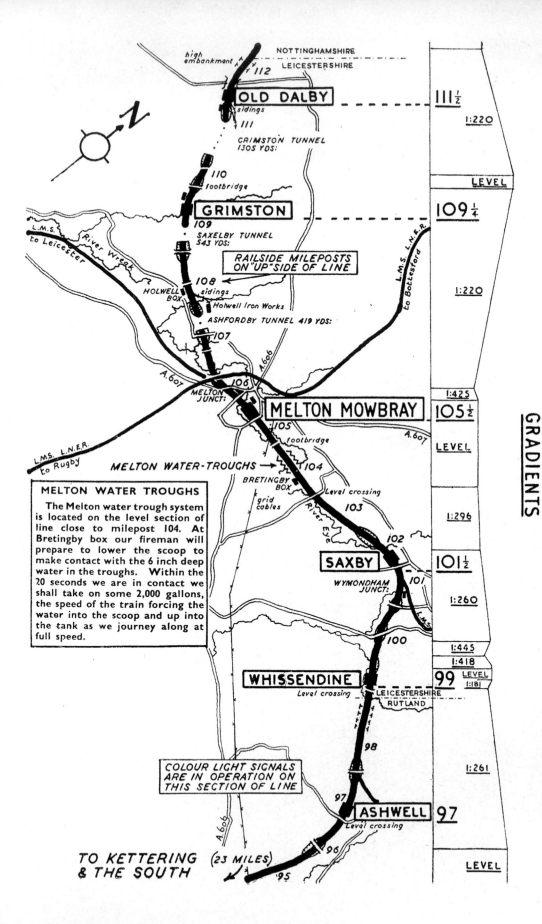

NOTTINGHAMSHIRE
LEICESTERSHIRE

high embankment

112

OLD DALBY

sidings

111

GRIMSTON TUNNEL 1305 YDS:

110
footbridge

GRIMSTON

109

SAXELBY TUNNEL 543 YDS:

RAILSIDE MILEPOSTS ON "UP" SIDE OF LINE

L.M.S. to Leicester

River Wreak

108
HOLWELL BOX
sidings
Holwell Iron Works

ASHFORDBY TUNNEL 419 YDS:

107

A.607

A.606

106
MELTON JUNCT:

MELTON MOWBRAY

L.M.S. L.N.E.R. to Rugby

105

footbridge

MELTON WATER-TROUGHS →

104
BRETINGBY BOX

grid cables

Level crossing

103

River Eye

102

SAXBY
WYMONDHAM JUNCT:

101

100

L.M.S.

L.M.S. L.N.E.R. to Bottesford

MELTON WATER TROUGHS

The Melton water trough system is located on the level section of line close to milepost 104. At Bretingby box our fireman will prepare to lower the scoop to make contact with the 6 inch deep water in the troughs. Within the 20 seconds we are in contact we shall take on some 2,000 gallons, the speed of the train forcing the water into the scoop and up into the tank as we journey along at full speed.

WHISSENDINE
Level crossing
LEICESTERSHIRE
RUTLAND

98

COLOUR LIGHT SIGNALS ARE IN OPERATION ON THIS SECTION OF LINE

97

ASHWELL
Level crossing

A.606

96

TO KETTERING (23 MILES) & THE SOUTH

95

GRADIENTS

1:220

LEVEL

111½

109¼

1:220

105½

1:425

LEVEL

1:296

101½

1:260

1:445
1:418

99   LEVEL
1:181

1:261

97

LEVEL

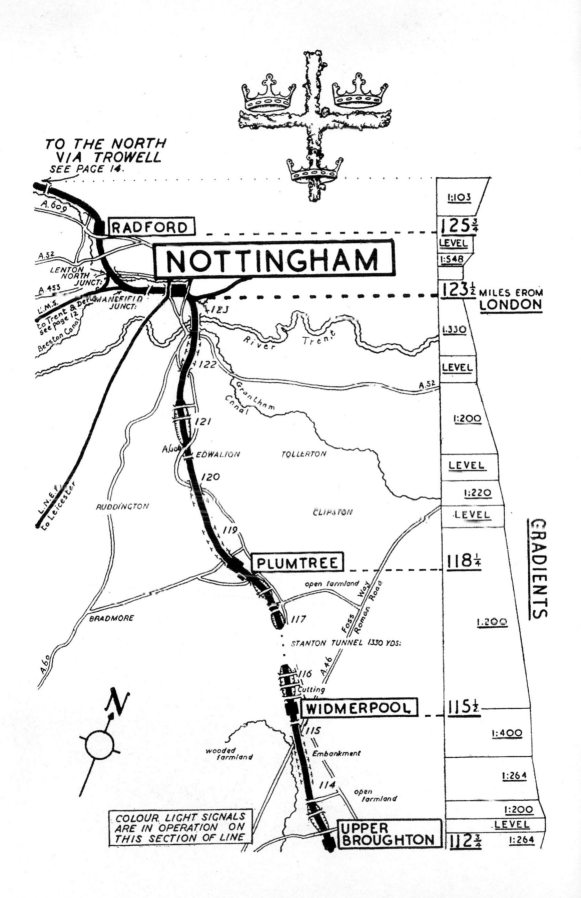

TO THE NORTH
VIA TROWELL
SEE PAGE 14.

A.609

RADFORD

A.52

LENTON
NORTH
JUNCT:

A.453

L.M.S.
to Trent & Derby
see page 12

Beeston Canal

MANSFIELD
JUNCT:

NOTTINGHAM

123

122

121

A.606 EDWALTON

120

River Trent

Grantham Canal

TOLLERTON

A.52

L.N.E.R.
to Leicester

RUDDINGTON

119

CLIPSTON

PLUMTREE

open farmland

Foss Way
Roman Road

BRADMORE

117

A.60

STANTON TUNNEL 1330 YDS:

116 A.46

Cutting

WIDMERPOOL

115

wooded
farmland

Embankment

114

open
farmland

**UPPER
BROUGHTON**

N

COLOUR LIGHT SIGNALS
ARE IN OPERATION ON
THIS SECTION OF LINE

1:103

125¾

LEVEL

1:548

123½ MILES FROM
LONDON

1:330

LEVEL

1:200

LEVEL

1:220

LEVEL

118¼

1:200

115½

1:400

1:264

1:200

LEVEL

112¾ 1:264

GRADIENTS

121

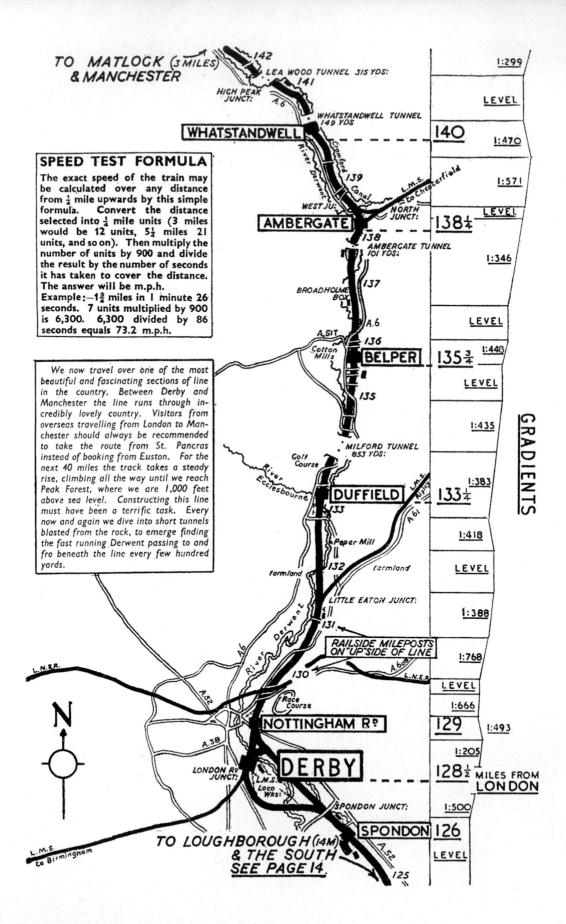

TO MATLOCK (3 MILES) & MANCHESTER

LEA WOOD TUNNEL 315 YDS:
142
141
HIGH PEAK JUNCT:
A.6

WHATSTANDWELL TUNNEL 149 YDS:
WHATSTANDWELL

River Derwent
Cromford Canal
L.M.S. to Chesterfield
139
WEST JU:
NORTH JUNCT:
AMBERGATE
138
AMBERGATE TUNNEL 101 YDS:
137
BROADHOLME BOX
A.6
A.517
136
Cotton Mills
BELPER
135
MILFORD TUNNEL 853 YDS:
Golf Course
River Ecclesbourne
DUFFIELD
133
L.M.S. to ...bury
A.61
Paper Mill
farmland
132
farmland
LITTLE EATON JUNCT:
131
RAILSIDE MILEPOSTS ON "UP" SIDE OF LINE
A.6
River Derwent
130
A.608
L.N.E.R.
L.N.E.R.
A.52
Race Course
NOTTINGHAM RD
A.38
DERBY
LONDON RD JUNCT:
L.M.S. Loco Wks:
SPONDON JUNCT:
SPONDON
TO LOUGHBOROUGH (14M) & THE SOUTH SEE PAGE 14.
L.M.S. to Birmingham
A.52
125

GRADIENTS

1:299
LEVEL
140 — 1:470
1:571
LEVEL
138¼ — 1:346
LEVEL
135¾ — 1:446
LEVEL
1:435
133¼ — 1:383
1:418
LEVEL
1:388
1:768
LEVEL
1:666
129 — 1:493
1:205
128½ — MILES FROM LONDON
1:500
126
LEVEL

SEE PAGE 14.

SPEED TEST FORMULA

The exact speed of the train may be calculated over any distance from ¼ mile upwards by this simple formula. Convert the distance selected into ¼ mile units (3 miles would be 12 units, 5¼ miles 21 units, and so on). Then multiply the number of units by 900 and divide the result by the number of seconds it has taken to cover the distance. The answer will be m.p.h.
Example:—1¾ miles in 1 minute 26 seconds. 7 units multiplied by 900 is 6,300. 6,300 divided by 86 seconds equals 73.2 m.p.h.

We now travel over one of the most beautiful and fascinating sections of line in the country. Between Derby and Manchester the line runs through incredibly lovely country. Visitors from overseas travelling from London to Manchester should always be recommended to take the route from St. Pancras instead of booking from Euston. For the next 40 miles the track takes a steady rise, climbing all the way until we reach Peak Forest, where we are 1,000 feet above sea level. Constructing this line must have been a terrific task. Every now and again we dive into short tunnels blasted from the rock, to emerge finding the fast running Derwent passing to and fro beneath the line every few hundred yards.

122

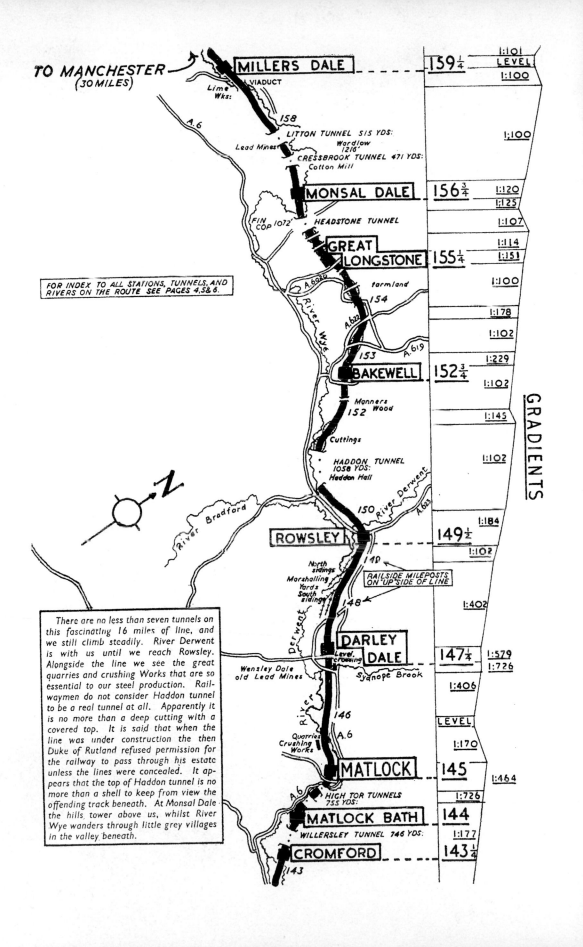

TO MANCHESTER (30 MILES)

MILLERS DALE — 159¼

LITTON TUNNEL 515 YDS.
Wardlow 1216'
CRESSBROOK TUNNEL 471 YDS.
Cotton Mill

MONSAL DALE — 156¾

HEADSTONE TUNNEL
FIN COP 1072'

GREAT LONGSTONE — 155¼

FOR INDEX TO ALL STATIONS, TUNNELS, AND RIVERS ON THE ROUTE SEE PAGES 4, 5 & 6.

BAKEWELL — 152¾

Manners Wood

Cuttings

HADDON TUNNEL 1058 YDS.
Haddon Hall

ROWSLEY — 149½

North sidings
Marshalling Yards
South sidings

RAILSIDE MILEPOSTS ON 'UP' SIDE OF LINE

DARLEY DALE — 147¼
Level crossing

Wensley Dale old Lead Mines
Sydnope Brook

MATLOCK — 145

HIGH TOR TUNNELS 755 YDS.

MATLOCK BATH — 144

WILLERSLEY TUNNEL 746 YDS.

CROMFORD — 143¼

GRADIENTS

1:101 LEVEL
1:100
1:100
1:120
1:125
1:107
1:114
1:151
1:100
1:178
1:102
1:229
1:102
1:145
1:102
1:184
1:102
1:402
1:579
1:726
1:406
LEVEL
1:170
1:464
1:726
1:177

There are no less than seven tunnels on this fascinating 16 miles of line, and we still climb steadily. River Derwent is with us until we reach Rowsley. Alongside the line we see the great quarries and crushing Works that are so essential to our steel production. Railwaymen do not consider Haddon tunnel to be a real tunnel at all. Apparently it is no more than a deep cutting with a covered top. It is said that when the line was under construction the then Duke of Rutland refused permission for the railway to pass through his estate unless the lines were concealed. It appears that the top of Haddon tunnel is no more than a shell to keep from view the offending track beneath. At Monsal Dale the hills tower above us, whilst River Wye wanders through little grey villages in the valley beneath.

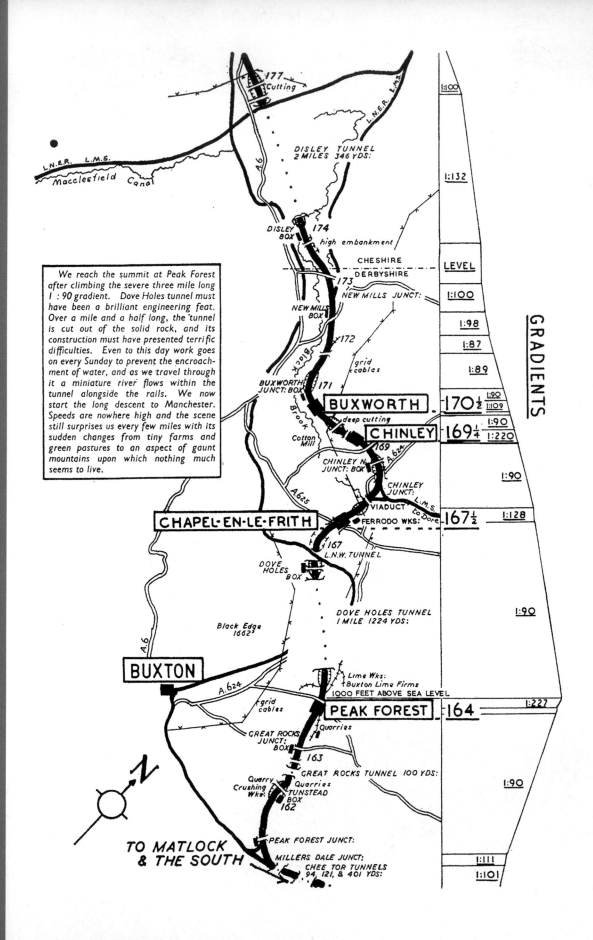

We reach the summit at Peak Forest after climbing the severe three mile long 1 : 90 gradient. Dove Holes tunnel must have been a brilliant engineering feat. Over a mile and a half long, the tunnel is cut out of the solid rock, and its construction must have presented terrific difficulties. Even to this day work goes on every Sunday to prevent the encroachment of water, and as we travel through it a miniature river flows within the tunnel alongside the rails. We now start the long descent to Manchester. Speeds are nowhere high and the scene still surprises us every few miles with its sudden changes from tiny farms and green pastures to an aspect of gaunt mountains upon which nothing much seems to live.

177 Cutting

L.N.E.R. L.M.S.

Macclesfield Canal

DISLEY TUNNEL 2 MILES 346 YDS:

L.N.E.R. L.M.S.

DISLEY BOX 174

high embankment

CHESHIRE

DERBYSHIRE

173

NEW MILLS JUNCT:

NEW MILLS BOX

172

grid cables

BUXWORTH JUNCT: BOX 171

Brook

Cotton Mill

deep cutting

BUXWORTH

CHINLEY 169

CHINLEY N. JUNCT: BOX

A.624

CHINLEY JUNCT:

VIADUCT

L.M.S. to Dore

FERRODO WKS:

CHAPEL-EN-LE-FRITH

167

L.N.W. TUNNEL

DOVE HOLES BOX

DOVE HOLES TUNNEL 1 MILE 1224 YDS:

Black Edge 1662'

A.6

BUXTON

A.624

grid cables

Lime Wks: Buxton Lime Firms
1000 FEET ABOVE SEA LEVEL

PEAK FOREST

Quarries

GREAT ROCKS JUNCT: BOX

163

GREAT ROCKS TUNNEL 100 YDS:

Quarry Crushing Wks:

Quarries

TUNSTEAD BOX

162

PEAK FOREST JUNCT:

TO MATLOCK & THE SOUTH

MILLERS DALE JUNCT:
CHEE TOR TUNNELS 94, 121, & 401 YDS:

GRADIENTS

1:100

1:132

LEVEL

1:100

1:98

1:87

1:89

170½ 1:90
1:109

169¾ 1:90
1:220

1:90

167½ 1:128

1:90

164 1:227

1:90

1:111

1:101

MANCHESTER

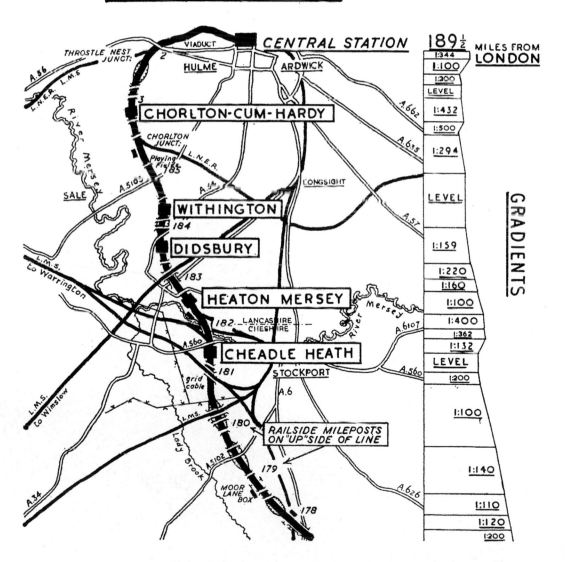

CENTRAL STATION

189½ MILES FROM LONDON

THROSTLE NEST JUNCT:

VIADUCT

HULME   ARDWICK

A.56

L.N.E.R. L.M.S.

River Mersey

CHORLTON-CUM-HARDY

CHORLTON JUNCT:

L.N.E.R.

Playing Fields

SALE

A.5103

LONGSIGHT

A.662

A.6.13

A.57

WITHINGTON

DIDSBURY

L.M.S. to Warrington

HEATON MERSEY

River Mersey

A.6107

LANCASHIRE CHESHIRE

CHEADLE HEATH

A.560

STOCKPORT

grid cable

A.6

A.560

L.M.S. to Wimslow

L.M.S.

RAILSIDE MILEPOSTS ON "UP" SIDE OF LINE

A.626

A.5102

MOOR LANE BOX

Lady Brook

A.34

GRADIENTS

1:344
1:100
1:200
LEVEL
1:432
1:500
1:294
LEVEL
1:159
1:220
1:160
1:100
1:400
1:362
1:132
LEVEL
1:200
1:100
1:140
1:110
1:120
1:200

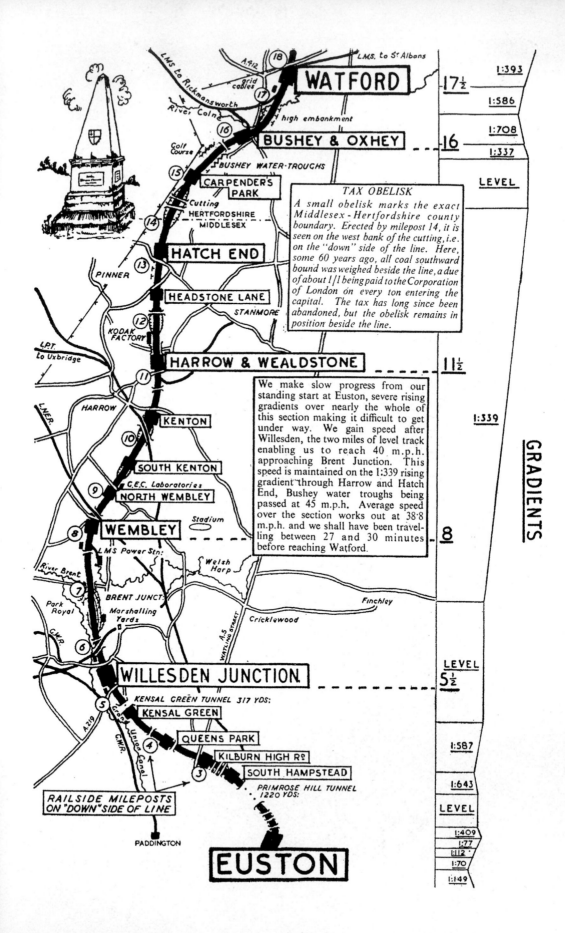

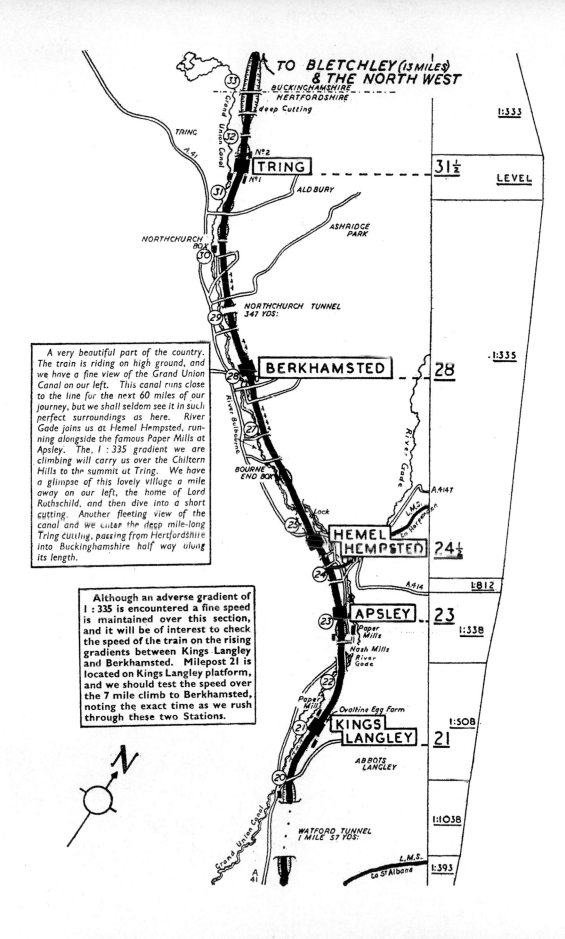

TO BLETCHLEY (13 MILES) & THE NORTH WEST

BUCKINGHAMSHIRE
HERTFORDSHIRE

33

deep Cutting

32

Grand Union Canal

TRING
A.41

Nº 2

TRING

31½

Nº 1

LEVEL

ALD BURY

31

ASHRIDGE PARK

NORTHCHURCH BOX

30

1:333

NORTHCHURCH TUNNEL 347 YDS:

29

River Gade

River Bulbourne

.1:335

28

BERKHAMSTED

28

> A very beautiful part of the country. The train is riding on high ground, and we have a fine view of the Grand Union Canal on our left. This canal runs close to the line for the next 60 miles of our journey, but we shall seldom see it in such perfect surroundings as here. River Gade joins us at Hemel Hempsted, running alongside the famous Paper Mills at Apsley. The, 1 : 335 gradient we are climbing will carry us over the Chiltern Hills to the summit at Tring. We have a glimpse of this lovely village a mile away on our left, the home of Lord Rothschild, and then dive into a short cutting. Another fleeting view of the canal and we enter the deep mile-long Tring cutting, passing from Hertfordshire into Buckinghamshire half way along its length.

27

BOURNE END BOX

A.4147

to Harpenden

L.M.S.

Lock

26

HEMEL HEMPSTED

24½

24

A.414

1:812

> Although an adverse gradient of 1 : 335 is encountered a fine speed is maintained over this section, and it will be of interest to check the speed of the train on the rising gradients between Kings Langley and Berkhamsted. Milepost 21 is located on Kings Langley platform, and we should test the speed over the 7 mile climb to Berkhamsted, noting the exact time as we rush through these two Stations.

23

APSLEY

23

Paper Mills

1:338

Nash Mills River Gade

22

Paper Mills

Ovaltine Egg Farm

21

KINGS LANGLEY

21

1:508

ABBOTS LANGLEY

20

1:1038

Grand Union Canal

WATFORD TUNNEL 1 MILE 57 YDS:

L.M.S. to St Albans

1:393

A.41

N

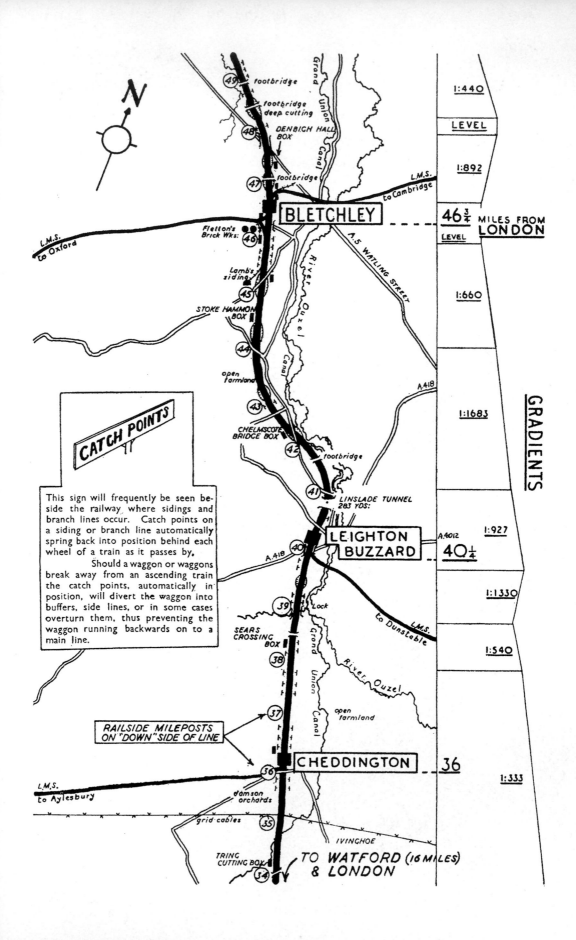

128

N

footbridge

49

footbridge
deep cutting

48

DENBIGH HALL
BOX

47 footbridge

L.M.S.
to Cambridge

1:440

LEVEL

1:892

BLETCHLEY - - - 46¾ MILES FROM
LONDON
LEVEL

L.M.S.
to Oxford

Fletton's
Brick Wks:

46

Lamb's
siding

45

STOKE HAMMOND
BOX

44

open
farmland

43

CHELMSCOTE
BRIDGE BOX

42 footbridge

41

LINSLADE TUNNEL
283 YDS:

A.5 WATLING STREET

River Ouzel

Canal

A.418

1:660

1:1683

CATCH POINTS

This sign will frequently be seen beside the railway where sidings and
branch lines occur. Catch points on
a siding or branch line automatically
spring back into position behind each
wheel of a train as it passes by.
     Should a waggon or waggons
break away from an ascending train
the catch points, automatically in
position, will divert the waggon into
buffers, side lines, or in some cases
overturn them, thus preventing the
waggon running backwards on to a
main line.

40

A.418

**LEIGHTON
BUZZARD** - - 40¼

A.4012

1:927

39 Lock

Grand Union Canal

to Dunstable

L.M.S.

1:1330

SEARS
CROSSING
BOX

38

1:540

37

**RAILSIDE MILEPOSTS
ON "DOWN" SIDE OF LINE**

open
farmland

River Ouzel

36

CHEDDINGTON - - 36

1:333

L.M.S.
to Aylesbury

damson
orchards

grid cables

35

IVINGHOE

TRING
CUTTING BOX

34

**TO WATFORD (16 MILES)
& LONDON**

GRADIENTS

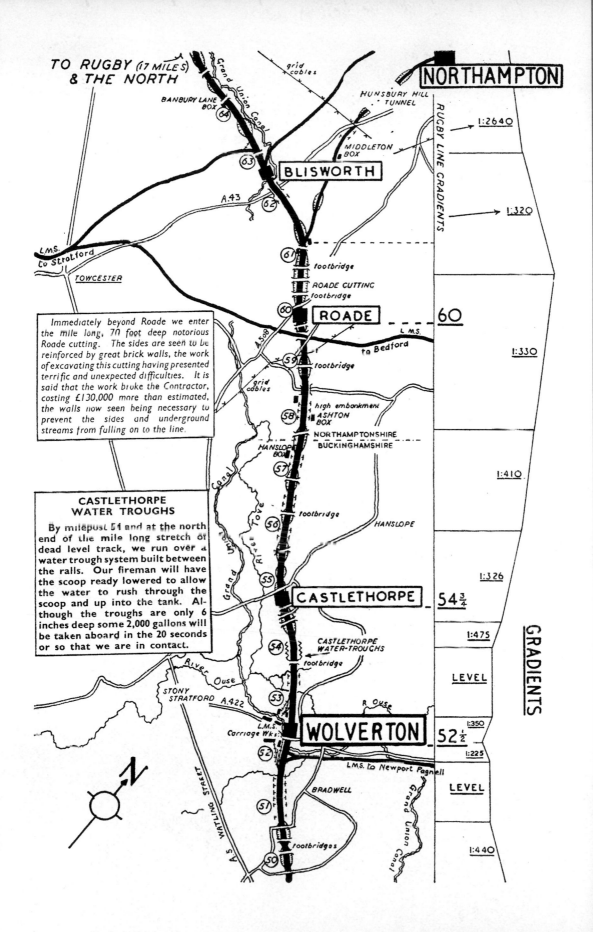

TO RUGBY (17 MILES) & THE NORTH

Grand Union Canal

grid cables

NORTHAMPTON

BANBURY LANE BOX

64

HUNSBURY HILL TUNNEL

63

MIDDLETON BOX

BLISWORTH

A.43

62

LMS. to Stratford

TOWCESTER

61

footbridge

ROADE CUTTING
footbridge

60

ROADE

L.M.S. to Bedford

Immediately beyond Roade we enter the mile long, 70 foot deep notorious Roade cutting. The sides are seen to be reinforced by great brick walls, the work of excavating this cutting having presented terrific and unexpected difficulties. It is said that the work broke the Contractor, costing £130,000 more than estimated, the walls now seen being necessary to prevent the sides and underground streams from falling on to the line.

59
footbridge

grid cables

58
high embankment
ASHTON BOX

NORTHAMPTONSHIRE
BUCKINGHAMSHIRE

HANSLOPE BOX

57

**CASTLETHORPE
WATER TROUGHS**

By milepost 54 and at the north end of the mile long stretch of dead level track, we run over a water trough system built between the rails. Our fireman will have the scoop ready lowered to allow the water to rush through the scoop and up into the tank. Although the troughs are only 6 inches deep some 2,000 gallons will be taken aboard in the 20 seconds or so that we are in contact.

56
footbridge

HANSLOPE

55

CASTLETHORPE

CASTLETHORPE
WATER-TROUGHS

54
footbridge

River Ouse

STONY STRATFORD   A.422

53

R. Ouse

WOLVERTON

L.M.S.
Carriage Wks.

52

LMS. to Newport Pagnell

BRADWELL

51

A.5 WATLING STREET

50
footbridges

Grand Union Canal

Rugby Line Gradients

Gradient	Milepost
1:2640	
1:320	
	60
1:330	
1:410	
1:326	
	54¾
1:475	
LEVEL	
	52½
1:350	
1:225	
LEVEL	
1:440	

GRADIENTS

129

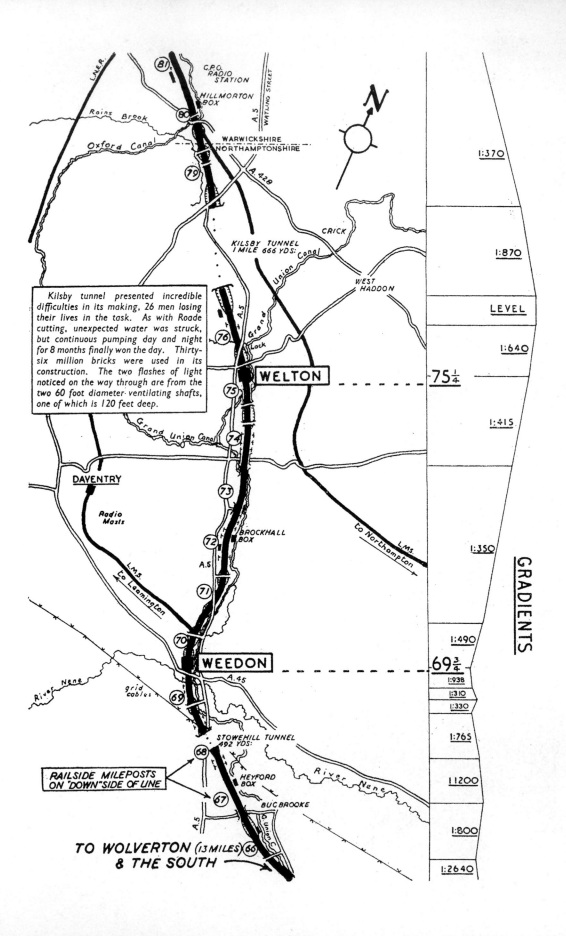

L.N.E.R.

81

C.P.O. RADIO STATION

HILLMORTON BOX

WATLING STREET

Rains Brook

80

WARWICKSHIRE
NORTHAMPTONSHIRE

Oxford Canal

A.5

N

79

A.428

CRICK

KILSBY TUNNEL
1 MILE 666 YDS.

Union Canal

WEST HADDON

Kilsby tunnel presented incredible difficulties in its making, 26 men losing their lives in the task. As with Roade cutting, unexpected water was struck, but continuous pumping day and night for 8 months finally won the day. Thirty-six million bricks were used in its construction. The two flashes of light noticed on the way through are from the two 60 foot diameter ventilating shafts, one of which is 120 feet deep.

76

A.5

Grand Union

Lock

WELTON

75

74

Grand Union Canal

to Northampton

L.M.S.

73

DAVENTRY

Radio Masts

72

BROCKHALL BOX

A.5

L.M.S. to Leamington

71

70

WEEDON

A.45

River Nene

grid cables

69

STOWEHILL TUNNEL
492 YDS.

HEYFORD BOX

River Nene

RAILSIDE MILEPOSTS
ON "DOWN" SIDE OF LINE

68

BUGBROOKE

67

A.5

Union C.

TO WOLVERTON (13 MILES) 66
& THE SOUTH

GRADIENTS

1:370

1:870

LEVEL

1:640

$75\frac{1}{4}$

1:415

1:350

1:490

$69\frac{3}{4}$

1:938

1:310

1:330

1:765

1:1200

1:800

1:2640

130

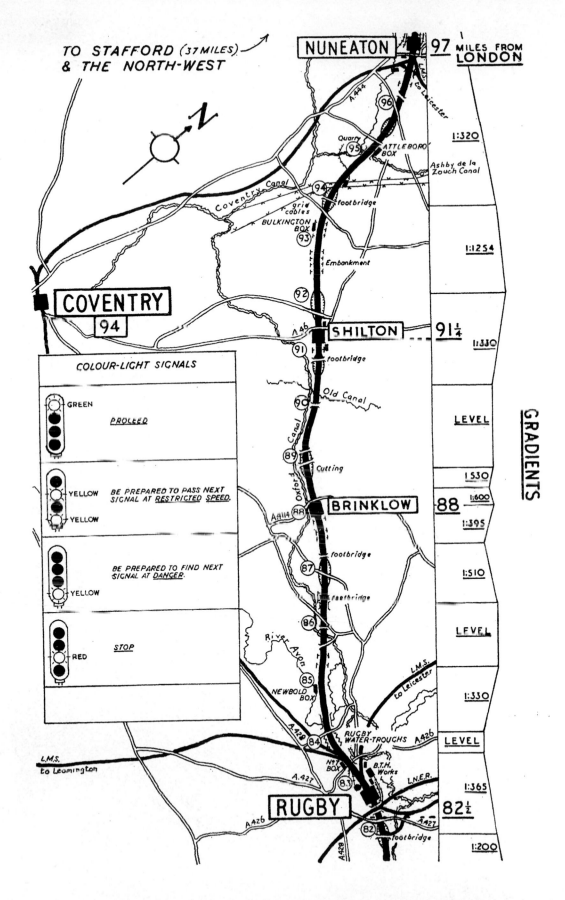

TO STAFFORD (37 MILES)
& THE NORTH-WEST

N

NUNEATON

97 MILES FROM LONDON

A.444

96

1:320

Quarry
95 ATTLEBORO'
BOX

Ashby de la
Zouch Canal

Coventry Canal

94

footbridge

grid
cables

BULKINGTON
BOX

1:1254

93

Embankment

COVENTRY
94

92

A46

SHILTON

91¼

1:330

91

footbridge

Old Canal

90

LEVEL

89

Cutting

1:530

A4114
88

BRINKLOW

88

1:600

1:395

footbridge

87

1:510

footbridge

86

LEVEL

River Avon

85

NEWBOLD
BOX

L.M.S.
to Leicester

1:330

A.428

84

RUGBY
WATER-TROUGHS

A.426

LEVEL

L.M.S.
to Leamington

A.427

No.7
BOX

B.T.H.
Works

L.N.E.R.

1:365

83

RUGBY

82½

A.426

82

A.427

footbridge

1:200

A.428

GRADIENTS

131

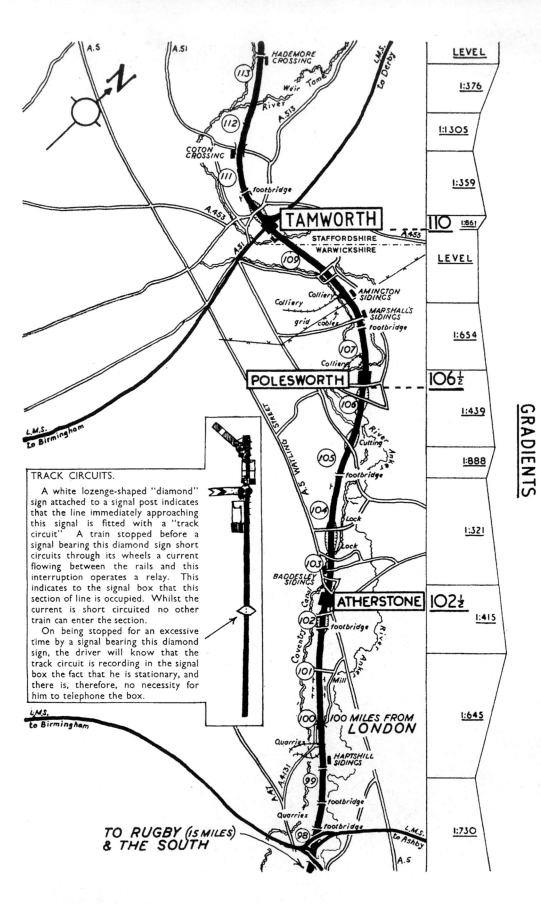

LEVEL

1:376

1:1305

1:359

110   1:861

LEVEL

1:654

106½

1:439

1:888

1:321

102½

1:415

1:645

1:730

GRADIENTS

A.S
A.51
A.51
L.M.S. to Derby

HADEMORE CROSSING
113
112
River Weir Tame
A.513
COTON CROSSING
111
footbridge
A.453
A.453

TAMWORTH
STAFFORDSHIRE
WARWICKSHIRE
109
AMINGTON SIDINGS
Colliery Colliery
Colliery
grid cables
MARSHALL'S SIDINGS
footbridge
107
Colliery

POLESWORTH
106
River Anker
Cutting
105
footbridge
104
Lock
Lock
103
BADDESLEY SIDINGS

ATHERSTONE
102
footbridge
River Anker
101
Mill

100 100 MILES FROM LONDON
Quarries
HARTSHILL SIDINGS
99
footbridge
Quarries
98
footbridge
L.M.S. to Ashby
A.S

WATLING STREET A.5
Coventry Canal

L.M.S. to Birmingham

L.M.S. to Birmingham

TO RUGBY (15 MILES) & THE SOUTH

132

TRACK CIRCUITS.

A white lozenge-shaped "diamond" sign attached to a signal post indicates that the line immediately approaching this signal is fitted with a "track circuit" A train stopped before a signal bearing this diamond sign short circuits through its wheels a current flowing between the rails and this interruption operates a relay. This indicates to the signal box that this section of line is occupied. Whilst the current is short circuited no other train can enter the section.

On being stopped for an excessive time by a signal bearing this diamond sign, the driver will know that the track circuit is recording in the signal box the fact that he is stationary, and there is, therefore, no necessity for him to telephone the box.

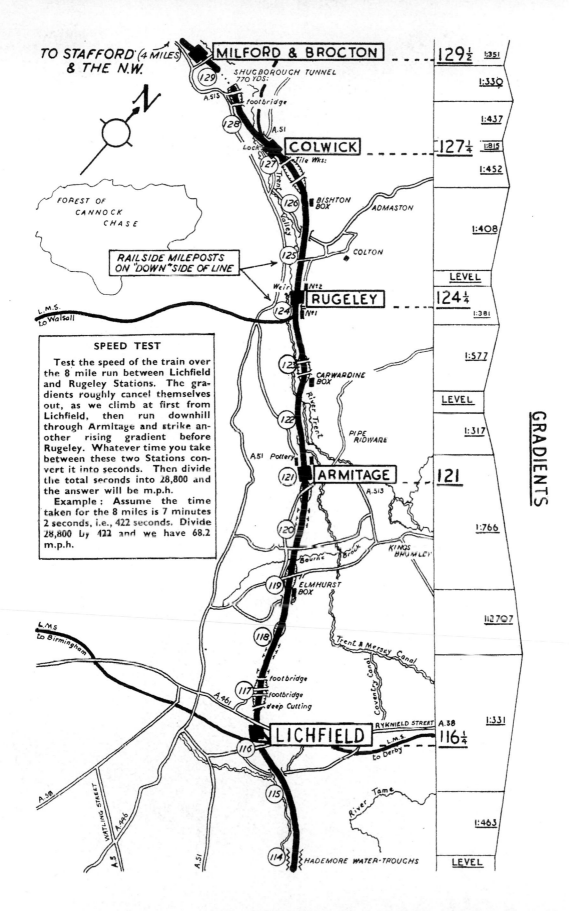

TO STAFFORD (4 MILES)
& THE N.W.

MILFORD & BROCTON

SHUGBOROUGH TUNNEL
770 YDS:

129

A.513

footbridge

128

A.51

COLWICK

Lock

127

Tile Wks:

Trent Valley

126

BISHTON BOX

ADMASTON

125

COLTON

FOREST OF
CANNOCK
CHASE

RAILSIDE MILEPOSTS
ON "DOWN" SIDE OF LINE

Weir

No 2

RUGELEY

124

No 1

L.M.S.
to Walsall

123

CARWARDINE
BOX

SPEED TEST

Test the speed of the train over the 8 mile run between Lichfield and Rugeley Stations. The gradients roughly cancel themselves out, as we climb at first from Lichfield, then run downhill through Armitage and strike another rising gradient before Rugeley. Whatever time you take between these two Stations convert it into seconds. Then divide the total seconds into 28,800 and the answer will be m.p.h.

Example : Assume the time taken for the 8 miles is 7 minutes 2 seconds, i.e., 422 seconds. Divide 28,800 by 422 and we have 68.2 m.p.h.

River Trent

122

PIPE RIDWARE

A.51 Pottery

121

ARMITAGE

A.513

120

KINGS BROMLEY

Bourne Brook

119

ELMHURST BOX

L.M.S
to Birmingham

118

A.461

Trent & Mersey Canal

117

footbridge

footbridge

deep Cutting

A.38

WATLING STREET

A.5

A.51

116

LICHFIELD

RYKNIELD STREET   A.38

L.M.S.
to Derby

115

River Tame

114

HADEMORE WATER-TROUGHS

Gradients column (right side)

129½ 1:351

1:330

1:437

127¼ 1:815

1:452

1:408

LEVEL

124¼

1:381

1:577

LEVEL

1:317

121

1:766

1:2707

1:331

116¼

1:463

LEVEL

GRADIENTS

133

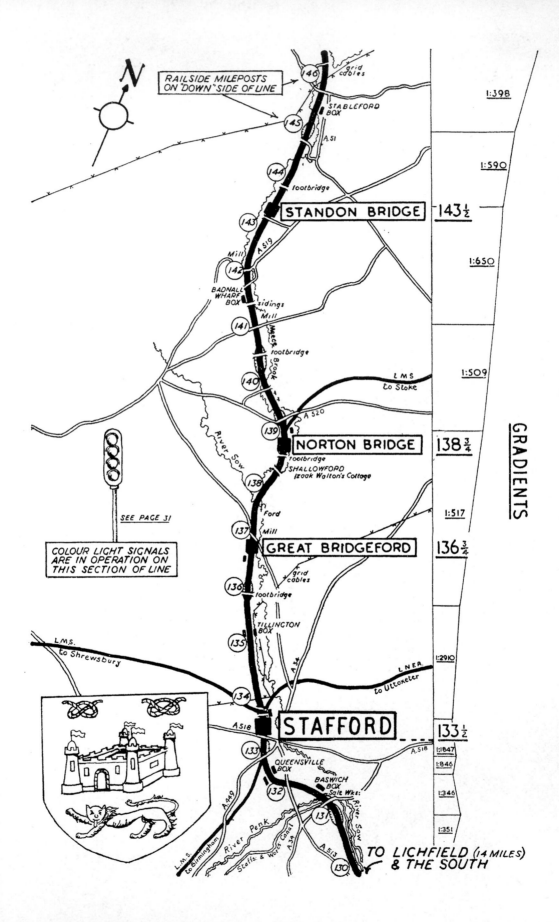

134

RAILSIDE MILEPOSTS
ON "DOWN" SIDE OF LINE

grid cables

146

STABLEFORD BOX

145

A.51

1:398

144

1:590

footbridge

STANDON BRIDGE   143½

143

Mill   A.519

1:650

142

BADNALL WHARF BOX

sidings

Mill

141

footbridge

Meece Brook

LMS to Stoke

1:509

140

A.520

139

NORTON BRIDGE   138¾

footbridge

SHALLOWFORD
Izaak Walton's Cottage

138

SEE PAGE 31

1:517

Ford

137   Mill

GREAT BRIDGEFORD   136¾

COLOUR LIGHT SIGNALS
ARE IN OPERATION ON
THIS SECTION OF LINE

grid cables

136   footbridge

TILLINGTON BOX

135

L.M.S.
to Shrewsbury

L.N.E.R.
to Uttoxeter

1:2910

134

A.518

STAFFORD   133½

1:847

133   QUEENSVILLE BOX   A.518

1:846

132   BASWICH BOX
Salt Wks.

1:346

River Sow

131

L.M.S.
to Birmingham   River Penk   Staffs. & Worcs Canal   A.3A   A.513

1:351

TO LICHFIELD (14 MILES)
& THE SOUTH

130

GRADIENTS

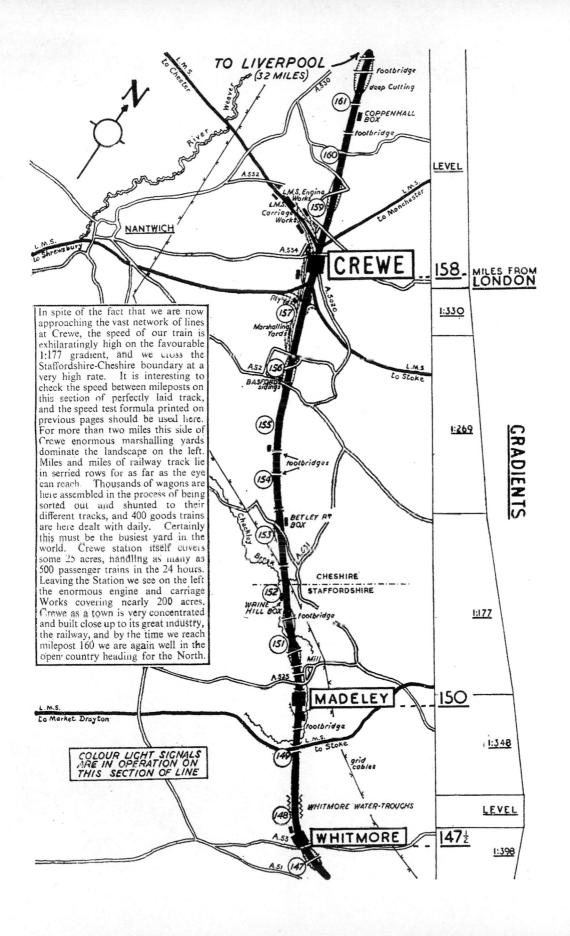

TO LIVERPOOL
(32 MILES)

footbridge

deep Cutting

161

COPPENHALL BOX

footbridge

160

L.M.S. To Chester

Weaver

River

N

A.530

LEVEL

A.532

L.M.S. Engine Works

L.M.S. Carriage Works

159

L.M.S. To Manchester

NANTWICH

A.534

L.M.S. To Shrewsbury

CREWE

158 MILES FROM LONDON

Rly.

157

1:330

Marshalling Yards

A.5020

AS2 156

L.M.S To Stoke

BASFORD sidings

155

1:269

footbridges

154

Checkley Brook

BETLEY R⁺ BOX

153

A.51

CHESHIRE

STAFFORDSHIRE

152

1:177

WAINE HILL BOX

footbridge

151

Mill

A.525

MADELEY 150

L.M.S. To Market Drayton

footbridge

L.M.S. To Stoke

1:348

149

grid cables

COLOUR LIGHT SIGNALS ARE IN OPERATION ON THIS SECTION OF LINE

LEVEL

WHITMORE WATER-TROUGHS

148

A.53

WHITMORE 147½

1:398

A.51 147

GRADIENTS

In spite of the fact that we are now approaching the vast network of lines at Crewe, the speed of our train is exhilaratingly high on the favourable 1:177 gradient, and we cross the Staffordshire-Cheshire boundary at a very high rate. It is interesting to check the speed between mileposts on this section of perfectly laid track, and the speed test formula printed on previous pages should be used here. For more than two miles this side of Crewe enormous marshalling yards dominate the landscape on the left. Miles and miles of railway track lie in serried rows for as far as the eye can reach. Thousands of wagons are here assembled in the process of being sorted out and shunted to their different tracks, and 400 goods trains are here dealt with daily. Certainly this must be the busiest yard in the world. Crewe station itself covers some 25 acres, handling as many as 500 passenger trains in the 24 hours. Leaving the Station we see on the left the enormous engine and carriage Works covering nearly 200 acres. Crewe as a town is very concentrated and built close up to its great industry, the railway, and by the time we reach milepost 160 we are again well in the open country heading for the North.

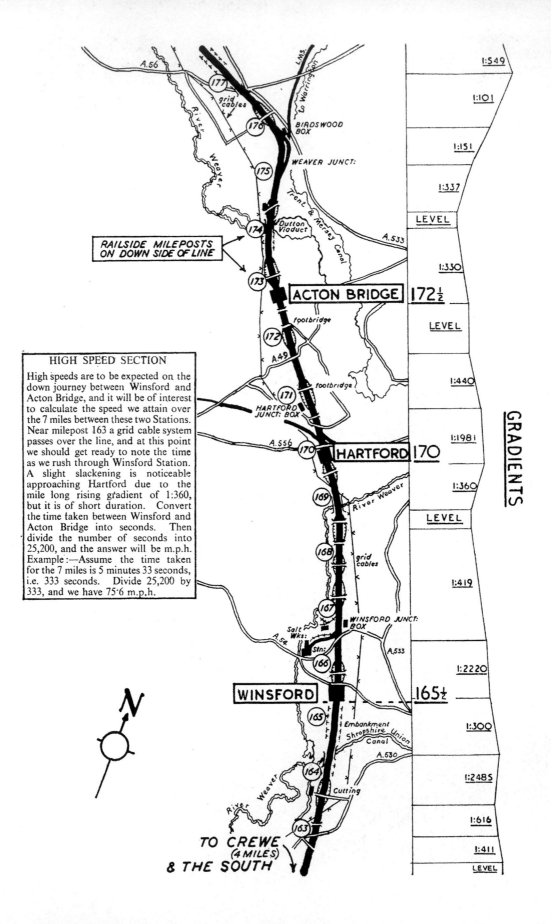

136

A.56

177

grid cables

176

BIRDSWOOD BOX

to Warrington

LMS

WEAVER JUNCT:

175

Trent & Mersey Canal

174

River Weaver

Dutton Viaduct

A.533

RAILSIDE MILEPOSTS ON DOWN SIDE OF LINE

173

ACTON BRIDGE 172½

172

footbridge

A.49

171

footbridge

Hartford JUNCT: BOX

A.556

170

HARTFORD 170

169

River Weaver

168

grid cables

167

WINSFORD JUNCT: BOX

Salt Wks:

A.54

Stn:

166

A.533

WINSFORD 165¼

165

Embankment

Shropshire Union Canal

A.530

164

Cutting

River Weaver

163

TO CREWE
(4 MILES)
& THE SOUTH

N

HIGH SPEED SECTION

High speeds are to be expected on the down journey between Winsford and Acton Bridge, and it will be of interest to calculate the speed we attain over the 7 miles between these two Stations. Near milepost 163 a grid cable system passes over the line, and at this point we should get ready to note the time as we rush through Winsford Station. A slight slackening is noticeable approaching Hartford due to the mile long rising gradient of 1:360, but it is of short duration. Convert the time taken between Winsford and Acton Bridge into seconds. Then divide the number of seconds into 25,200, and the answer will be m.p.h. Example :—Assume the time taken for the 7 miles is 5 minutes 33 seconds, i.e. 333 seconds. Divide 25,200 by 333, and we have 75·6 m.p.h.

GRADIENTS

| 1:549 |
| 1:101 |
| 1:151 |
| 1:337 |
| LEVEL |
| 1:330 |
| LEVEL |
| 1:440 |
| 1:1981 |
| 1:360 |
| LEVEL |
| 1:419 |
| 1:2220 |
| 1:300 |
| 1:2485 |
| 1:616 |
| 1:411 |
| LEVEL |

LIVERPOOL

LIME STREET STATION 193¾ MILES FROM LONDON

BIRKENHEAD

RIVER

PORT SUNLIGHT

MERSEY

193

TUNNELS

EDGE HILL

192

EDGE HILL N°3 BOX
WAVERTREE JUNCT:

RAILSIDE MILEPOSTS ON "DOWN" SIDE OF LINE

WAVERTREE

191

SEFTON PARK

A.5058

190

MOSSLEY HILL

WEST ALLERTON

189

DOCKS

188

ALLERTON

SPEKE JUNCT:

LIVERPOOL AIRPORT (SPEKE)

187

A.57

N

186

SPEKE

Cheshire Lines

A.5080

185

A.562

WOODSIDE SIDINGS BOX

184

HALEBANK

HALEBANK WATER-TROUGHS

183

DITTON JUNCT:

HALE

Ditton Marsh

182

Fisons Wks:

LANCASHIRE

181

VIADUCT

CHESHIRE

Manchester Ship Canal

180

RUNCORN 180½

HALTON JUNC: BOX

A.557

Mersey

Manchester Ship Canal

River Weaver Canal

179

deep Cutting

A.558

A.553

178

Embankment

River Weaver

Runcorn town lies far below the line and on passing over the bridge we see the famous Manchester Ship Canal and River Mersey running together beneath; the one tidal, the other taking the largest of vessels through its series of locks on to Manchester. On the shore of the Mersey a bewildering array of Chemical Works greet the eye with their thousands of barrels of acid, mysterious tanks, and mounds of brilliantly coloured chemicals. After the vast railway yards at Ditton we run into open country again, and pass over the Halebank water-trough system just before that Station. A glimpse of the vast airfield at Speke and we near journey's end. For the last 1½ miles we travel through a series of tunnels or deep cuttings carved out of the solid rock. Lime Street Station is ideally situated in the centre of the City, the famous Art Gallery facing us across the busy square as we leave the station.

GRADIENTS

1:83
1:93
1:136
LEVEL
1:93
1:200
1:445
1:345
1:113
1:331
1:1660
1:305
1:296
1:399
LEVEL
1:220
1:187
1:448
1:180
1:254
LEVEL
1:161
LEVEL
1:114
LEVEL
1:145
1:101
1:115
1:158
1:323
1:549

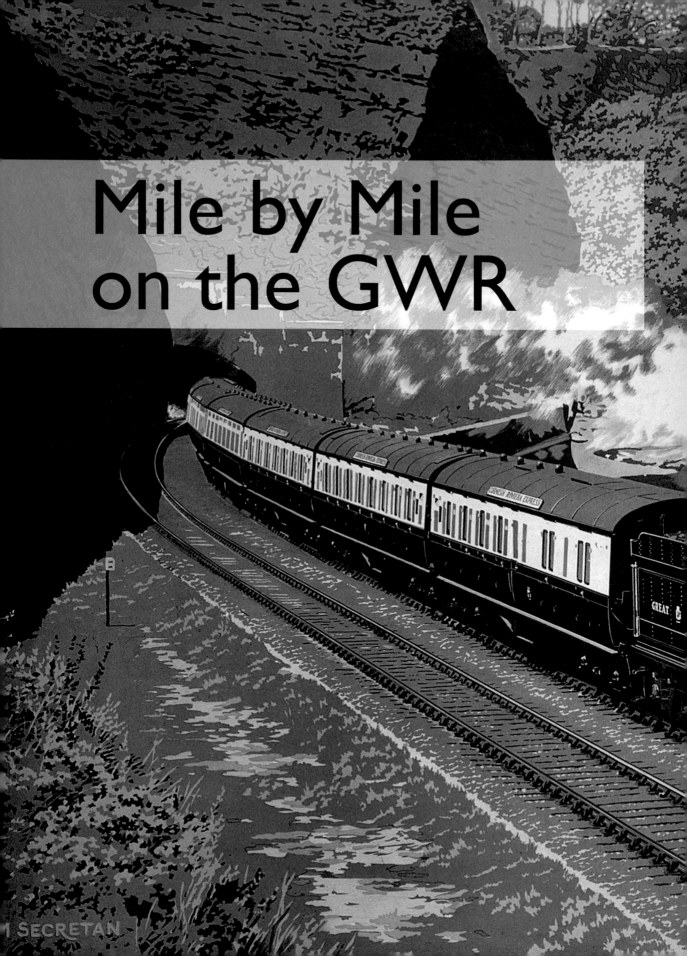

Mile by Mile on the GWR

The GWR Story

For the GWR – known to its admirers as 'God's Wonderful Railway' – the Grouping was chiefly a matter of welcoming some Welsh neighbours into the Paddington fold. The land of 'Kings', 'Castles', 'Halls' and 'Manors' – and Brunel's billiard table railway – had to bear little change.

Compared to the in-fighting and rivalries elsewhere, the gestation of the Great Western was painless. It retained its pre-Grouping identity, its locomotive numbering system – and its independent streak – and seamlessly absorbed seventeen far smaller companies into its structure. Fifteen of those were in South Wales, chiefly connecting the valleys and colliery towns with the docks of, principally, Cardiff, Barry, Newport and Swansea. The outcome was to make the GWR the largest docks operator in the world. The

Cambrian Railway, serving mid- and North Wales, and the Midland & South Western Junction, linking Cheltenham with Swindon and Andover, also came into the GWR fold. The Andover connection gave the GWR a second gateway, Southampton, along with the link from Reading through Basingstoke.

At 331 miles (532.6km), the Cambrian was the largest of the acquisitions, which together added a modest 922 miles (1,483.8km) to the network and took the GWR's route mileage to 4,053 (6,522.6km). A collection of sturdy, six-coupled Welsh tank engines was the most useful addition to the GWR locomotive stock which, in 1921, totalled 3,089, a figure exceeded only by the London & North Western Railway.

Anticipating the relative ease with which the GWR's transition could be accomplished, and hoping to learn lessons that might prove useful in subsequent, more complex amalgamations, the government brought forward its incorporation to 1 January 1922. Little of value was learned from the following twelve months other than that, under General Manager Felix Pole, Paddington's people knew how to run a railway.

◀ GWR's Swindon works built and overhauled the company's principal passenger locomotives for over a century. Here, in 1935, one 'Hall' class loco is about to be wheeled, while another – brand-new no.5956 *Horsley Hall* – is readied for service.

Along with the main routes from London to Bristol, Exeter, Plymouth and Penzance, which are the focus here, the GWR extended its service through the Severn Tunnel (and via Gloucester and Chepstow) into South Wales and along the coast to Swansea and Fishguard. It served Birmingham, Wolverhampton, Shrewsbury and Chester and extended as far north as Birkenhead. Other routes served Oxford, Banbury, Leamington Spa, Kidderminster, Great Malvern, Hereford, Gloucester and Worcester.

Churchward's Claim to Fame

In 1892 the GWR had been compelled to abandon Brunel's broad gauge and scrap a legion of locomotives. Undeterred, in the ensuing thirty years it not only rebuilt its locomotive fleet but, under George Jackson Churchward, took it to a level unmatched elsewhere. Churchward was not solely a remarkable engineer but one who looked to France and the United States for ideas and was open to adopting them. Standardisation united his designs. Boilers, wheel sets, cylinders and a host of smaller components were interchangeable among a number of classes; self-recommending now, but not in 1902, when Churchward became the GWR's Chief Mechanical Engineer.

Passengers continued to dominate the GWR's receipts, but coal traffic from the West Midlands and South Wales was growing. China clay for the porcelain industry was brought out of Cornwall, and perishables traffic – fish, fruit, vegetables, dairy products, milk and cattle – was also increasing. The growth in freight, principally minerals, led Churchward to introduce Britain's first 2-8-0. The '2800' class of 1903 was one of several ground-breaking designs to emerge during his tenure. The 'Star' class 4-cylinder 4-6-0, 'Saint' 2-cylinder 4-6-0, '4500' class 2-6-2 tank and '4300' 2-6-0 were others. Churchward retired in 1922 to be replaced by Charles Collett,

▲ A poster by Herbert Alker Tripp (1883-1954) promoting the splendour of the Cornish coast and the availability of monthly return tickets for holidaymakers. Eye-catching poster art was a key publicity tool for all the 'Big Four'.

who was content to build on the work of his predecessor. He developed the 'Star' into the celebrated 'Castle' class of 1923 and the 'Kings' of 1927. The 'Saint' class evolved into the 'Hall' class of 1928, the precursor of both a class of 330 and many hundreds of mixed-traffic 4-6-0s built for Britain's railways up to the 1950s.

For Felix Pole, image and publicity were important. Express services to the resorts of Somerset, Devon, Cornwall and south-west Wales, spearheaded by the 'Cornish Riviera Express' and the 'Torbay Express', were energetically promoted. In 1927, the introduction of the 'Kings' allowed the former's timing from Paddington to Plymouth

(226 miles/363.7km) to be cut to four hours, an average of 56.5mph (90.9kph). For speed, however, the 'Castle'-hauled 'Cheltenham Flyer' was unmatched anywhere. Its schedule of 65 minutes for the 77.25 miles (124.3km) between Swindon and Paddington at an average of 71.3mph (114.7kph) made it the fastest train in the world. On Monday 6 June 1932, the train shattered records with a time of 56 minutes 47 seconds for the journey, an average speed of 81.6mph (131.3kph). No faster time had been recorded. The GWR's success was reflected in revenues which peaked in 1924, when it carried over 140 million passengers and 81 million tons of freight.

As with every railway company, the GWR was not immune to the industrial downturn of the late 1920s and 1930s. The demand for coal fell dramatically and there was a broader reduction in freight and passenger revenues. One consequence of the Depression, however, did benefit the GWR. The Loans Act of 1929

Paddington's platform one bustles with activity on a day in 1931. A pannier tank has arrived with empty stock; amid the milling passengers, three heavily laden porters' trolleys await loading, while a refreshment trolley provides an oasis of calm.

was intended to stimulate employment by financing construction and similar projects. It was an opportunity to modernise Paddington, Bristol Temple Meads and Cardiff General stations, quadruple the main line through Taunton, and build new marshalling yards, goods depots and locomotive sheds.

At Swindon, the momentum in locomotive design of the 1920s was not sustained into the next decade. Charles Collett did not see the necessity to depart from Churchward's principles. Arguably Collett's most significant project was to create a series of diesel railcars, their popular appeal enhanced by their streamlined bodywork.

Collett retired in 1941, two years into the Second World War. His successor, Frederick

Hawksworth, had little scope for innovation, merely adding to the stock of pannier tanks and 4-6-0s. He was, though, instrumental in the GWR building experimental diesel shunters and ordering two pioneering gas turbine locomotives.

The Great Western Railway officially ceased to exist on 23 December 1949, but British Railways' Western Region did all it could to maintain its character and independent nature, something that continues today. In September 2015, First Great Western changed its identity to Great Western Railway, saying that it wanted 'to reinstate the ideals of our founder.' Isambard Kingdom Brunel could be allowed a wry smile.

▼ A 'Castle' class 4-6-0 crosses Liskeard viaduct with a Penzance-bound train in July 1935. One of many such structures on the Cornish main line, it is 150 feet (45.7m) high and 720 feet (219.4m) long, and stands on eleven piers. The Liskeard to Looe branch line passes below.

▲ Passengers enjoying a meal in one of the GWR's plush first-class dining cars, whose on-board kitchen was equipped to cook everything up to a three-course roast dinner. Savouring fine food while travelling through pleasant countryside was once one of the joys of rail travel.

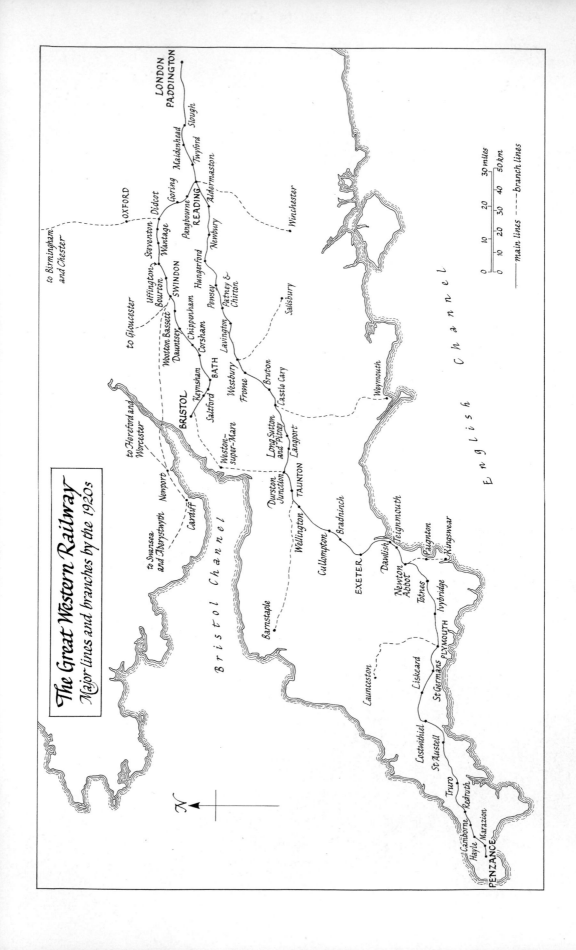

The Great Western Railway
Major lines and branches by the 1920s

LONDON PADDINGTON
Slough
Twyford
Maidenhead
Goring
Pangbourne
READING
Aldermaston
Newbury
Winchester
Didcot
Wantage
Steventon
Uffington
Bourton
SWINDON
Wootton Bassett
Dauntsey
Chippenham
Corsham
Hungerford
Pewsey
Patney & Chirton
Lavington
Westbury
Frome
Salisbury
Bruton
Castle Cary
Bath
Keynsham
Saltford
BRISTOL
Weston-super-Mare
Long Sutton and Pitney
Langport
Durston Junction
TAUNTON
Wellington
Cullompton
Bradninch
EXETER
Dawlish
Teignmouth
Newton Abbot
Paignton
Kingswear
Totnes
Ivybridge
PLYMOUTH
St Germans
Liskeard
Launceston
Lostwithiel
St Austell
Truro
Redruth
Camborne
Hayle
Marazion
PENZANCE
Barnstaple
Weymouth

to Birmingham and Chester
OXFORD
to Gloucester
to Hereford and Worcester
Newport
to Swansea and Aberystwyth
Cardiff

B r i s t o l   C h a n n e l

E n g l i s h   C h a n n e l

N

0   10   20   30 miles
0 10 20 30 40 50 km
——— main lines   ----- branch lines

146

Mile by Mile

ON THE G.W.R.

Maps by Reginald Piggott; research by Matt Thompson

PADDINGTON EDITION

The journey between London and the South-West
described in detail:–

- ● GRADIENTS OF THE LINE
- ● MILEAGES
- ● VIADUCTS, BRIDGES AND EMBANKMENTS
- ● TUNNELS, CUTTINGS AND CROSSOVERS
- ● STREAMS, RIVERS AND ROADS
- ● TOWNS, VILLAGES AND CHURCHES
- ● MINES, FACTORIES AND WORKS

With an account of features of interest and beauty
to be seen from the train.

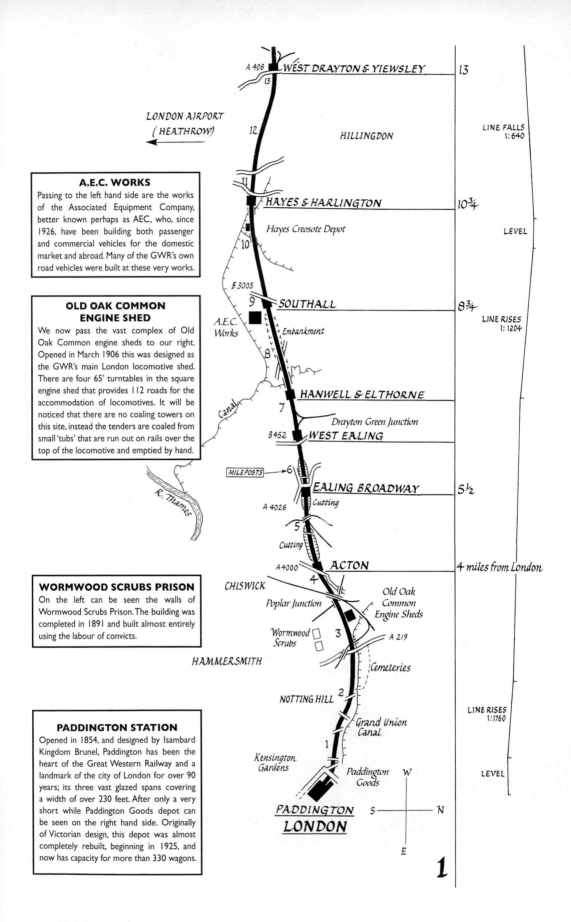

148

A 408 WEST DRAYTON & YIEWSLEY 13
13

LONDON AIRPORT
(HEATHROW)

12

HILLINGDON

LINE FALLS
1:640

11

A.E.C. WORKS
Passing to the left hand side are the works of the Associated Equipment Company, better known perhaps as AEC, who, since 1926, have been building both passenger and commercial vehicles for the domestic market and abroad. Many of the GWR's own road vehicles were built at these very works.

HAYES & HARLINGTON 10¾

Hayes Creosote Depot

LEVEL

10

B 3005

OLD OAK COMMON ENGINE SHED
We now pass the vast complex of Old Oak Common engine sheds to our right. Opened in March 1906 this was designed as the GWR's main London locomotive shed. There are four 65' turntables in the square engine shed that provides 112 roads for the accommodation of locomotives. It will be noticed that there are no coaling towers on this site, instead the tenders are coaled from small 'tubs' that are run out on rails over the top of the locomotive and emptied by hand.

9 SOUTHALL 8¾

A.E.C.
Works

Embankment

LINE RISES
1:1204

8

Canal

HANWELL & ELTHORNE

7

Drayton Green Junction

B 452 WEST EALING

R. Thames

MILEPOSTS → 6

EALING BROADWAY 5½

A 4026 Cutting

5

Cutting

WORMWOOD SCRUBS PRISON
On the left can be seen the walls of Wormwood Scrubs Prison. The building was completed in 1891 and built almost entirely using the labour of convicts.

A4000 ACTON 4 miles from London

4

CHISWICK

Poplar Junction

Old Oak
Common
Engine Sheds

A 219

Wormwood
Scrubs 3

HAMMERSMITH

Cemeteries

NOTTING HILL 2

LINE RISES
1:1760

Grand Union
Canal

PADDINGTON STATION
Opened in 1854, and designed by Isambard Kingdom Brunel, Paddington has been the heart of the Great Western Railway and a landmark of the city of London for over 90 years; its three vast glazed spans covering a width of over 230 feet. After only a very short while Paddington Goods depot can be seen on the right hand side. Originally of Victorian design, this depot was almost completely rebuilt, beginning in 1925, and now has capacity for more than 330 wagons.

1

Kensington
Gardens

Paddington
Goods

W

LEVEL

PADDINGTON
LONDON

S —— N

E

1

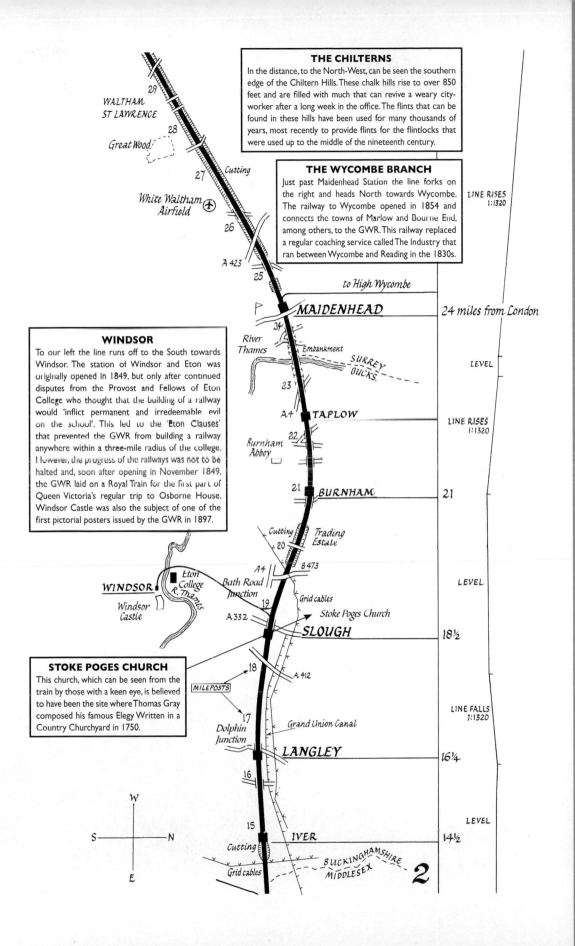

WALTHAM
ST LAWRENCE

Great Wood

29

28

27 Cutting

White Waltham
Airfield

26

A 423

25

THE CHILTERNS

In the distance, to the North-West, can be seen the southern edge of the Chiltern Hills. These chalk hills rise to over 850 feet and are filled with much that can revive a weary city-worker after a long week in the office. The flints that can be found in these hills have been used for many thousands of years, most recently to provide flints for the flintlocks that were used up to the middle of the nineteenth century.

THE WYCOMBE BRANCH

Just past Maidenhead Station the line forks on the right and heads North towards Wycombe. The railway to Wycombe opened in 1854 and connects the towns of Marlow and Bourne End, among others, to the GWR. This railway replaced a regular coaching service called The Industry that ran between Wycombe and Reading in the 1830s.

LINE RISES
1:1320

to High Wycombe

MAIDENHEAD   24 miles from London

24

River
Thames   Embankment   SURREY   LEVEL
BUCKS.

23

A4 **TAPLOW**   LINE RISES
1:1320

22

Burnham
Abbey

WINDSOR

To our left the line runs off to the South towards Windsor. The station of Windsor and Eton was originally opened in 1849, but only after continued disputes from the Provost and Fellows of Eton College who thought that the building of a railway would 'inflict permanent and irredeemable evil on the school'. This led to the 'Eton Clauses' that prevented the GWR from building a railway anywhere within a three-mile radius of the college. However, the progress of the railways was not to be halted and, soon after opening in November 1849, the GWR laid on a Royal Train for the first part of Queen Victoria's regular trip to Osborne House. Windsor Castle was also the subject of one of the first pictorial posters issued by the GWR in 1897.

21 **BURNHAM**   21

Cutting Trading
Estate

20

A4 B 473
Bath Road
Junction   LEVEL

WINDSOR Eton
College
R. Thames

Windsor
Castle

19   Grid cables

A 332   Stoke Poges Church

SLOUGH   18½

18   A 412

STOKE POGES CHURCH

This church, which can be seen from the train by those with a keen eye, is believed to have been the site where Thomas Gray composed his famous Elegy Written in a Country Churchyard in 1750.

MILEPOSTS

17   Grand Union Canal   LINE FALLS
1:1320
Dolphin
Junction

LANGLEY   16¼

16

W

S   N   LEVEL

15   **IVER**   14½

E   Cutting

Grid cables   BUCKINGHAMSHIRE
MIDDLESEX   **2**

149

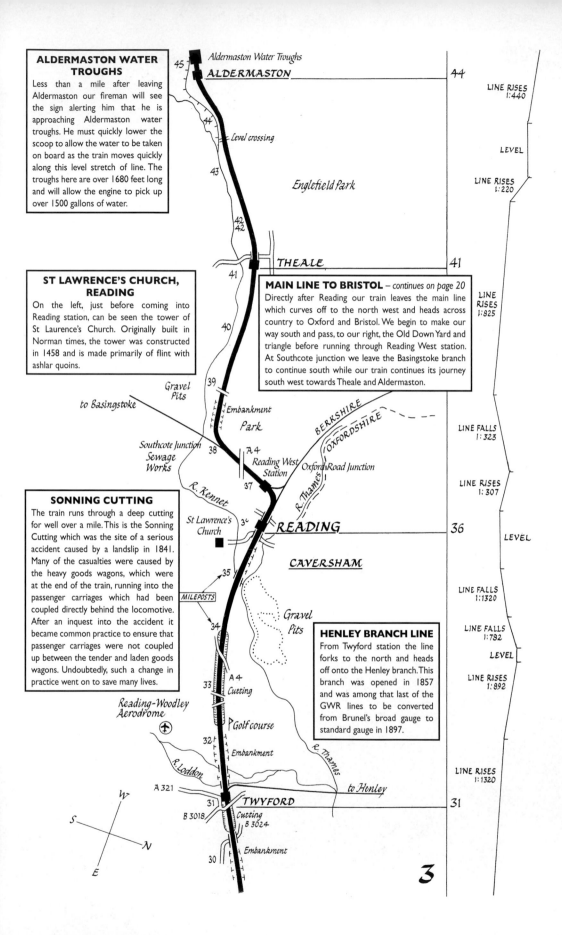

ALDERMASTON WATER TROUGHS

Less than a mile after leaving Aldermaston our fireman will see the sign alerting him that he is approaching Aldermaston water troughs. He must quickly lower the scoop to allow the water to be taken on board as the train moves quickly along this level stretch of line. The troughs here are over 1680 feet long and will allow the engine to pick up over 1500 gallons of water.

ST LAWRENCE'S CHURCH, READING

On the left, just before coming into Reading station, can be seen the tower of St Laurence's Church. Originally built in Norman times, the tower was constructed in 1458 and is made primarily of flint with ashlar quoins.

SONNING CUTTING

The train runs through a deep cutting for well over a mile. This is the Sonning Cutting which was the site of a serious accident caused by a landslip in 1841. Many of the casualties were caused by the heavy goods wagons, which were at the end of the train, running into the passenger carriages which had been coupled directly behind the locomotive. After an inquest into the accident it became common practice to ensure that passenger carriages were not coupled up between the tender and laden goods wagons. Undoubtedly, such a change in practice went on to save many lives.

MAIN LINE TO BRISTOL – continues on page 20

Directly after Reading our train leaves the main line which curves off to the north west and heads across country to Oxford and Bristol. We begin to make our way south and pass, to our right, the Old Down Yard and triangle before running through Reading West station. At Southcote junction we leave the Basingstoke branch to continue south while our train continues its journey south west towards Theale and Aldermaston.

HENLEY BRANCH LINE

From Twyford station the line forks to the north and heads off onto the Henley branch. This branch was opened in 1857 and was among that last of the GWR lines to be converted from Brunel's broad gauge to standard gauge in 1897.

Aldermaston Water Troughs
ALDERMASTON
Level crossing
Englefield Park
THEALE
to Basingstoke
Gravel Pits
Embankment
Park
BERKSHIRE
OXFORDSHIRE
Southcote Junction
Sewage Works
R. Kennet
Reading West Station
Oxford Road Junction
R. Thames
St Lawrence's Church
READING
CAVERSHAM
MILEPOSTS
Gravel Pits
A4 Cutting
Reading-Woodley Aerodrome
Golf course
R. Thames
Embankment
R. Loddon
to Henley
A 321
TWYFORD
B 3018
Cutting
B 3024
Embankment

LINE RISES 1:440
LEVEL
LINE RISES 1:220
LINE RISES 1:825
LINE FALLS 1:323
LINE RISES 1:307
LEVEL
LINE FALLS 1:1320
LINE FALLS 1:782
LEVEL
LINE RISES 1:892
LINE RISES 1:1320

W
S
N
E

3

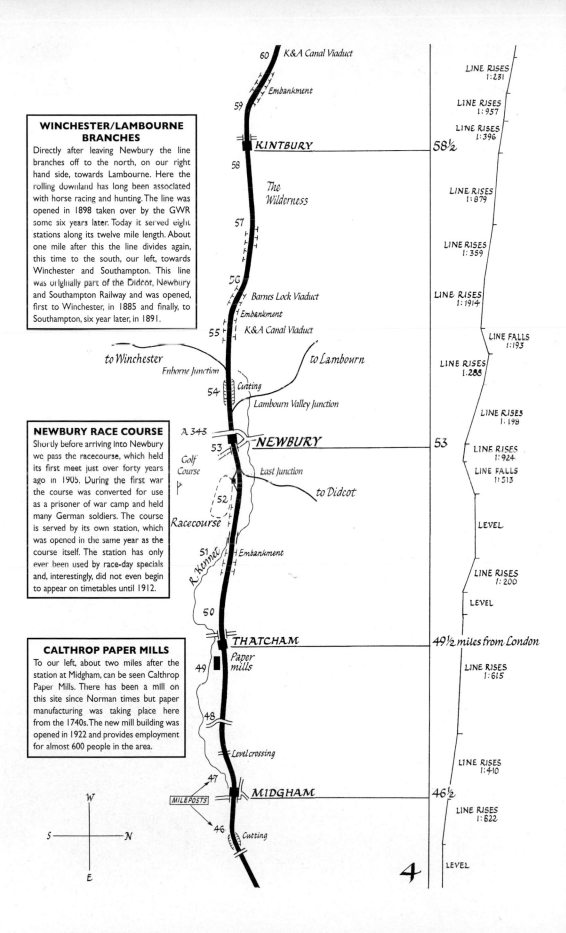

WINCHESTER/LAMBOURNE BRANCHES

Directly after leaving Newbury the line branches off to the north, on our right hand side, towards Lambourne. Here the rolling downland has long been associated with horse racing and hunting. The line was opened in 1898 taken over by the GWR some six years later. Today it served eight stations along its twelve mile length. About one mile after this the line divides again, this time to the south, our left, towards Winchester and Southampton. This line was originally part of the Didcot, Newbury and Southampton Railway and was opened, first to Winchester, in 1885 and finally, to Southampton, six year later, in 1891.

NEWBURY RACE COURSE

Shortly before arriving into Newbury we pass the racecourse, which held its first meet just over forty years ago in 1905. During the first war the course was converted for use as a prisoner of war camp and held many German soldiers. The course is served by its own station, which was opened in the same year as the course itself. The station has only ever been used by race-day specials and, interestingly, did not even begin to appear on timetables until 1912.

CALTHROP PAPER MILLS

To our left, about two miles after the station at Midgham, can be seen Calthrop Paper Mills. There has been a mill on this site since Norman times but paper manufacturing was taking place here from the 1740s. The new mill building was opened in 1922 and provides employment for almost 600 people in the area.

60 — K&A Canal Viaduct

Embankment

59

KINTBURY — 58½

58

The Wilderness

57

56 — Barnes Lock Viaduct

Embankment

55 — K&A Canal Viaduct

to Winchester — Enborne Junction — to Lambourn

54 — Cutting — Lambourn Valley Junction

A 343

53 — **NEWBURY** — 53

Golf Course — East Junction

52 — to Didcot

Racecourse

R. Kennet

51 — Embankment

50

THATCHAM — 49½ miles from London

49 — Paper mills

48

Level crossing

47 — MILEPOSTS — **MIDGHAM** — 46½

46 — Cutting

LINE RISES 1:231

LINE RISES 1:957

LINE RISES 1:396

LINE RISES 1:879

LINE RISES 1:359

LINE RISES 1:1914

LINE FALLS 1:193

LINE RISES 1:285

LINE RISES 1:198

LINE RISES 1:924

LINE FALLS 1:513

LEVEL

LINE RISES 1:200

LEVEL

LINE RISES 1:615

LINE RISES 1:410

LINE RISES 1:522

LEVEL

W
S — N
E

4

151

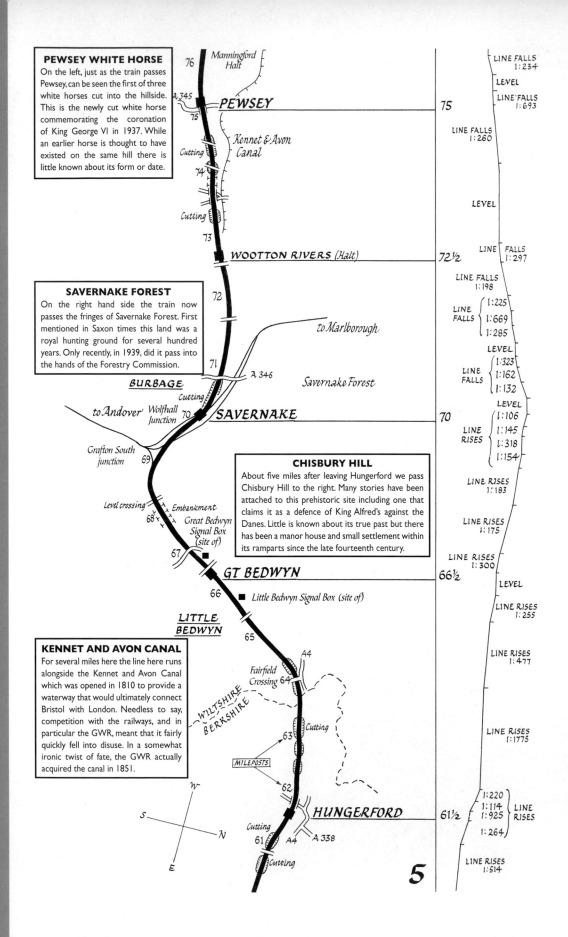

PEWSEY WHITE HORSE
On the left, just as the train passes Pewsey, can be seen the first of three white horses cut into the hillside. This is the newly cut white horse commemorating the coronation of King George VI in 1937. While an earlier horse is thought to have existed on the same hill there is little known about its form or date.

SAVERNAKE FOREST
On the right hand side the train now passes the fringes of Savernake Forest. First mentioned in Saxon times this land was a royal hunting ground for several hundred years. Only recently, in 1939, did it pass into the hands of the Forestry Commission.

CHISBURY HILL
About five miles after leaving Hungerford we pass Chisbury Hill to the right. Many stories have been attached to this prehistoric site including one that claims it as a defence of King Alfred's against the Danes. Little is known about its true past but there has been a manor house and small settlement within its ramparts since the late fourteenth century.

KENNET AND AVON CANAL
For several miles here the line here runs alongside the Kennet and Avon Canal which was opened in 1810 to provide a waterway that would ultimately connect Bristol with London. Needless to say, competition with the railways, and in particular the GWR, meant that it fairly quickly fell into disuse. In a somewhat ironic twist of fate, the GWR actually acquired the canal in 1851.

Manningford Halt

PEWSEY

Kennet & Avon Canal

Cutting

Cutting

WOOTTON RIVERS (Halt)

to Marlborough

Savernake Forest

BURBAGE

Cutting

to Andover · Wolfhall Junction

SAVERNAKE

Grafton South junction

Level crossing

Embankment

Great Bedwyn Signal Box (site of)

GT BEDWYN

Little Bedwyn Signal Box (site of)

LITTLE BEDWYN

Fairfield Crossing

WILTSHIRE / BERKSHIRE

Cutting

MILEPOSTS

HUNGERFORD

Cutting

Cutting

LINE FALLS 1:234
LEVEL
LINE FALLS 1:693
LINE FALLS 1:260
LEVEL
LINE FALLS 1:297
LINE FALLS 1:198
LINE FALLS { 1:225 / 1:669 / 1:285 }
LEVEL
LINE FALLS { 1:323 / 1:162 / 1:132 }
LEVEL
LINE RISES { 1:106 / 1:145 / 1:318 / 1:154 }
LINE RISES 1:183
LINE RISES 1:175
LINE RISES 1:300
LEVEL
LINE RISES 1:255
LINE RISES 1:477
LINE RISES 1:1775
LINE RISES { 1:220 / 1:114 / 1:925 / 1:264 }
LINE RISES 1:514

5

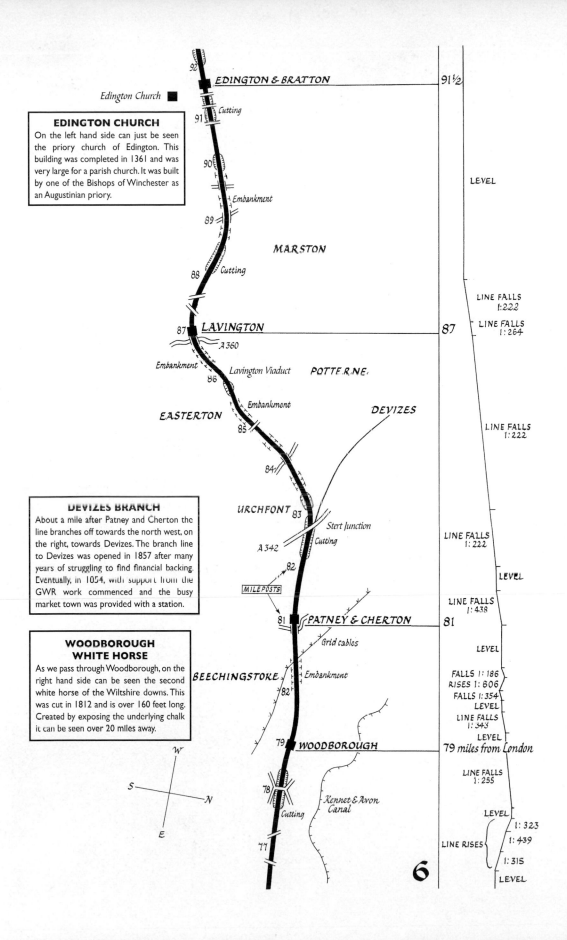

EDINGTON & BRATTON

Edington Church ■

EDINGTON CHURCH

On the left hand side can just be seen the priory church of Edington. This building was completed in 1361 and was very large for a parish church. It was built by one of the Bishops of Winchester as an Augustinian priory.

Cutting

Embankment

MARSTON

Cutting

LAVINGTON

A 360

Embankment *Lavington Viaduct*

POTTERNE

EASTERTON

Embankment

DEVIZES

URCHFONT

Stert Junction

A 342 *Cutting*

DEVIZES BRANCH

About a mile after Patney and Cherton the line branches off towards the north west, on the right, towards Devizes. The branch line to Devizes was opened in 1857 after many years of struggling to find financial backing. Eventually, in 1854, with support from the GWR work commenced and the busy market town was provided with a station.

MILEPOSTS

PATNEY & CHERTON

Grid cables

WOODBOROUGH WHITE HORSE

As we pass through Woodborough, on the right hand side can be seen the second white horse of the Wiltshire downs. This was cut in 1812 and is over 160 feet long. Created by exposing the underlying chalk it can be seen over 20 miles away.

BEECHINGSTOKE

Embankment

WOODBOROUGH

W

S

N

E

Cutting

Kennet & Avon Canal

91½

LEVEL

LINE FALLS 1:222

LINE FALLS 1:264

87

LINE FALLS 1:222

LINE FALLS 1:222

LEVEL

LINE FALLS 1:438

81

LEVEL

FALLS 1:186
RISES 1:606
FALLS 1:354
LEVEL
LINE FALLS 1:343
LEVEL

79 miles from London

LINE FALLS 1:255

LEVEL

1:323

LINE RISES { 1:439

1:315

LEVEL

6

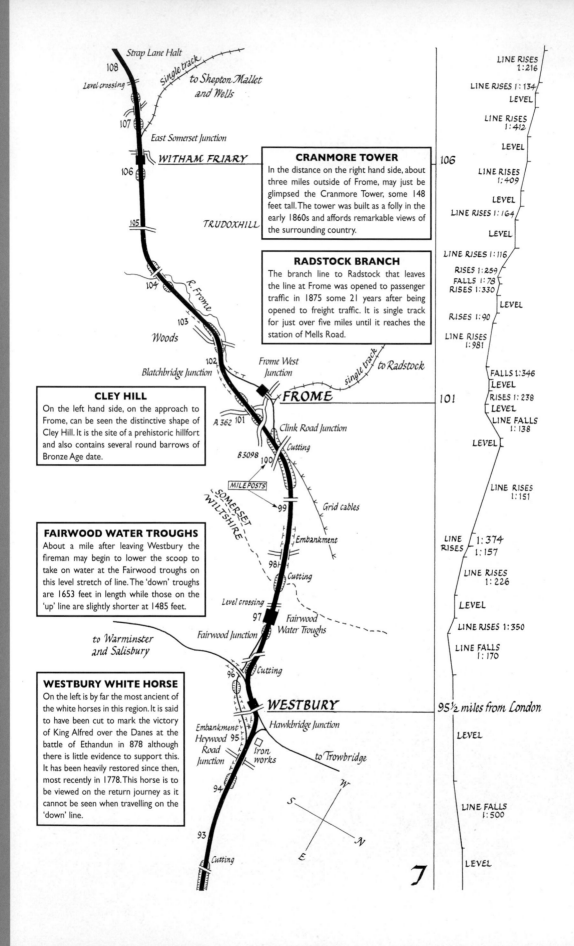

108
Strap Lane Halt
Level crossing
single track
to Shepton Mallet
and Wells

107

East Somerset Junction
WITHAM FRIARY
106

105

TRUDOXHILL

104
R. Frome

103
Woods

102
Blatchbridge Junction
Frome West Junction
single track
to Radstock

FROME

A 362 101
Clink Road Junction
B3098 100
Cutting
MILE POSTS
99
Grid cables
SOMERSET
WILTSHIRE
Embankment
98
Cutting
Level crossing
97
Fairwood Junction
Fairwood Water Troughs
to Warminster
and Salisbury

96
Cutting

WESTBURY
Hawkbridge Junction
Embankment
Heywood 95
Road
Junction
Iron works
to Trowbridge

94

93
Cutting

CRANMORE TOWER
In the distance on the right hand side, about three miles outside of Frome, may just be glimpsed the Cranmore Tower, some 148 feet tall. The tower was built as a folly in the early 1860s and affords remarkable views of the surrounding country.

RADSTOCK BRANCH
The branch line to Radstock that leaves the line at Frome was opened to passenger traffic in 1875 some 21 years after being opened to freight traffic. It is single track for just over five miles until it reaches the station of Mells Road.

CLEY HILL
On the left hand side, on the approach to Frome, can be seen the distinctive shape of Cley Hill. It is the site of a prehistoric hillfort and also contains several round barrows of Bronze Age date.

FAIRWOOD WATER TROUGHS
About a mile after leaving Westbury the fireman may begin to lower the scoop to take on water at the Fairwood troughs on this level stretch of line. The 'down' troughs are 1653 feet in length while those on the 'up' line are slightly shorter at 1485 feet.

WESTBURY WHITE HORSE
On the left is by far the most ancient of the white horses in this region. It is said to have been cut to mark the victory of King Alfred over the Danes at the battle of Ethandun in 878 although there is little evidence to support this. It has been heavily restored since then, most recently in 1778. This horse is to be viewed on the return journey as it cannot be seen when travelling on the 'down' line.

154

LINE RISES 1:216
LINE RISES 1:134
LEVEL
LINE RISES 1:412
LEVEL
106
LINE RISES 1:409
LEVEL
LINE RISES 1:164
LEVEL
LINE RISES 1:116
RISES 1:259
FALLS 1:78
RISES 1:330
LEVEL
RISES 1:90
LINE RISES 1:981
FALLS 1:346
LEVEL
101
RISES 1:238
LEVEL
LINE FALLS 1:138
LEVEL
LINE RISES 1:151
LINE RISES 1:374
1:157
LINE RISES 1:226
LEVEL
LINE RISES 1:350
LINE FALLS 1:170
95½ miles from London
LEVEL
LINE FALLS 1:500
LEVEL

7

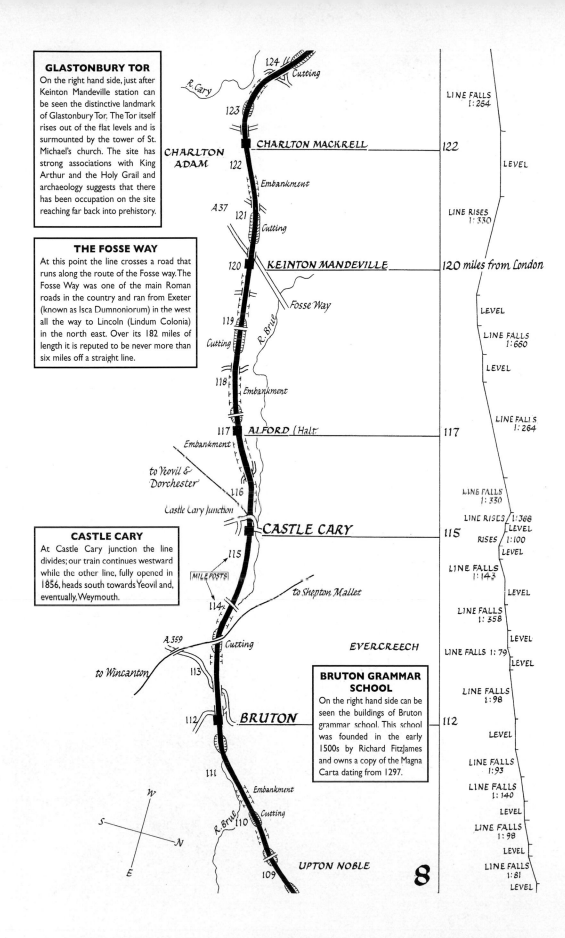

GLASTONBURY TOR

On the right hand side, just after Keinton Mandeville station can be seen the distinctive landmark of Glastonbury Tor. The Tor itself rises out of the flat levels and is surmounted by the tower of St. Michael's church. The site has strong associations with King Arthur and the Holy Grail and archaeology suggests that there has been occupation on the site reaching far back into prehistory.

THE FOSSE WAY

At this point the line crosses a road that runs along the route of the Fosse way. The Fosse Way was one of the main Roman roads in the country and ran from Exeter (known as Isca Dumnoniorum) in the west all the way to Lincoln (Lindum Colonia) in the north east. Over its 182 miles of length it is reputed to be never more than six miles off a straight line.

CASTLE CARY

At Castle Cary junction the line divides; our train continues westward while the other line, fully opened in 1856, heads south towards Yeovil and, eventually, Weymouth.

BRUTON GRAMMAR SCHOOL

On the right hand side can be seen the buildings of Bruton grammar school. This school was founded in the early 1500s by Richard FitzJames and owns a copy of the Magna Carta dating from 1297.

R. Cary

124 — Cutting

123

CHARLTON MACKRELL — 122

CHARLTON ADAM 122

Embankment

A37

121 Cutting

120 KEINTON MANDEVILLE — 120 miles from London

Fosse Way

R. Brue

119 Cutting

118 Embankment

117 ALFORD (Halt — 117

Embankment

to Yeovil & Dorchester

116

Castle Cary Junction

CASTLE CARY — 115

115

MILEPOSTS

to Shepton Mallet

114½

A359 Cutting

EVERCREECH

to Wincanton 113

112 BRUTON — 112

111

Embankment

R. Brue 110 Cutting

W
S
E
N

UPTON NOBLE

109

8

LINE FALLS 1:264

LEVEL

LINE RISES 1:330

LEVEL

LINE FALLS 1:660

LEVEL

LINE FALLS 1:264

LINE FALLS 1:330

LINE RISES 1:368

LEVEL

RISES 1:100

LEVEL

LINE FALLS 1:143

LEVEL

LINE FALLS 1:358

LEVEL

LINE FALLS 1:79

LEVEL

LINE FALLS 1:98

LEVEL

LINE FALLS 1:93

LINE FALLS 1:140

LEVEL

LINE FALLS 1:98

LEVEL

LINE FALLS 1:81

LEVEL

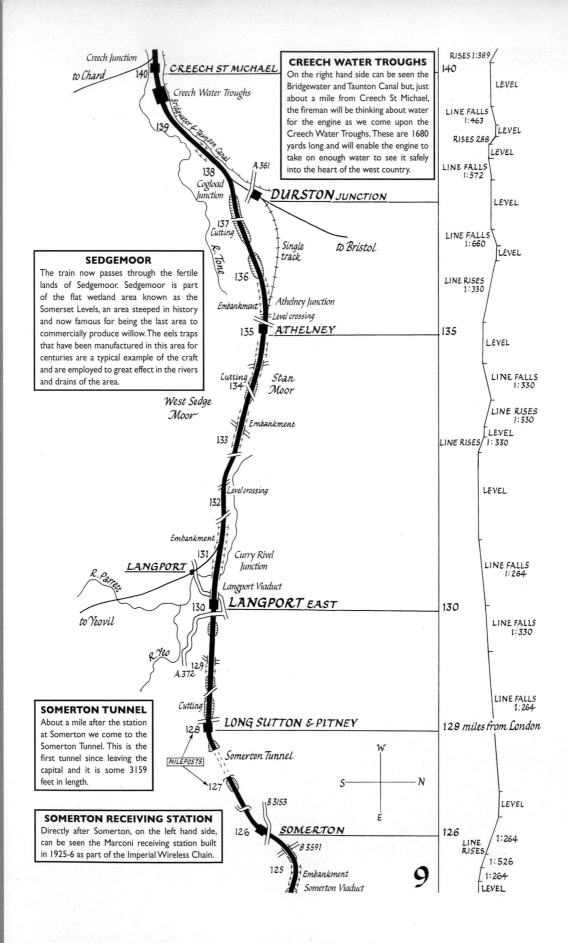

CREECH WATER TROUGHS

On the right hand side can be seen the Bridgewater and Taunton Canal but, just about a mile from Creech St Michael, the fireman will be thinking about water for the engine as we come upon the Creech Water Troughs. These are 1680 yards long and will enable the engine to take on enough water to see it safely into the heart of the west country.

SEDGEMOOR

The train now passes through the fertile lands of Sedgemoor. Sedgemoor is part of the flat wetland area known as the Somerset Levels, an area steeped in history and now famous for being the last area to commercially produce willow. The eels traps that have been manufactured in this area for centuries are a typical example of the craft and are employed to great effect in the rivers and drains of the area.

SOMERTON TUNNEL

About a mile after the station at Somerton we come to the Somerton Tunnel. This is the first tunnel since leaving the capital and it is some 3159 feet in length.

SOMERTON RECEIVING STATION

Directly after Somerton, on the left hand side, can be seen the Marconi receiving station built in 1925-6 as part of the Imperial Wireless Chain.

Creech Junction
to Chard
140
CREECH ST MICHAEL
Creech Water Troughs
139
Bridgewater & Taunton Canal
138
Cogload Junction
A 361
DURSTON JUNCTION
137
Cutting
to Bristol
R. Tone
Single track
136
Embankment
Athelney Junction
Level crossing
135
ATHELNEY
Cutting
134
Stan Moor
West Sedge Moor
Embankment
133
Level crossing
132
Embankment
131
Curry Rivel Junction
LANGPORT
R. Parrett
Langport Viaduct
130
LANGPORT EAST
to Yeovil
R. Yeo
129
A 372
Cutting
128
LONG SUTTON & PITNEY
MILEPOSTS
Somerton Tunnel
127
B 3153
W
S — N
E
126
SOMERTON
B 3591
125
Embankment
Somerton Viaduct

RISES 1:389
140
LEVEL
LINE FALLS 1:463
LEVEL
RISES 288
LEVEL
LINE FALLS 1:572
LEVEL
LINE FALLS 1:660
LEVEL
LINE RISES 1:330
135
LEVEL
LINE FALLS 1:330
LINE RISES 1:330
LEVEL
LINE RISES 1:330
LEVEL
LINE FALLS 1:264
130
LINE FALLS 1:330
LINE FALLS 1:264
128 miles from London
LEVEL
126
1:264
LINE RISES
1:526
1:264
LEVEL

9

156

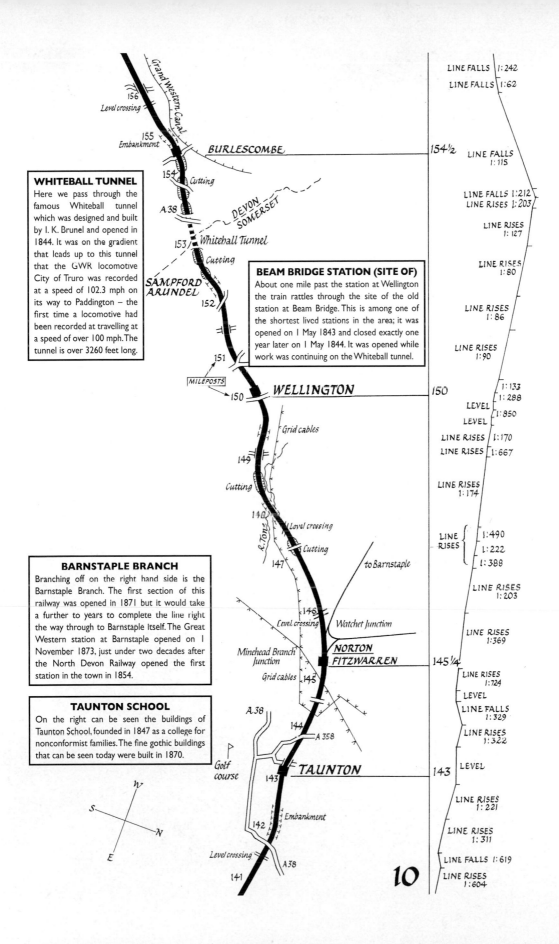

WHITEBALL TUNNEL

Here we pass through the famous Whiteball tunnel which was designed and built by I. K. Brunel and opened in 1844. It was on the gradient that leads up to this tunnel that the GWR locomotive City of Truro was recorded at a speed of 102.3 mph on its way to Paddington – the first time a locomotive had been recorded at travelling at a speed of over 100 mph. The tunnel is over 3260 feet long.

BEAM BRIDGE STATION (SITE OF)

About one mile past the station at Wellington the train rattles through the site of the old station at Beam Bridge. This is among one of the shortest lived stations in the area; it was opened on 1 May 1843 and closed exactly one year later on 1 May 1844. It was opened while work was continuing on the Whiteball tunnel.

BARNSTAPLE BRANCH

Branching off on the right hand side is the Barnstaple Branch. The first section of this railway was opened in 1871 but it would take a further to years to complete the line right the way through to Barnstaple itself. The Great Western station at Barnstaple opened on 1 November 1873, just under two decades after the North Devon Railway opened the first station in the town in 1854.

TAUNTON SCHOOL

On the right can be seen the buildings of Taunton School, founded in 1847 as a college for nonconformist families. The fine gothic buildings that can be seen today were built in 1870.

BURLESCOMBE

WHITEBALL TUNNEL

SAMPFORD ARUNDEL

WELLINGTON

NORTON FITZWARREN

TAUNTON

10

LINE FALLS 1:242
LINE FALLS 1:62
LINE FALLS 1:115
LINE FALLS 1:212
LINE RISES 1:203
LINE RISES 1:127
LINE RISES 1:80
LINE RISES 1:86
LINE RISES 1:90
1:133
1:288
LEVEL
1:850
LINE RISES 1:170
LINE RISES 1:667
LINE RISES 1:174
LINE RISES 1:490 1:222 1:388
LINE RISES 1:203
LINE RISES 1:369
LINE RISES 1:724
LEVEL
LINE FALLS 1:329
LINE RISES 1:322
LEVEL
LINE RISES 1:221
LINE RISES 1:311
LINE FALLS 1:619
LINE RISES 1:604

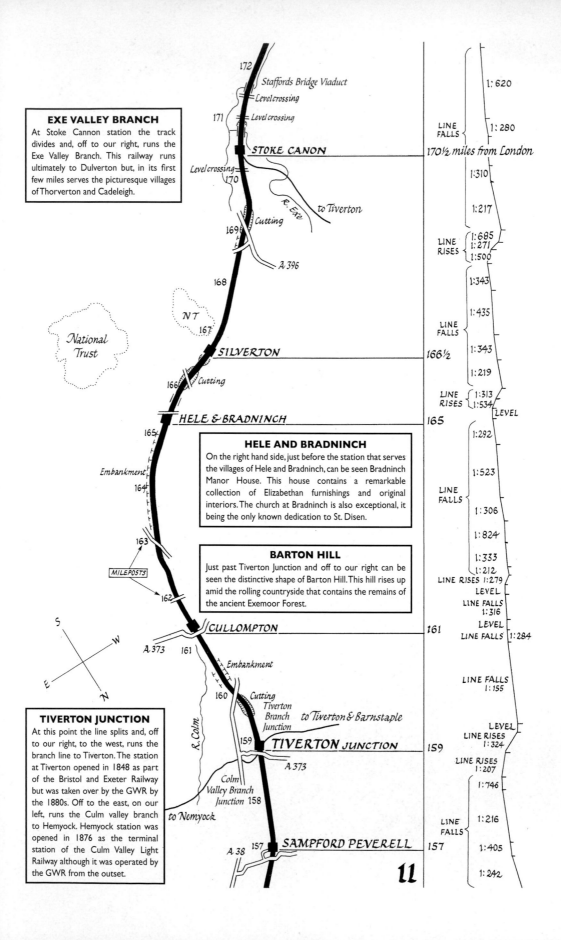

EXE VALLEY BRANCH

At Stoke Cannon station the track divides and, off to our right, runs the Exe Valley Branch. This railway runs ultimately to Dulverton but, in its first few miles serves the picturesque villages of Thorverton and Cadeleigh.

HELE AND BRADNINCH

On the right hand side, just before the station that serves the villages of Hele and Bradninch, can be seen Bradninch Manor House. This house contains a remarkable collection of Elizabethan furnishings and original interiors. The church at Bradninch is also exceptional, it being the only known dedication to St. Disen.

BARTON HILL

Just past Tiverton Junction and off to our right can be seen the distinctive shape of Barton Hill. This hill rises up amid the rolling countryside that contains the remains of the ancient Exemoor Forest.

TIVERTON JUNCTION

At this point the line splits and, off to our right, to the west, runs the branch line to Tiverton. The station at Tiverton opened in 1848 as part of the Bristol and Exeter Railway but was taken over by the GWR by the 1880s. Off to the east, on our left, runs the Culm valley branch to Hemyock. Hemyock station was opened in 1876 as the terminal station of the Culm Valley Light Railway although it was operated by the GWR from the outset.

172
Staffords Bridge Viaduct
Level crossing
171
Level crossing
STOKE CANON
Level crossing
170
R. Exe
to Tiverton
169
Cutting
A 396
168
N T
167
SILVERTON
166
Cutting
HELE & BRADNINCH
165
Embankment
164
163
MILEPOSTS
162
CULLOMPTON
A 373
161
Embankment
160
Cutting
Tiverton Branch Junction
to Tiverton & Barnstaple
159
TIVERTON JUNCTION
A 373
R. Colm
Colm Valley Branch Junction 158
to Nemyock
157
A 38
SAMPFORD PEVERELL

National Trust

S
W
E
N

1:620
1:280
LINE FALLS
170½ miles from London
1:310
1:217
LINE RISES
1:685
1:271
1:500
1:343
1:435
LINE FALLS
1:343
166½
1:219
LINE RISES
1:313
1:534
LEVEL
165
1:292
1:523
LINE FALLS
1:306
1:824
1:333
1:212
LINE RISES 1:279
LEVEL
LINE FALLS 1:316
LEVEL
LINE FALLS 1:284
161
LINE FALLS 1:155
LEVEL
LINE RISES 1:324
LINE RISES 1:207
159
1:746
1:216
LINE FALLS
1:405
157
1:242

11

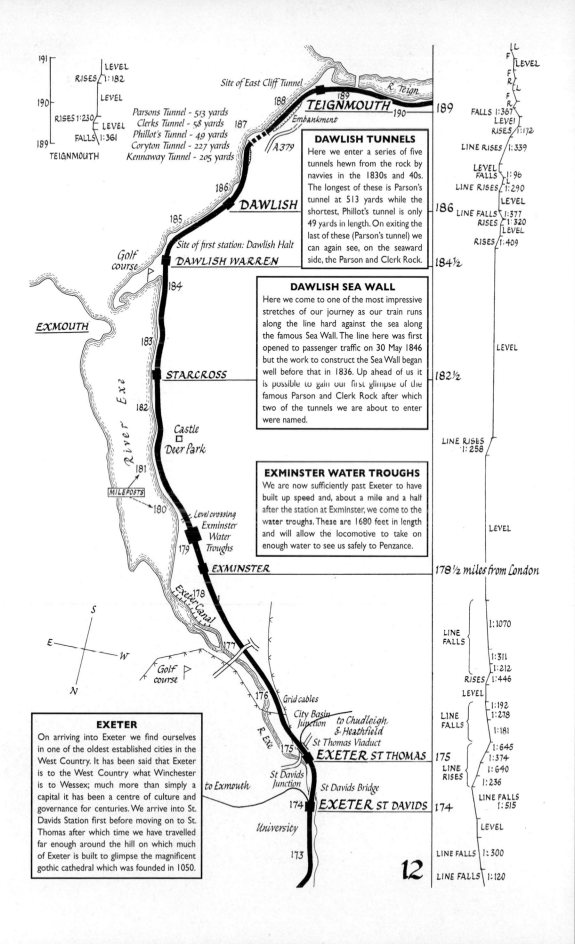

191

LEVEL

RISES 1:182

LEVEL

190

RISES 1:230

LEVEL

189

FALLS 1:361

TEIGNMOUTH

Parsons Tunnel - 513 yards
Clerks Tunnel - 58 yards
Phillot's Tunnel - 49 yards
Coryton Tunnel - 227 yards
Kennaway Tunnel - 205 yards

187

Site of East Cliff Tunnel

188   189

TEIGNMOUTH

Embankment   190

R. Teign

189

A379

186

DAWLISH

185

Site of first station: Dawlish Halt

DAWLISH WARREN

Golf course

184

183

182

Castle

Deer Park

181

MILEPOSTS

180

Level crossing
Exminster
Water
Troughs

179

EXMINSTER

178

Exeter Canal

177

Golf course

176   Grid cables

City Basin
Junction

St Thomas Viaduct

175

EXETER ST THOMAS

175

St Davids
Junction

to Exmouth

St Davids Bridge

174

EXETER ST DAVIDS

174

University

173

R. Exe

to Chudleigh
& Heathfield

EXMOUTH

River Exe

S
E — W
N

DAWLISH TUNNELS

Here we enter a series of five tunnels hewn from the rock by navvies in the 1830s and 40s. The longest of these is Parson's tunnel at 513 yards while the shortest, Phillot's tunnel is only 49 yards in length. On exiting the last of these (Parson's tunnel) we can again see, on the seaward side, the Parson and Clerk Rock.

DAWLISH SEA WALL

Here we come to one of the most impressive stretches of our journey as our train runs along the line hard against the sea along the famous Sea Wall. The line here was first opened to passenger traffic on 30 May 1846 but the work to construct the Sea Wall began well before that in 1836. Up ahead of us it is possible to gain our first glimpse of the famous Parson and Clerk Rock after which two of the tunnels we are about to enter were named.

EXMINSTER WATER TROUGHS

We are now sufficiently past Exeter to have built up speed and, about a mile and a half after the station at Exminster, we come to the water troughs. These are 1680 feet in length and will allow the locomotive to take on enough water to see us safely to Penzance.

EXETER

On arriving into Exeter we find ourselves in one of the oldest established cities in the West Country. It has been said that Exeter is to the West Country what Winchester is to Wessex; much more than simply a capital it has been a centre of culture and governance for centuries. We arrive into St. Davids Station first before moving on to St. Thomas after which time we have travelled far enough around the hill on which much of Exeter is built to glimpse the magnificent gothic cathedral which was founded in 1050.

L
F
R
L
F
R
LEVEL
FALLS 1:367
LEVEL
RISES 1:172
LINE RISES 1:339
LEVEL
FALLS 1:96
LINE RISES 1:290
LEVEL
186   LINE FALLS 1:377
RISES 1:320
LEVEL
RISES 1:409

184½

LEVEL

182½

LINE RISES 1:258

LEVEL

178½ miles from London

1:1070
LINE FALLS
1:311
1:212
RISES 1:446
LEVEL
1:192
LINE FALLS 1:278
1:181
1:645
1:374
LINE RISES 1:640
1:236
LINE FALLS 1:515
LEVEL
LINE FALLS 1:300
LINE FALLS 1:120

12

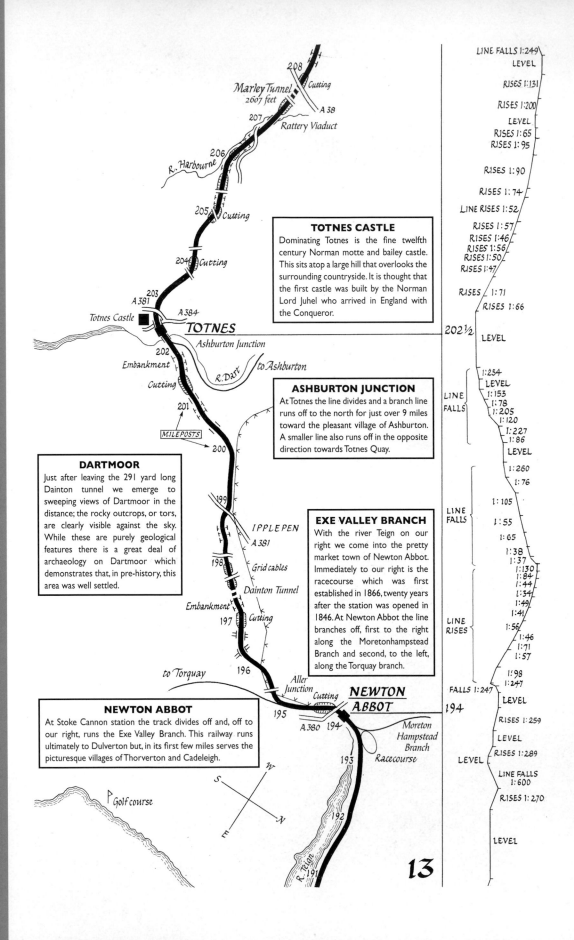

208

Marley Tunnel
2607 feet

Cutting

A 38

207

Rattery Viaduct

206

R. Harbourne

205 *Cutting*

204 *Cutting*

203
A 381

Totnes Castle

A 384

TOTNES

Ashburton Junction

202

Embankment

R. Dart *to Ashburton*

Cutting

201

MILEPOSTS

200

199

IPPLEPEN
A 381

198

Grid cables

Dainton Tunnel

Embankment

197 *Cutting*

to Torquay

196

Aller
Junction *Cutting*

NEWTON
ABBOT

195

A 380 *194*

Moreton
Hampstead
Branch
Racecourse

194

193

192

R. Teign
191

Golf course

W
S
N
E

13

TOTNES CASTLE

Dominating Totnes is the fine twelfth century Norman motte and bailey castle. This sits atop a large hill that overlooks the surrounding countryside. It is thought that the first castle was built by the Norman Lord Juhel who arrived in England with the Conqueror.

ASHBURTON JUNCTION

At Totnes the line divides and a branch line runs off to the north for just over 9 miles toward the pleasant village of Ashburton. A smaller line also runs off in the opposite direction towards Totnes Quay.

DARTMOOR

Just after leaving the 291 yard long Dainton tunnel we emerge to sweeping views of Dartmoor in the distance; the rocky outcrops, or tors, are clearly visible against the sky. While these are purely geological features there is a great deal of archaeology on Dartmoor which demonstrates that, in pre-history, this area was well settled.

EXE VALLEY BRANCH

With the river Teign on our right we come into the pretty market town of Newton Abbot. Immediately to our right is the racecourse which was first established in 1866, twenty years after the station was opened in 1846. At Newton Abbot the line branches off, first to the right along the Moretonhampstead Branch and second, to the left, along the Torquay branch.

NEWTON ABBOT

At Stoke Cannon station the track divides off and, off to our right, runs the Exe Valley Branch. This railway runs ultimately to Dulverton but, in its first few miles serves the picturesque villages of Thorverton and Cadeleigh.

LINE FALLS 1:249
LEVEL
RISES 1:131
RISES 1:200
LEVEL
RISES 1:65
RISES 1:95
RISES 1:90
RISES 1:74
LINE RISES 1:52
RISES 1:57
RISES 1:46
RISES 1:56
RISES 1:50
RISES 1:47
RISES 1:71
RISES 1:66
202½ LEVEL
1:254
LEVEL
1:153
1:78
1:205
1:120
1:227
1:86
LEVEL
LINE FALLS
1:260
1:76
1:105
LINE FALLS
1:55
1:65
1:38
1:37
1:130
1:84
1:44
1:34
1:49
1:41
LINE RISES
1:56
1:46
1:71
1:57
1:98
1:247
FALLS 1:247
LEVEL
194
RISES 1:259
LEVEL
RISES 1:289
LEVEL
LINE FALLS
1:600
RISES 1:270
LEVEL

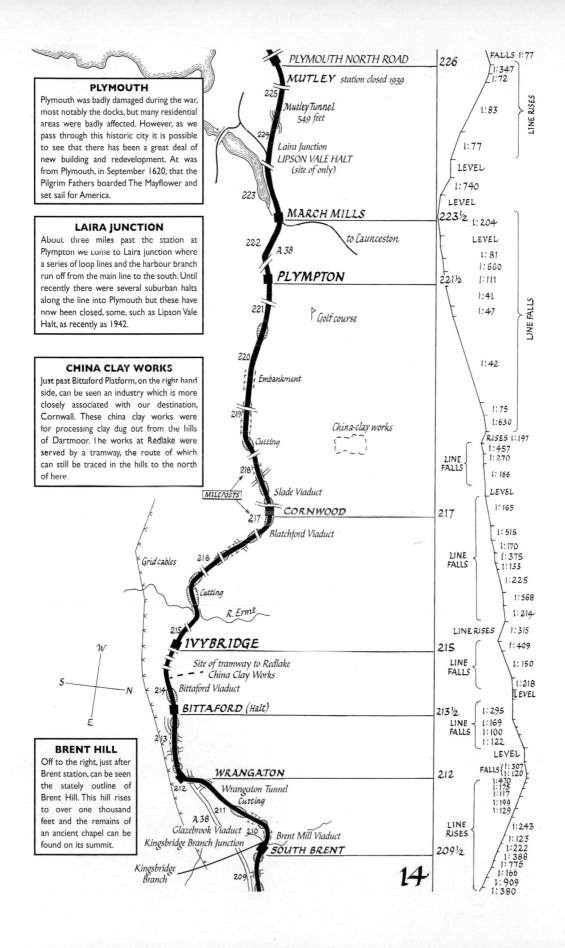

PLYMOUTH

Plymouth was badly damaged during the war, most notably the docks, but many residential areas were badly affected. However, as we pass through this historic city it is possible to see that there has been a great deal of new building and redevelopment. At was from Plymouth, in September 1620, that the Pilgrim Fathers boarded The Mayflower and set sail for America.

LAIRA JUNCTION

About three miles past the station at Plympton we come to Laira junction where a series of loop lines and the harbour branch run off from the main line to the south. Until recently there were several suburban halts along the line into Plymouth but these have now been closed, some, such as Lipson Vale Halt, as recently as 1942.

CHINA CLAY WORKS

Just past Bittaford Platform, on the right hand side, can be seen an industry which is more closely associated with our destination, Cornwall. These china clay works were for processing clay dug out from the hills of Dartmoor. The works at Redlake were served by a tramway, the route of which can still be traced in the hills to the north of here.

BRENT HILL

Off to the right, just after Brent station, can be seen the stately outline of Brent Hill. This hill rises to over one thousand feet and the remains of an ancient chapel can be found on its summit.

PLYMOUTH NORTH ROAD — 226 — FALLS 1:77 / 1:347 / 1:72

MUTLEY station closed 1939 — 225 / 1:83

Mutley Tunnel 549 feet — 224 / 1:77

Laira Junction LIPSON VALE HALT (site of only) — LEVEL / 1:740

223 — LEVEL

MARCH MILLS — 223½ / 1:204

to Launceston — LEVEL / 1:81 / 1:660

222 / A38 / 1:111

PLYMPTON — 221½ / 1:41 / 1:47

221 — Golf course

220 / 1:42

Embankment

219 / 1:75 / 1:630

Cutting — RISES 1:197 / 1:457 / 1:270 — LINE FALLS / 1:166

218 — LEVEL

Slade Viaduct — 1:165

217 — CORNWOOD — 217

Blatchford Viaduct — 1:515 / 1:170 / 1:375 / 1:133

216 — LINE FALLS

Grid cables

Cutting — 1:225 / 1:568 / 1:214

R. Erme — LINE RISES / 1:315

215 — IVYBRIDGE — 215 / 1:409

Site of tramway to Redlake China Clay Works — LINE FALLS / 1:150

214 — Bittaford Viaduct — 1:218 / LEVEL

BITTAFORD (Halt) — 213½ / 1:295 / LINE FALLS / 1:169 / 1:100 / 1:122

213 — LEVEL

WRANGATON — 212 — FALLS {1:307 / 1:120}

212 — Wrangaton Tunnel Cutting — 1:470 / 1:175 / 1:117 / 1:199 / 1:129

211 — LINE RISES / 1:243 / 1:123

A38 / Glazebrook Viaduct — 210 — Brent Mill Viaduct

Kingsbridge Branch Junction / SOUTH BRENT — 209½ — 1:222 / 1:388 / 1:775 / 1:166

Kingsbridge Branch — 209 / 1:909 / 1:380

MILEPOSTS

W / S / N / E

14

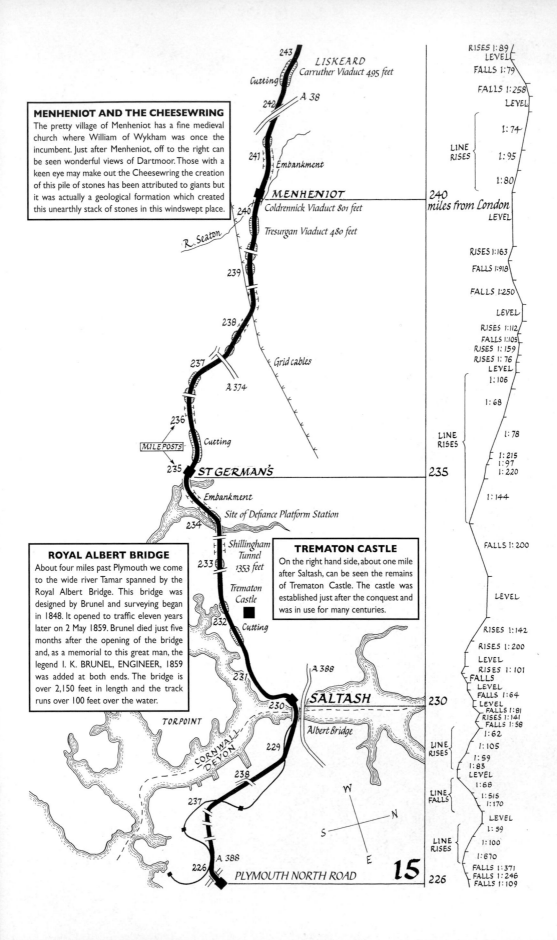

MENHENIOT AND THE CHEESEWRING

The pretty village of Menheniot has a fine medieval church where William of Wykham was once the incumbent. Just after Menheniot, off to the right can be seen wonderful views of Dartmoor. Those with a keen eye may make out the Cheesewring the creation of this pile of stones has been attributed to giants but it was actually a geological formation which created this unearthly stack of stones in this windswept place.

ROYAL ALBERT BRIDGE

About four miles past Plymouth we come to the wide river Tamar spanned by the Royal Albert Bridge. This bridge was designed by Brunel and surveying began in 1848. It opened to traffic eleven years later on 2 May 1859. Brunel died just five months after the opening of the bridge and, as a memorial to this great man, the legend I. K. BRUNEL, ENGINEER, 1859 was added at both ends. The bridge is over 2,150 feet in length and the track runs over 100 feet over the water.

TREMATON CASTLE

On the right hand side, about one mile after Saltash, can be seen the remains of Trematon Castle. The castle was established just after the conquest and was in use for many centuries.

243
LISKEARD
Carruther Viaduct 495 feet
Cutting
242
A 38
241
Embankment
MENHENIOT
Coldrennick Viaduct 801 feet
240
Tresurgan Viaduct 480 feet
R. Seaton
239
238
237
Grid cables
A 374
236
Cutting
MILEPOSTS
235
ST GERMAN'S
Embankment
Site of Defiance Platform Station
234
Shillingham Tunnel 1353 feet
233
Trematon Castle
232
Cutting
231
A 388
230
SALTASH
229
Albert Bridge
238
237
TORPOINT
CORNWALL DEVON
226
A 388
PLYMOUTH NORTH ROAD

15

RISES 1:89
LEVEL
FALLS 1:79
FALLS 1:258
LEVEL
1:74
LINE RISES
1:95
1:80
240 miles from London
LEVEL
RISES 1:163
FALLS 1:918
FALLS 1:250
LEVEL
RISES 1:112
FALLS 1:105
RISES 1:159
RISES 1:76
LEVEL
1:106
1:68
235
1:78
LINE RISES
1:215
1:97
1:220
1:144
FALLS 1:200
LEVEL
RISES 1:142
RISES 1:200
LEVEL
RISES 1:101
FALLS
LEVEL
FALLS 1:64
LEVEL
FALLS 1:81
RISES 1:141
FALLS 1:58
230
1:62
1:105
LINE RISES
1:59
1:83
LEVEL
1:68
LINE FALLS
1:515
1:170
LEVEL
1:59
LINE RISES
1:100
1:670
FALLS 1:371
FALLS 1:246
226
FALLS 1:109

W
N
S
E

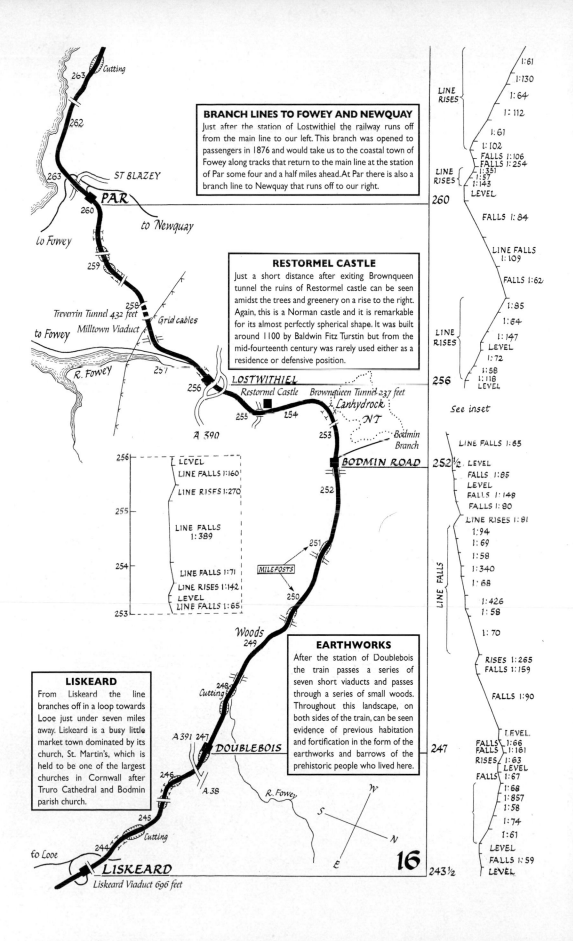

263 *Cutting*

262

263 ST BLAZEY

PAR

260

to Newquay

to Fowey

259

258

Treverrin Tunnel 432 feet · *Milltown Viaduct* · *Grid cables*

to Fowey

R. Fowey

257

256 **LOSTWITHIEL**

Restormel Castle · *Brownqueen Tunnel 237 feet* · *Lanhydrock*

255 254

A 390

253

NT

Bodmin Branch

BODMIN ROAD

252

251

MILEPOSTS

250

Woods
249

248
Cutting

A 391 247

DOUBLEBOIS

246

A 38 · *R. Fowey*

245

244 *Cutting*

to Looe

LISKEARD
Liskeard Viaduct 696 feet

16

BRANCH LINES TO FOWEY AND NEWQUAY
Just after the station of Lostwithiel the railway runs off from the main line to our left. This branch was opened to passengers in 1876 and would take us to the coastal town of Fowey along tracks that return to the main line at the station of Par some four and a half miles ahead. At Par there is also a branch line to Newquay that runs off to our right.

RESTORMEL CASTLE
Just a short distance after exiting Brownqueen tunnel the ruins of Restormel castle can be seen amidst the trees and greenery on a rise to the right. Again, this is a Norman castle and it is remarkable for its almost perfectly spherical shape. It was built around 1100 by Baldwin Fitz Turstin but from the mid-fourteenth century was rarely used either as a residence or defensive position.

EARTHWORKS
After the station of Doublebois the train passes a series of seven short viaducts and passes through a series of small woods. Throughout this landscape, on both sides of the train, can be seen evidence of previous habitation and fortification in the form of the earthworks and barrows of the prehistoric people who lived here.

LISKEARD
From Liskeard the line branches off in a loop towards Looe just under seven miles away. Liskeard is a busy little market town dominated by its church, St. Martin's, which is held to be one of the largest churches in Cornwall after Truro Cathedral and Bodmin parish church.

Inset (right gradient profile):

LINE RISES — 1:61 / 1:130 / 1:64 / 1:112 / 1:61 / 1:102
FALLS 1:106 / FALLS 1:254 / 1:351 / 1:57 / 1:143
LINE RISES — LEVEL
260
FALLS 1:84
LINE FALLS 1:109
FALLS 1:62
1:85 / 1:64 / 1:147 / LEVEL / 1:72 / 1:58 / 1:118 / LEVEL
LINE RISES
256

See inset

Gradient profile (lower right):

LINE FALLS 1:65
252½ LEVEL
FALLS 1:85
LEVEL
FALLS 1:148
FALLS 1:80
LINE RISES 1:81
1:94 / 1:69 / 1:58 / 1:340 / 1:68
1:426 / 1:58
1:70
RISES 1:265
FALLS 1:159
FALLS 1:90
LEVEL
FALLS 1:66
FALLS 1:161
RISES 1:63
LEVEL
FALLS 1:67
1:68 / 1:857 / 1:58 / 1:74 / 1:61
LEVEL
FALLS 1:59
LEVEL
LINE FALLS
247
243½

Inset box (left centre):

256 — LEVEL / LINE FALLS 1:160 / LINE RISES 1:270
255
LINE FALLS 1:389
254 — LINE FALLS 1:71 / LINE RISES 1:142 / LEVEL / LINE FALLS 1:65
253

Compass:
W / S / N / E

163

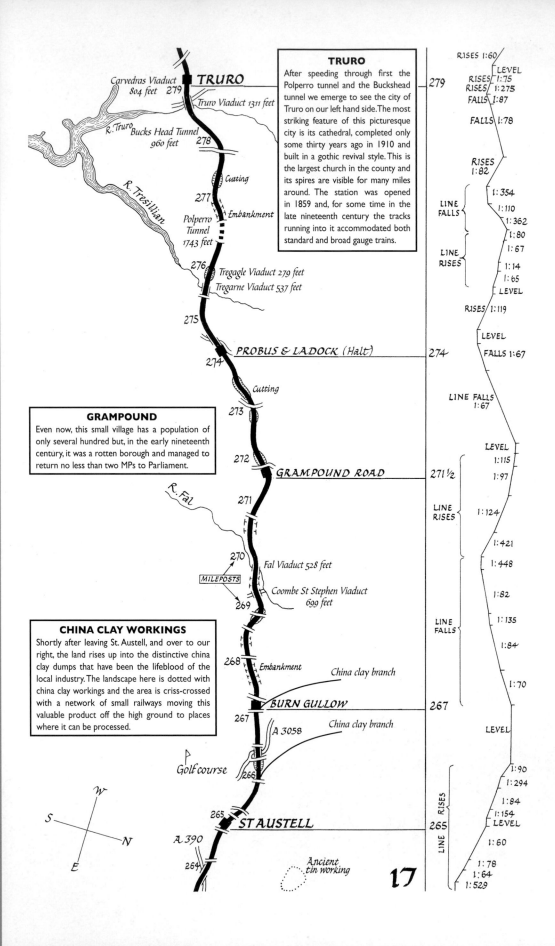

TRURO

Carvedras Viaduct 804 feet 279
Truro Viaduct 1311 feet
R. Truro Bucks Head Tunnel 960 feet 278
R. Tresillian
Cutting
277
Embankment
Polperro Tunnel 1743 feet
276
Tregagle Viaduct 279 feet
Tregarne Viaduct 537 feet
275
PROBUS & LADOCK (Halt) 274
Cutting
273
272
GRAMPOUND ROAD
R. Fal 271
270
MILEPOSTS
Fal Viaduct 528 feet
Coombe St Stephen Viaduct 699 feet
269
268 Embankment
China clay branch
BURN GULLOW
267
A 3058 China clay branch
Golf course 266
265 ST AUSTELL
A 390
264
Ancient tin working

W
S
N
E

17

TRURO

After speeding through first the Polperro tunnel and the Buckshead tunnel we emerge to see the city of Truro on our left hand side. The most striking feature of this picturesque city is its cathedral, completed only some thirty years ago in 1910 and built in a gothic revival style. This is the largest church in the county and its spires are visible for many miles around. The station was opened in 1859 and, for some time in the late nineteenth century the tracks running into it accommodated both standard and broad gauge trains.

GRAMPOUND

Even now, this small village has a population of only several hundred but, in the early nineteenth century, it was a rotten borough and managed to return no less than two MPs to Parliament.

CHINA CLAY WORKINGS

Shortly after leaving St. Austell, and over to our right, the land rises up into the distinctive china clay dumps that have been the lifeblood of the local industry. The landscape here is dotted with china clay workings and the area is criss-crossed with a network of small railways moving this valuable product off the high ground to places where it can be processed.

279
RISES 1:60
LEVEL
RISES 1:75
RISES 1:275
FALLS 1:87
FALLS 1:78
RISES 1:82
1:354
LINE FALLS 1:110
1:362
1:80
1:67
LINE RISES 1:14
1:65
LEVEL
RISES 1:119
LEVEL
274 FALLS 1:67
LINE FALLS 1:67
LEVEL
271½ 1:115
1:97
LINE RISES 1:124
1:421
1:448
1:82
LINE FALLS 1:135
1:84
1:70
267
LEVEL
1:90
1:294
1:84
LINE RISES 1:154
265 LEVEL
1:60
1:78
1:64
1:529

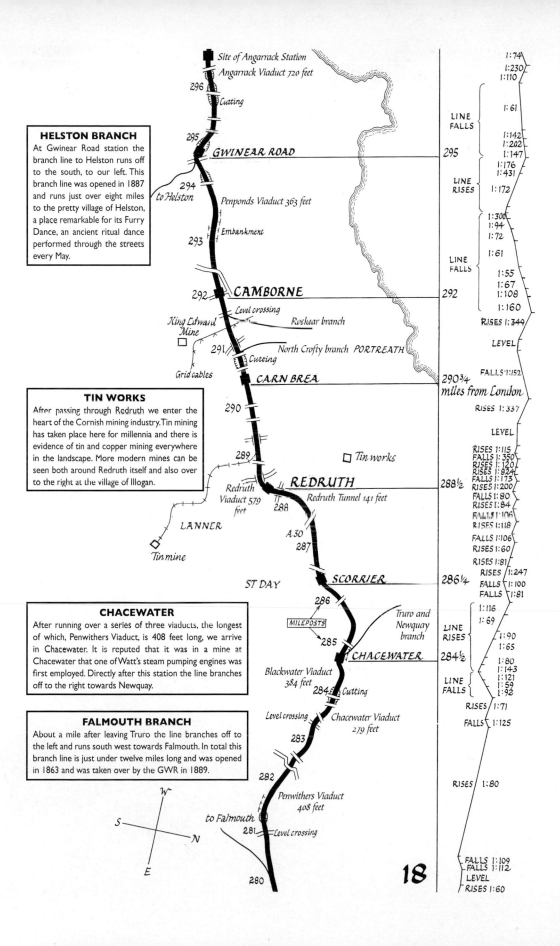

HELSTON BRANCH

At Gwinear Road station the branch line to Helston runs off to the south, to our left. This branch line was opened in 1887 and runs just over eight miles to the pretty village of Helston, a place remarkable for its Furry Dance, an ancient ritual dance performed through the streets every May.

TIN WORKS

After passing through Redruth we enter the heart of the Cornish mining industry. Tin mining has taken place here for millennia and there is evidence of tin and copper mining everywhere in the landscape. More modern mines can be seen both around Redruth itself and also over to the right at the village of Illogan.

CHACEWATER

After running over a series of three viaducts, the longest of which, Penwithers Viaduct, is 408 feet long, we arrive in Chacewater. It is reputed that it was in a mine at Chacewater that one of Watt's steam pumping engines was first employed. Directly after this station the line branches off to the right towards Newquay.

FALMOUTH BRANCH

About a mile after leaving Truro the line branches off to the left and runs south west towards Falmouth. In total this branch line is just under twelve miles long and was opened in 1863 and was taken over by the GWR in 1889.

Site of Angarrack Station
Angarrack Viaduct 720 feet
296
Cutting
295
GWINEAR ROAD
295
to Helston
294
Penponds Viaduct 363 feet
293
Embankment
CAMBORNE
292
292
Level crossing
King Edward Mine
Roskear branch
291
North Crofty branch PORTREATH
Cutting
Grid cables
CARN BREA
290¾ miles from London
290
289
Tin works
REDRUTH
288½
Redruth Viaduct 579 feet
Redruth Tunnel 141 feet
288
LANNER
A 30
287
Tin mine
ST DAY
SCORRIER
286¼
286
MILEPOSTS
Truro and Newquay branch
285
CHACEWATER
284½
Blackwater Viaduct 384 feet
284½ Cutting
Level crossing
Chacewater Viaduct 279 feet
283
282
Penwithers Viaduct 408 feet
to Falmouth
281
Level crossing
280

W
S
N
E

18

LINE FALLS
1:74
1:230
1:110
1:61
1:142
1:202
1:147
1:176
1:431
LINE RISES
1:172
1:300
1:94
1:72
1:61
LINE FALLS
1:55
1:67
1:108
1:160
RISES 1:349
LEVEL
FALLS 1:152
RISES 1:337
LEVEL
RISES 1:115
FALLS 1:350
RISES 1:120
RISES 1:824
FALLS 1:173
RISES 1:200
FALLS 1:80
RISES 1:84
FALLS 1:106
RISES 1:118
FALLS 1:106
RISES 1:60
RISES 1:81
RISES 1:247
FALLS 1:100
FALLS 1:81
1:116
1:69
LINE RISES
1:90
1:65
1:80
1:143
1:121
1:59
1:92
RISES 1:71
FALLS 1:125
RISES 1:80
FALLS 1:109
FALLS 1:112
LEVEL
RISES 1:60

165

PENZANCE

We arrive at our destination after over 300 miles of travel through the varied landscapes of many of the most beautiful counties in the country. The station was first opened in 1852 but a more modern building was erected in 1879 and since that time it has served many tens of thousands of holiday makers and countless tons of freight. From here the tourist may explore the villages in the surrounding countryside, visit the Lands End or even travel across the water to the Scilly Isles. Our journey at an end, we disembark and set out to enjoy what has been known for generations as The Cornish Riviera.

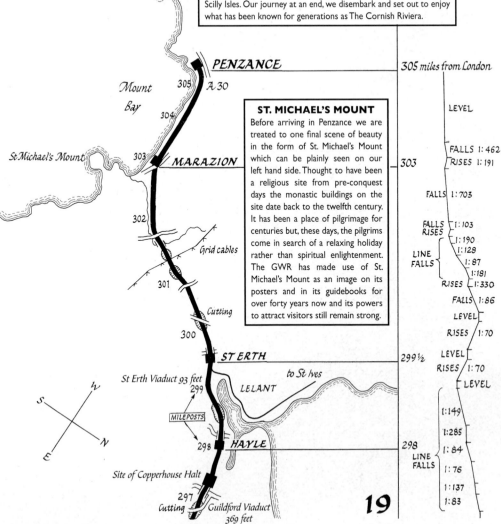

NEWLYN

PENZANCE

305 miles from London

Mount Bay

305   A 30

304

St Michael's Mount

303   *MARAZION*

302

Grid cables

301

Cutting

300

ST ERTH   299½

St Erth Viaduct 93 feet
299

to St Ives

LELANT

MILEPOSTS

298   *HAYLE*   298

Site of Copperhouse Halt

297
Cutting   *Guildford Viaduct 369 feet*

ST. MICHAEL'S MOUNT

Before arriving in Penzance we are treated to one final scene of beauty in the form of St. Michael's Mount which can be plainly seen on our left hand side. Thought to have been a religious site from pre-conquest days the monastic buildings on the site date back to the twelfth century. It has been a place of pilgrimage for centuries but, these days, the pilgrims come in search of a relaxing holiday rather than spiritual enlightenment. The GWR has made use of St. Michael's Mount as an image on its posters and in its guidebooks for over forty years now and its powers to attract visitors still remain strong.

LEVEL

FALLS 1:462
RISES 1:191

303

FALLS 1:703

FALLS 1:103
RISES

1:190
1:128
1:87
1:181
RISES 1:330

FALLS 1:86

LEVEL

RISES 1:70

LEVEL
RISES 1:70

LEVEL

1:149

1:285

1:84
LINE
FALLS
1:76

1:137

1:83

LINE
FALLS

19

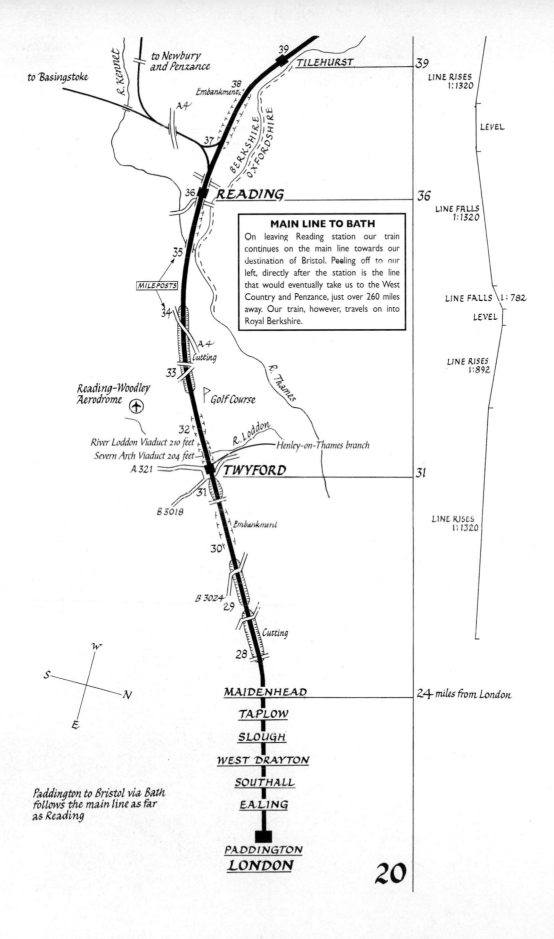

to Newbury
and Penzance

to Basingstoke

R. Kennet

TILEHURST

39

39

LINE RISES
1:1320

LEVEL

38
Embankment

A4

37

BERKSHIRE / OXFORDSHIRE

36

36

MAIN LINE TO BATH

On leaving Reading station our train continues on the main line towards our destination of Bristol. Peeling off to our left, directly after the station is the line that would eventually take us to the West Country and Penzance, just over 260 miles away. Our train, however, travels on into Royal Berkshire.

READING

LINE FALLS
1:1320

35

MILEPOSTS

34

A4
Cutting

33

R. Thames

LINE FALLS   1:782

LEVEL

Reading-Woodley
Aerodrome

Golf Course

32

R. Loddon

River Loddon Viaduct 210 feet
Severn Arch Viaduct 204 feet

Henley-on-Thames branch

A 321

TWYFORD

31

31

LINE RISES
1:892

B 3018

Embankment

30

LINE RISES
1:1320

B 3024

29

Cutting

28

MAIDENHEAD

24 miles from London

TAPLOW

SLOUGH

WEST DRAYTON

SOUTHALL

W

EALING

S

N

E

PADDINGTON
LONDON

20

Paddington to Bristol via Bath
follows the main line as far
as Reading

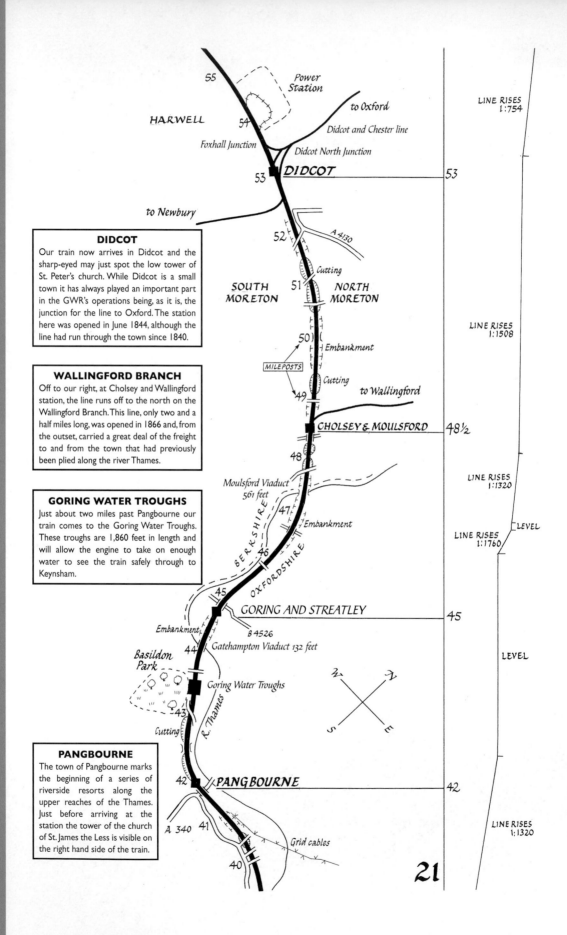

55

Power Station

HARWELL

54

to Oxford

Didcot and Chester line

Foxhall Junction

Didcot North Junction

53 DIDCOT 53

to Newbury

52

A4130

DIDCOT

Our train now arrives in Didcot and the sharp-eyed may just spot the low tower of St. Peter's church. While Didcot is a small town it has always played an important part in the GWR's operations being, as it is, the junction for the line to Oxford. The station here was opened in June 1844, although the line had run through the town since 1840.

Cutting

51

SOUTH MORETON

NORTH MORETON

50

Embankment

MILEPOSTS

Cutting

49

to Wallingford

WALLINGFORD BRANCH

Off to our right, at Cholsey and Wallingford station, the line runs off to the north on the Wallingford Branch. This line, only two and a half miles long, was opened in 1866 and, from the outset, carried a great deal of the freight to and from the town that had previously been plied along the river Thames.

CHOLSEY & MOULSFORD 48½

48

Moulsford Viaduct 561 feet

47

Embankment

GORING WATER TROUGHS

Just about two miles past Pangbourne our train comes to the Goring Water Troughs. These troughs are 1,860 feet in length and will allow the engine to take on enough water to see the train safely through to Keynsham.

BERKSHIRE

46

OXFORDSHIRE

45

GORING AND STREATLEY 45

Embankment

44

B4526

Gatehampton Viaduct 132 feet

Basildon Park

43

Goring Water Troughs

R. Thames

Cutting

PANGBOURNE

The town of Pangbourne marks the beginning of a series of riverside resorts along the upper reaches of the Thames. Just before arriving at the station the tower of the church of St. James the Less is visible on the right hand side of the train.

42 PANGBOURNE 42

A340 41

Grid cables

40

21

LINE RISES 1:754

LINE RISES 1:1508

LINE RISES 1:1320

LEVEL

LINE RISES 1:1760

LEVEL

LINE RISES 1:1320

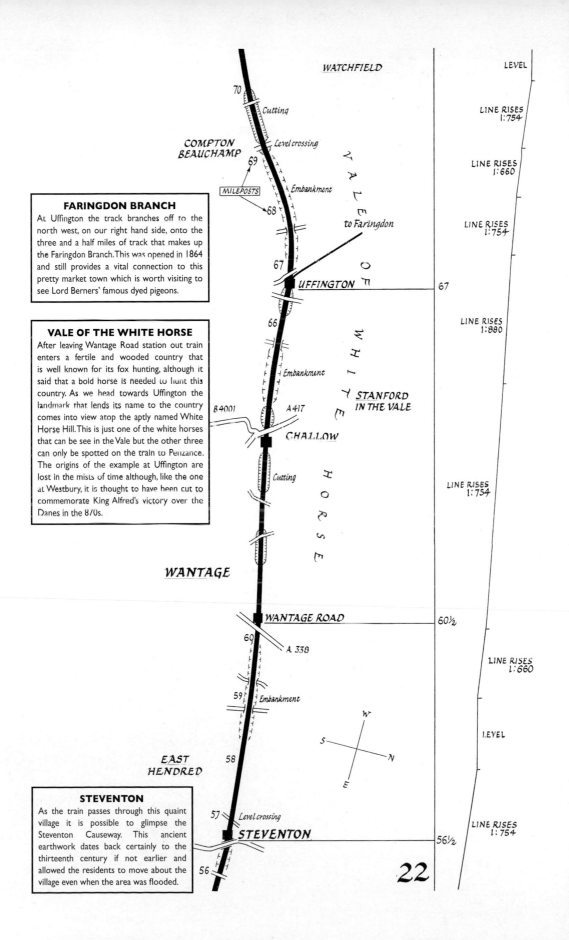

WATCHFIELD

LEVEL

70

Cutting

LINE RISES
1:754

COMPTON
BEAUCHAMP

Level crossing

LINE RISES
1:660

69

MILEPOSTS

Embankment

LINE RISES
1:754

68

to Faringdon

V
A
L
E

O
F

67

UFFINGTON

67

FARINGDON BRANCH

At Uffington the track branches off to the north west, on our right hand side, onto the three and a half miles of track that makes up the Faringdon Branch. This was opened in 1864 and still provides a vital connection to this pretty market town which is worth visiting to see Lord Berners' famous dyed pigeons.

LINE RISES
1:880

66

W
H
I
T
E

VALE OF THE WHITE HORSE

After leaving Wantage Road station out train enters a fertile and wooded country that is well known for its fox hunting, although it said that a bold horse is needed to hunt this country. As we head towards Uffington the landmark that lends its name to the country comes into view atop the aptly named White Horse Hill. This is just one of the white horses that can be see in the Vale but the other three can only be spotted on the train to Penzance. The origins of the example at Uffington are lost in the mists of time although, like the one at Westbury, it is thought to have been cut to commemorate King Alfred's victory over the Danes in the 870s.

Embankment

STANFORD
IN THE VALE

B4001

A417

CHALLOW

Cutting

H
O
R
S
E

LINE RISES
1:754

169

WANTAGE

WANTAGE ROAD

60½

60

A 338

LINE RISES
1:660

59½

Embankment

LEVEL

W

S

N

E

EAST
HENDRED

58

STEVENTON

As the train passes through this quaint village it is possible to glimpse the Steventon Causeway. This ancient earthwork dates back certainly to the thirteenth century if not earlier and allowed the residents to move about the village even when the area was flooded.

57

Level crossing

STEVENTON

56½

LINE RISES
1:754

56

22

WOOTTON BASSETT

To the right of the line can be seen the town of Wootton Bassett and, from here, the track divides with the line running off to our right being the Badminton Line that heads off to South Wales via Chipping Sodbury. This line was opened in 1903 and, finally, put paid to the GWR's nickname the 'Great Way Round'. Our journey, however, takes us to Bristol via the beautiful Avon valley and the city of Bath.

SWINDON WORKS

The train now arrives into what can only be called the beating heart of the GWR. Swindon is a railway town that has its roots back in 1840 when Daniel Gooch commented in a letter to Brunel that Swindon was 'by far the best point we have for a Central Engine Station'. As Swindon Works grew, so did the town, New Swindon, that was built to house its workers and, by 1900, it had swallowed the village of Old Swindon. At its height, just a decade ago, there were almost 14,000 workers employed at the Works and, at times, more than 50 locomotives a year were being built. The South Wales Main line runs off on the right hand side directly after the station and, on the same side, can be seen the locomotive Works where engines, in various stages of repair, might be seen.

ERMINE STREET

Although not visible from the train, directly after passing through Stratton Park Halt, the line crosses the route of the Roman road of Ermine Street. This ancient highway connected London with the important military centres of York and Lincoln in the north. Its presence reminds us that, long before the railways, people were travelling great distances throughout the country.

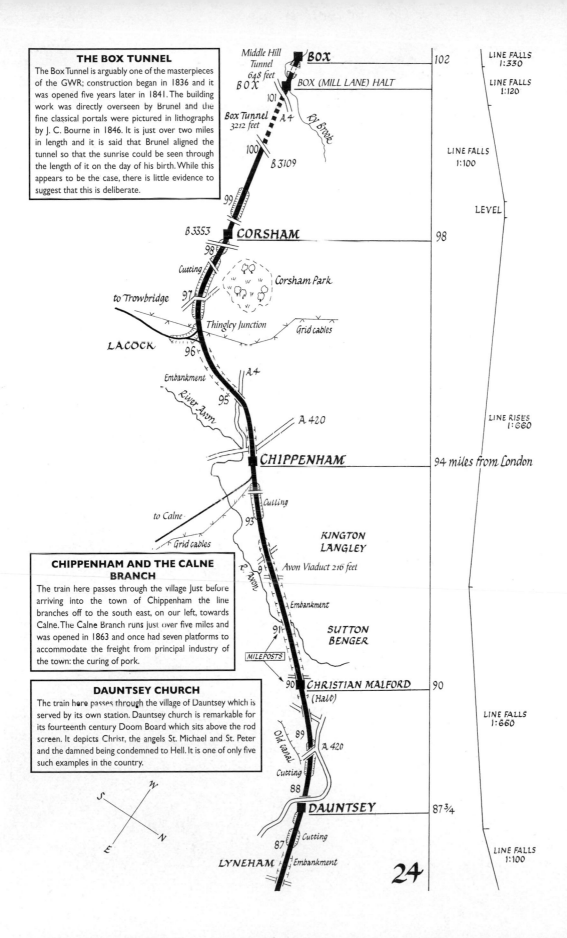

THE BOX TUNNEL

The Box Tunnel is arguably one of the masterpieces of the GWR; construction began in 1836 and it was opened five years later in 1841. The building work was directly overseen by Brunel and the fine classical portals were pictured in lithographs by J. C. Bourne in 1846. It is just over two miles in length and it is said that Brunel aligned the tunnel so that the sunrise could be seen through the length of it on the day of his birth. While this appears to be the case, there is little evidence to suggest that this is deliberate.

CHIPPENHAM AND THE CALNE BRANCH

The train here passes through the village just before arriving into the town of Chippenham the line branches off to the south east, on our left, towards Calne. The Calne Branch runs just over five miles and was opened in 1863 and once had seven platforms to accommodate the freight from principal industry of the town: the curing of pork.

DAUNTSEY CHURCH

The train here passes through the village of Dauntsey which is served by its own station. Dauntsey church is remarkable for its fourteenth century Doom Board which sits above the rod screen. It depicts Christ, the angels St. Michael and St. Peter and the damned being condemned to Hell. It is one of only five such examples in the country.

BOX

Middle Hill Tunnel 648 feet

BOX (MILL LANE) HALT

BOX

101

By Brook

A 4

Box Tunnel 3212 feet

100

B 3109

99

B 3353 CORSHAM

98

Cutting

Corsham Park

97

to Trowbridge

Thingley Junction

Grid cables

LACOCK

96

Embankment

River Avon

95

A 4

A 420

CHIPPENHAM

Cutting

to Calne

93

Grid cables

KINGTON LANGLEY

R. Avon

Avon Viaduct 216 feet

Embankment

91

SUTTON BENGER

MILEPOSTS

90 CHRISTIAN MALFORD

(Halt)

89

Old canal

A 420

Cutting

88

DAUNTSEY

87

Cutting

LYNEHAM

Embankment

102

LINE FALLS 1:330

LINE FALLS 1:120

LINE FALLS 1:100

LEVEL

98

LINE RISES 1:660

94 miles from London

171

LINE FALLS 1:660

90

87¾

LINE FALLS 1:100

24

W
N
S
E

BRISTOL

After passing through the two tunnels at St. Anne's Park and the lines to Frome and South Wales we arrive at our destination of Bristol. This city has a long and illustrious maritime tradition but it is also the original home of the Great Western Railway Company. A proposal to link Bristol to London by railway was suggested in the early 1830s but it was in 1833 that a committee of Bristol businessmen met to discuss the serious possibility of building a line. It was at this meeting that the name of Isambard Kingdom Brunel was suggested as the engineer. Although the company now resides in London, Bristol has always been seen as its birthplace. It is a fine city with much to recommend it to the tourist. It is here that we alight, our journey of over 118 miles at an end.

KEYNSHAM WATER TROUGHS

About one mile after the station at Keynsham we come to the water troughs where the engine can take on enough water to see it safely to South Wales. The troughs here are 1,860 feet long.

BATH

After passing through Bathampton and the Bradford Branch, which runs off to the south, out train arrives in Bath. The station here was opened in 1840 and served one of the most famous spa towns in the world. The town, founded by the Romans as Aquae Sulis, has been famous for its waters for almost two thousand years and still draws many people in search of a health and relaxation. Although badly bombed during the war the town is still a fine example of Georgian architecture.

BRISTOL TEMPLE MEADS

to Weston-super-Mare

Frome and North Somerset line

Severe speed restriction from milepost 117

Golf Course

St Anne's Park No.3 Tunnel 3051 feet

St Anne's Park No.2 Tunnel 468 feet

ST ANNE'S PARK

R. Avon

118½ — LEVEL — LINE RISES 1:264

LEVEL

116½ — LINE FALLS 1:1320

LEVEL

Cutting
A 4

Keynsham Water Troughs

R. Chew

KEYNSHAM AND SOMERDALE

B 4427

to Gloucester

Embankment

Cutting

Golf Course

SALTFORD

A 4

Cutting

Twerton Long Tunnel 786 feet
Twerton Short Tunnel 135 feet

LMSR line

SOUTH TWERTON

OLDFIELD PARK
MILEPOSTS

Bath LMSR station (Green Park) Airfield ✈

BATH

A 36
Embankment

△ Solsbury Hill Fort

Golf course

BATHAMPTON

Bradford branch
to Salisbury

R. Avon
A 363

SOMERSET / WILTSHIRE

Cutting

113½

LINE FALLS 1:1320

111 — LEVEL

LEVEL

108 miles from London

LINE FALLS 1:1320

107 — LINE FALLS 1:3441

LEVEL

104½ — LINE FALLS 1:1320

25

W
N
S
E

Principal Stations of the GWR

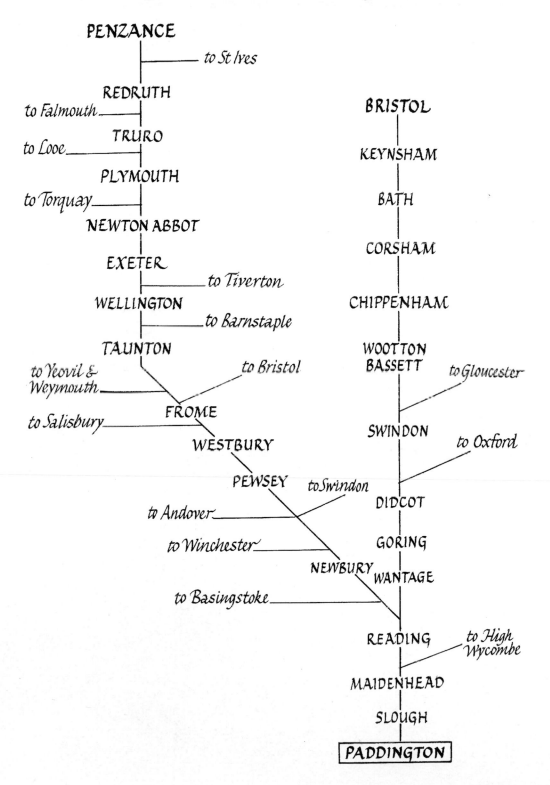

Page 1: Streamlined LMSR 'Princess Coronation' class Pacific no.6220 *Coronation* attacks the 1 in 75 climb to Shap Summit in the Cumbrian fells with the Glasgow-bound 'Coronation Scot.' At 1,036 feet (315.7m), this is the highest point on the route from Euston to Carlisle.

Page 3: Far from Southern Railway territory, in Leicestershire, but appropriately paired with a rake of Southern green stock, Maunsell 'Schools' class 4-4-0 no.925 *Cheltenham* heads south past Swithland Sidings on the Great Central Railway with a photographers' charter on 17 October 2012.

Page 53: One of six preserved 'A4' Pacifics, no.4464 *Bittern* entered service in December 1937, and was among the last to be withdrawn in 1966. Now privately owned, it hauls main-line specials, and visits preserved railways. Here, on the Severn Valley Railway, it is appropriately harnessed to a rake of Gresley teak-bodied carriages.

Page 62: The freight equivalent of the 'King Arthur', the 'S15' 4-6-0 was introduced by the L&SWR in 1920 and enlarged to a class of 45 by the Southern. Here, no.847, owned by the Maunsell Society, approaches Horsted Keynes on Sussex's Bluebell Railway at the head of vintage stock.

Page 93: A poster produced for Southern Railway to promote rail services from cities in Germany to London via Ostende and Dover. This poster is among many reproduced from a snapshot taken in 1924 by commercial photographer Charles E. Brown on a platform at Waterloo Station, London.

Pages 138–139: Stanier designed the '5XP' or 'Jubilee' class 4-6-0 for secondary express and semi-fast services. After initial steaming problems were resolved, they became widely used. Here, no.5690 *Leander* – one of four survivors – is at the head of 'The Fellsman', passing Settle before climbing through the Yorkshire Dales to Carlisle.

Pages 174–175: Whether 'City' class 4-4-0 no.3440 *City of Truro* was actually the first-ever steam locomotive to achieve 100mph (160.9kph) – on its journey from Plymouth to London heading the 'Ocean Mails Express' on 9 May 1904 – remains disputed. Nevertheless, the 1903-built engine was returned to steam, and to main-line working order, to mark the centenary. It also visited many preserved railways, and is shown here on GWR territory, approaching Furnace Sidings on the Pontypool & Blaenavon Railway in South Wales.